"In the packed pages of *UFO W...* impressive breadth of knowledg(........ous and intriguing UFO encounters. He also reveals the sheer number and diversity of UFO reports that Wisconsin has received across the decades. Whether you are a resident of Wisconsin or not, this is a book that is guaranteed to appeal to UFO enthusiasts everywhere."

—Nick Redfern, author of *On the Trail of the Saucer Spies,* and *Memoirs of a Monster Hunter*

****

"Voss provides a fascinating handbook to five of the state's UFO hotspots, as well as his own candid insights on the phenomena. A meticulously compiled must-have for anyone serious about studying aerial weirdness. Lots of info in a handy, take-with size!"

—Linda Godfrey, author *The Beast of Bray Road, Hunting The American Werewolf, Strange Wisconsin,* and co-author of *Weird Wisconsin*

****

"The *UFO Wisconsin* book has arrived. To me it's a great find and a huge step forward for UFO research in the state."

—Jim Aho, author of *EARS: Book One, The Evidence*

UFO

WISCONSIN

A PROGRESS REPORT

Watch
the
Sky

UFO
WISCONSIN
A PROGRESS REPORT

By NOAH VOSS

Research Publishing Company
A Division of Unexplained Research LLC

Library of Congress Control Number: 2007905842
ISBN-10: 0-9762099-7-7
ISBN-13: 978-0-9762099-7-3

Printed in the United States by Documation

Unexplained Research Publishing Company
A Division of Unexplained Research LLC
P.O. Box 2173, Eau Claire, WI 54702-2173
Email: info@unexplainedresearch.com
www.unexplainedresearch.com

DEDICATION

To Jennifer Voss

Table of Contents
"Nothing can be known, not even this." Attributed to Carneades

Here you get to meet my personality, read some of my thoughts, and gain some insight on my perspective and background. "Nothing would be done at all if one waited until one could do it so well that no one could find fault with it." —John Henry Newman (Cardinal)

A brief discussion of a few UFO field specific terms and ideas used in this book. "Ignorance more frequently begets confidence than does knowledge." —Charles Darwin

The top five areas of UFO activity in the state. "After success has been reached in anything, the necessary things seem obvious enough to all. The discovery of the obvious is a slow and costly process." —Inventor A.E. Dolbear Professor of Physics, Astronomy and Natural Sciences

Currently weighing in with more than 60 UFO reports online at UFOwisconsin.com, Milwaukee covers a lot of land.

At 40-plus reports on www.UFOwisconsin.com, Madison has it all: wooded hills, open prairies, large lakes, small ponds, and swamps, with plenty of cement and urban development to round it out.

Winter of 1987 may have changed Belleville, Wisconsin forever.

This area has an intriguing connection with UFOs over the last 50 years and about 430 million years of odd events starting with a 600 foot wide meteor striking just miles from where Elmwood now sits.

From unexplainable lights in the nighttime sky, to daylight clear discs, UFO crafts sitting on the ground in front of you, or coming face-to-face with little green men; you can find or hear about it here.

This Time Around Above all else be inquisitive and have fun; remember adventures come to the adventuresome! "Be ashamed to die until you have won some victory for humanity." Horace Mann

Any details, theories, or images that didn't fit into the body were kept and placed neatly and in order for you here

Foreword

As a life-long resident of Wisconsin, I have become accustom to the weird reputation that the state has garnered from the national media. We have gotten used to being known as the state of cheese heads and beer drinkers. Thanks to the likes of Ed Gein (The Butcher of Plainfield) and Jeffrey Dahmer (The Milwaukee Cannibal) many people think of Wisconsin as the home of crazy killers. Yet, a less known, and less sinister fact about the state is that we are home to the "UFO Capital of the World." Actually, Wisconsin is home to three UFO capitals of the World. The Wisconsin towns of Bellville, Dundee, and Elmwood all claim to be the home to the most UFOs sightings in the nation. I grew up in the city of Eau Claire, which is not too far from where the famous Elmwood UFO sightings took place in the 1970's and 80's. As a young high school student I traveled to the small rural town to see the spot where so many UFOs had been reported. While speaking with witnesses and residents, I soon found out that sightings of UFOs in Elmwood had not stopped appearing, they were just no longer reported by the media. Talking with witnesses about their amazing stories of odd ships and puzzling lights is what started my research into the paranormal.

Soon after my initial trip to Elmwood, the UFO craze of the mid 1990's spread throughout the country. Reports of UFOs and alien abductions skyrocketed. UFO and alien themes began appearing everywhere in movies, TV shows, and radio programs. The invasion of UFO and alien merchandise had also begun. From clothing to candy, you could not go anywhere without seeing the phenomenon throughout mainstream culture. Of course this set off a flood of UFO and alien themed books into the market. Authors widely speculated on every possible segment of the phenomenon. Each theory being more fascinating and bizarre than the previous. As the years passed, the more I read about UFOs, the more I found the subject had become stale and boring. Year after year it seemed like the same five people were putting out the same five books. The general public quickly became bored with the stagnant field and soon the subject was in need of something different.

Thankfully this is where UFO Wisconsin comes in, as Noah Voss has wisely discovered that UFOs are not exclusively a sit and read phenomenon. And he should know, because for over a decade Voss has traveled the world on adventures collecting, investigating, and chronicling reports of the strange and unexplained. Throughout the book Voss skillfully showcases his vast knowledge into the field of UFOs and alien abductions, while expertly guiding us through the history and basics of the fascinating subject. While exploring the numerous theories of UFOs and aliens Voss is conscious of never pushing a specific theory on us. This refreshing approach allows us to form our own ideas, thoughts, and possibilities on the subject.

UFO Wisconsin is the most innovative book to hit the field in years as Voss doesn't simply tell you about UFOs, he provides you with the all the necessary information in order for you to venture out in search of your own personal UFO encounter. Gone are the days of simply reading about UFOs. As more and more people seek out adventure, the idea of reading has shifted to the idea of doing, and Voss seems to welcome in this new era of "do it yourself" investigating. With UFO Wisconsin, the possibilities for adventure are endless. You can grab this book and head out to Madison to spot mysterious lights hovering silently in the dark night sky, or travel to Dundee, where out in the middle of nowhere you might just come face to face with a mysterious being not of this earth. Yet, maybe you are the type of person who has no intention of seeing UFOs up close and would prefer to sit back in the safety of your favorite reading chair and enjoy these stories with a nice cup of hot chocolate. Either way the only trouble you will have will be putting this book down long enough to gaze into the night sky in search of UFOs.

Of course there are numerous books on the shelf where you can read about mysterious reports of UFOs and terrifying abductions. Although it is fun to read about these cases in New York or California, it is a much different matter when these strange events happen in our own backyard. Finally a researcher has discovered that the most interesting cases take place in the areas where we live, work, and play. As you travel through the back roads of this book Voss brings to life the strangest UFO and alien encounters the Badger State has to offer. From the forests of the north woods to the busy streets of Milwaukee, UFO Wisconsin is overflowing with cases that will leave you wondering.

Voss has set the standard high with this guide and this book is a must have for anyone looking to delve into the bizarre world of UFOs and alien abductions and it sits in my car poised for yet another excursion in the unknown world of UFOs.

Keep an eye out,
Chad Lewis

Acknowledgments

To the first person in my support system, my lovely wife Jennifer. How many times I have focused on the paranormal topic that remains more distant from her heart than mine. The hours have had to become years by now. She remains an indispensable character in my endeavors. Add to that the countless times she has updated the websites in my absence, whether that be I'm on an adventure or simply need more time than the day allows. Thank you, as they say, even in this most impersonal medium — from the bottom of my heart.

To my fellow adventurers! You know who you are and you all have your own story to tell so I will not do you the dishonor of trying here. John Albrecht, Sean Bindley, Kevin Nelson, Rick Hendricks, Chad Lewis, Brandon St. Germain, Todd Roll, Linda Godfrey, Terry Fisk, and COTOE for whom nothing is out of the realm of discussion or debate, and no stance out of the possibility of change when exposed to reason, logic, and new data.

To Mr. Jim Aho who must be noted for collecting and organizing the original files that went on to create the W-Files.com and UFOwisconsin.com both. For without his tireless work I do not know where I might be today. Thank you Jim.

To all the persons who have bravely shared their very real, very personal experiences with me in person, or indirectly through www.UFOwisconsin.com. I thank you for coming forward with a situation not always easily done so with. To them all, I hold your decision to share the experience in high regards.

To all the people who have helped keep www.UFOwisconsin.com going until my personal path crossed with its own.

Despite a life time of continual studying, over two year's research, investigation, and writing of this book, at some point I'm guessing I was lead astray. Whether it was I, leading myself off course via a poor nights sleep, a stressful shift at the day job, or just imperfect procedures not catching all occurrences of imperfect research used as sources. I may have inadvertently transposed dates, causing experiences to fall out of chronological order. I may have melded two sightings together in my food deprived mind or left one out because it simply had not yet reached my ears. If I have, and I hope I haven't, please let me know. I am always open to constructive criticism of any portrayed facts in my work, so I might correct them in future printings.

As I strived to put forward in my book, there is nothing but possibilities and potentials at this point. It is entirely possible that there is some level of potential I made a mistake. I want to hear about it, and your proof that I have done so. Thank you in advance for your time and efforts in helping create an even additionally accurate following edition.

"Nothing would be done at all if one waited until one could do it so well that no one could find fault with it." John Henry Newman (Cardinal)

Introduction

Unidentified flying objects (UFOs) and Wisconsin skies…not an immediate connection for most people, including those actually living in the state. That is in part why I chose to write UFO Wisconsin: A Progress Report. Not to create a buzz, but rather to help spread an increased awareness of one already in existence; to produce another something that becomes an additional avenue for people to learn about their immediate surroundings wherever they may be in Wisconsin and beyond; not to craft or feature UFO conspiracy, or even get into great depth on UFO theory. That being said, of course, it is nearly impossible to have a UFO focused book without at least touching on some, if not all, of these areas. I aim to share some of the intriguing experiences that have been reported to UFOwisconsin.com and learned of through my own research and investigation.

Not just a couple of experiences either. There are over 100 separate experiences from over 100 different locations in Wisconsin documented in this book alone. This is just the tip of the iceberg, as they say; with currently well over 1,000 reports archived on www.UFOwisconsin.com. Those reports come from all over the world and from all walks of life.

I am inundated with stories told by nearly everyone I encounter: my banker, co-workers, tax preparers, journalists, the gas station attendant, landlords, family, and friends. Whenever I meet someone who learns of this particular interest of mine, there is a continuing process I have noticed over the years. I immediately take the stand as a key witness in the case of my credulity. The cross-examiner leads with probing questions, looking to find my stance and watching for any sign of me recording the conversation. Once comfortably establishing my viewpoint, the cross-examiner turns into storyteller; acting as if a youngster returning home from the first day of school. Some of my first, first days at school were full of new experiences, making the shyest amongst us bursting to share with anyone who has an interest and an empathetic ear. I have more than just a vested interest in the UFO field. I have a passion for watching people learn, for feeling myself learn from someone's experience, for taking that information and placing it neatly beside the overflowing filing cabinets in my mind of countless other accounts. Some are similar; some are different—really different. I am continually fascinated by the unique stories people choose to share with me. I love that everyone has a story to tell, unfortunately some never leave the dark confines of the discoverers mind. Those stories that break the silence I consider a great thing and find myself very fortunate to be in the position to document and learn from these experiences. I see my encounters with these people as an immense motivator in my work. It helps keep me driven to continue my efforts to research and investigate paranormal phenomena full-time.

The stories to follow in UFO Wisconsin are not fiction. Each documented experience has its own intriguing angle…some scary, others outright bewildering. Whatever you think of the experiences presented in UFO Wisconsin, I feel they do start to show how a wide demographic of Wisconsinites are, and have been experiencing something…a certain something that was so out of their ordinary, they felt compelled to take the extra time and effort to make sure their stories were told.

I do not make or hold any predispositions about divining answers in this book. I will put forth much information, in the form of witness testimony, photographic confirmation, artist re-creations and transcribed audio recordings. None of these will be irrefutable facts, but please look at them as data…or clues for you, now the researcher and investigator, to go out into the world and use, leap off of, change when needed, and build onto whenever possible. Included are some ideas for you to implement into your adventures, even pointers on practicing them as you read this book, should you find them deserving.

I will define some ideas and terms in ufology that have been postulated. I will give some of my insight gained through years of experience in the UFO and paranormal fields, but not in the form of answers. Rather than force my opinions I'd rather have my experience come through in my presentation of facts. After all, anyone's opinion, whether backed by a surplus of education or none to speak of, is just that—an opinion. This opinion was based, at least somewhat, on a belief system, for better or worse. Whether that belief system is none at all or the complete opposite of yours today, you hopefully can learn something from it. Learn yes, but not follow it blindly, mine included.

There are areas or parts that will simply not receive the full attention that is their potential. This thirst will be quenched in my following book, which picks up where this one leaves off. Where applicable, I do touch on relatable experiences outside of Wisconsin to help bring forward a point. With this method, you as the reader are given a wider scope of the UFO phenomena and a unique perspective on how it could relate back to Wisconsin.

It may help to look at UFO Wisconsin as not an investigation case book, question answering, phenomenon-predicting product, but rather more of a record, textbook and, or timeline of the experiences put forth as of now. It's a compellation of stories, events and people surrounding UFOs and what we can see with our present perspective on the past. Researchers often speak towards an "end." I don't see this end being so effortlessly reached. I see an ongoing, evolving issue of intellectual and critical thinking that includes rational but fair investigation and observation of simply everything. May this be a stepping-off point for researchers and investigators who follow after me.

With that very thought in the forefront of our minds I bid no more adieu to a clearinghouse of Wisconsin UFO related phenomena.

Thanks for taking the time to check out UFO Wisconsin, and please enjoy!

Sincerely,
Noah Voss

Ufology 101

"Ignorance more frequently begets confidence than does knowledge."
Charles Darwin

You have picked up this book, so most likely you have a certain level of understanding in the paranormal fields and are at least familiar with the term UFO (Unidentified Flying Object). However, in my pursuit of perfection, for the ideology of idealism while trying to captain the cause that this work may be held by anyone and speak to all, let's go over some terms. From Ufology 101 we will work our way into perhaps more complex or at least industry-specific thoughts in Ufology 102 presented not in this book but the one to follow. School's in session, so let's make sure everyone is on the same page before we jump into the lesson plan that is the top five.

What is ufology? The field of study related to UFOs can be simply called ufology. To me ufology has become an all-encompassing, slightly generic classification for anything directly or indirectly connected to the UFO phenomena, whether that be UFOs themselves, aliens, or top secret government disinformation conspiracies. Today they all seem to be conveniently categorized under ufology. Ufologist naysayers may be out there saying, not only is the entire field a scam, the word ufology itself is not even one.

The word ufology is a neologism, or words and phrases that are recent creations. Such is the case with ufology, or for another example, E-mail a neologism can be a new invention or a different understanding of an old belief, practice or system. So now that we've established that the word is actually one, what do these terms and titles, such as ufologist, really mean to the people using them?

Those people who have dedicated much time and many resources to the field of ufology have come to be called ufologists. This is a new word to many and pronounced by most as "u_FOL_ogist." The majority of ufologists are those who, by their own interests, have done the research and have become learned in the UFO field. This may seem a rudimentary idea hidden with a fancy title when one considers that any school-attending child could be then called an educational researcher instead of a more common term like student. A stipulation for this ufologist title seems to be that it is more accepted when deemed one by someone other than yourself. I know this seems like a relaxed method, but it is also a good insight as to where the field currently is in its own development and evolution.

To be a quality ufologist in today's world one must at least hold a minimal understanding of many fields. Areas of study not exclusive to, but including the inner workings of, governmental branches, many disciplines of physics, geology, aeronautics, history and space science. This to me helps keep the field elite and somewhat self-regulating as a working understanding of such a wide variety of topics can be difficult at best to achieve on one's own. Those in the industry who don't have a grasp on the varied industries become quite apparent over time.

The UFO field has been called a fringe area, studied by independent scientists, futurists, and those with curious minds and driven personalities. Of course, this field is not unlike any other area of study and is not impermeable to those that society may have additionally colorful names for, such as kooky or crazy. Regardless of what they're called, the more relatable people typically have read every related book they can find, researched the people who have had experiences and investigated all things the witnesses share with them. Those who become respected in the field have typically been able to remember, apply, and connect their research to workable, logical theories based on factual verifiable data. This of course does not happen overnight, rather years or lifetimes are invested to reach the level of ufologist. Before the Internet was what it is, and before the first books we now have on the UFO subject were written, the field was researched by an intrepid few. Telephoning, writing and visiting the witnesses forced the researcher to get fully involved with what they were investigating. Making hundreds of research phone calls a year racked up huge bills and large sighting databases. I must admit I find myself jealous of how it must have evoked a completely different experience for the ufologist. I could speculate an almost guttural response—one of complete confusion in many cases. There would be no degree of separation between you and the sometimes life-altering experiences being related. I place myself in that raw situation many times a year and feel it helps keep me grounded. It is easy to take an inaccurate view of the UFO phenomena when you keep yourself as a researcher constantly several degrees removed from the witness. Receiving numerous nameless UFO accounts through E-mail, signed sightings via my website reporting forms or even you, as the reader reviewing the situations listed later in this book: it is easy to disassociate an actual person is behind each of these reports. People of all demographics report these unexplainable situations and quite likely someone just like you or someone you know. Freelance writers, investigative journalists, and general seekers of the unknown and fortean covered the experiences as much as possible in the past. Those days are gone and a new, subject-focused form of researcher is evolving in the field of study.

What does it really mean to be a ufologist today? As a researcher or investigator in the UFO field, one does not have the structured support system available that a doctor or an engineer can have while attending school. Looking at the previous example of our forefather ufologists, you could start to picture an adventure-filled daily life. One with the unknown around every corner, consistently bounding head first into the inexpressible, encountering the indefinable and inadvertently passing by the imperceptible. Of course we all land feet square on the other side, every time. Well maybe not every time, however the unknown is not alone in my experience. Along with it, the next pile of bills, the occasional am I utilizing my resources in an irrational way that is followed by the opposite and constant yearning of what could I accomplish with just a few more resources if I continued down this same path. It's perhaps not as glamorous as one might first imagine. One could also consider the field of UFO research as one without college guide-lines most obviously due to the lack of high paying jobs awaiting those who put in the effort to become experienced on the subject. It is perchance this lack of structure that slows the evolution of UFO theory, research, and inves-tigation.

In this field there is not necessarily one successful method of oper-ation, procedure, or protocol to follow that ensures any specific level of suc-cess. This is not all that different than every other discipline in life, other-wise we might all be millionaires or working on a beach full time. It would seem the UFO and paranormal investigator needs to constantly adapt to the new information they encounter, some quite literally discovering for the first time. Freelance writer John A. Keel was instrumental in documenting the 1960s mysterious UFO encounters in West Virginia. The witnessed creature was dubbed "Mothman" and has since become the subject of a popular book and movie in which many UFO sightings were also documented. Eerily sim-ilar UFO sightings and creature reports have been reported as recently as 2006 from the western portions of Wisconsin. These experiences have not been greatly publicized however due to my continued research and industry contacts I catch wind of the reports. It makes me wonder what other experiences I have yet to hear about and at the same time it leaves me perplexed as how to move forward with this extremely difficult information to categorize. Each researcher and investigator can form a unique theory on UFO phenomena that is specific to their subjective perception or qualitative data, whatever their methods may be. This keeps current and ongoing theories diverse to say the least.

While not everyone in the UFO field believes a scientific approach is the best; one thing we can all agree on is the fact we will not always agree. Those that can agree on a scientific approach most likely will differ in understandings of the scientific method. When looking for the most thought-out and all encompassing definition to use for this book, I ended up at Wikipedia.org. According to the entry for "scientific method," it is "a body of techniques for investigating phenomena and acquiring new knowledge." Sounds basic enough, but it is those "techniques" that very noticeably vary between researchers in this field. Now this next portion of the definition is vital, "as well as for correcting and integrating previous knowledge. It is based on observable, empirical, measurable evidence, and subject to laws of reasoning." Dr. Carl Sagan, an American astronomer and astrobiologist had this to say about the scientific method, "Science is a way of thinking much more than it is a body of knowledge." To me, Dr. Sagan's words have always helped place into perspective that science is not something sitting out there, holding all the answers and doing so completely infallible—quite the opposite in reality. Dr. Sagan has too many accomplishments to list here, however, his work with the effect of radiation on amino acids may come to a new understanding in 2014. There is a planned space mission to land equipment designed by Uwe Meierhenrich that will mesure certain qualities of the amino acids on the surface of a meteor. What the scientists discover could lend additional support to a theory of basic life being nudged a certain direction, adding to the possibility that life has been seeded on other habitable planets. Not just life, but life perhaps very similar to that found on planet Earth. This is a topic we will discuss at greater depth, and how it actually relates to UFOs and Wisconsin, in my following book.

Let's get one thing very clear as early on as possible, a UFO or unidentified flying object means to me quite exactly that. For some, this may be a new way of thinking, no longer blindly grouping "alien" craft with a UFO sighting. Anything that is less than identifiable, perceived as flying and appearing to be an object would be categorized as a UFO. I do not make the leap to use "UFO" interchangeably with "alien," "advanced race of beings," or even "otherworldly." Let's look at a different situation now, one where a UFO is witnessed and the reportee has experienced what they perceived to be an alien race. This is substantiated when the witness reports a creature with an inhuman form. Such was the case on July 31, 1976 when Mark, who stood in his father's farm field near Long Lake, Wisconsin, watched two green figures as they "disappeared somehow", right before his eyes. This happened immediately after he and his father watched a camper-sized craft nearly miss hitting their silo. Ideally there may be some physical evidence left behind, such as a footprint in the soft soil. The physical evidence along with witness testimony would then allow the researcher to easily and clearly follow those paths of data to the possibility it may be more than a basic UFO. Simply put, follow the facts as we could logically recognize them at the time. Alien and extraterrestrial, while not synonymous with UFO, are used interchangeably in this book to allow for an increased natural flow. What would it take for a ufologist to be contacted immediately following a sighting, just like the previous one, to then allow for verification of any physical data left behind? Of course this means UFO researchers need to be known and trusted enough by simply everyone who might ever have an experience, be easily contacted, and constantly hold the resources to travel to a sighting at a moments notice; at which point they would instantly perform a flawless forensic investigation of the scene, conduct separate interviews and so on and so forth. This is a reality not currently overpopulated, perhaps not populated at all.

Whatever UFO means to you specifically, when and where did the unidentified flying object term come from? Let's look at that question most literally. Some trace the roots of the acronym UFO now so prevalent in linguistics back to the late Captain Edward J. Ruppelt. While working operations on a United States Air Force funded investigation into unknown aerial phenomena called Project Blue Book, and the earlier Project Grudge, Captain Ruppelt made open comments on wanting to replace the term "flying saucers" with "UFO." There is some confusion whether he was laying claim to the creation of the acronym itself or merely the use of it in 1951. Others believe it may very well have been some nameless Air Force employee pitching titles for early Project Grudge. This thought is held by some that believe the working title in 1949 may have been "Unidentified Flying Objects Project Grudge" which would place it several years earlier than Captain Ruppelt's known involvement.

Charles Fort, sometimes called the "father of ufology" noted the captains' log of F. Banner in some of his works published in the early 1900s. Captain Banner recorded his observations in 1870 of a cloudlike object in the sky that was of specific structure however did not behave or disappear from view like a cloud. He noted in his log detailed observations of geometric symmetry and how it was a cloud of circular form. This observation was made quite some time before the acronym UFO was being tossed about.

Reading the captains log it seemed to me that he was struggling with what it was he was seeing. He continually spoke of the object as a cloud, but equally so repeating that it was not cloud like. Perhaps it was nothing more than an odd lenticular cloud formation as pictured next.

Lenticular cloud formation in the upper left of photograph holding a classic-looking flying-saucer shape. Photograph courtesy of Sam Roberts of www.SRobertsPhoto.com.

In modern culture people say, "I saw a UFO," and the description of events typically ends there...as if all UFOs are the same, the people who see them are the same, and it is an all-encompassing experience of the same qualities and same characteristics. Of course you and I wouldn't make this presumption. We see with Captain F. Banner, how there was no clear category or well-known baseline for the phenomenon he was witnessing. He didn't have the easy out acronym and as a result, today we have a further descriptive analysis of what he saw. His continuing back and forth description of comparing it to a cloud, however making sure the reader new it wasn't any normal cloud afforded him the opportunity to record more details of the object, as apposed to have the simple, "it was a UFO." He recorded his observations in specifics, noting details like how it moved against the wind. Below is a reproduction of a sketch purportedly by Captain F. Banner.

This is an unusual looking "cloud" to be sure. From his description in writing we could almost say it was a lenticular cloud, however we have the above sketch. This seems to reduce the likely hood that Captain Banner saw a simple lenticular cloud and without that final piece of data from his experience we may never had thought twice about his experience. Indeed from his sketch what he witnessed in 1870 could be the same thing people report today as a UFO.

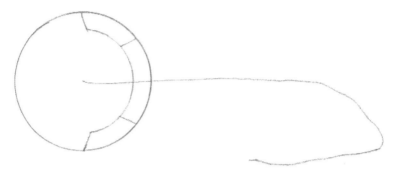

A reproduction of the original sketch by Captain F. Banner of the UFO he recorded in his log and later brought to light by Charles Fort. Redrawing by Noah Voss.

The predisposition of UFO meaning "alien" to most seems clear when I speak with pilots and air traffic controllers. The long hesitations and short answers reveal the true stigma for these professionals to have their name associated with UFO. Some of those in the field of aeronautics have moved from what most would straightforwardly call a UFO, to a UAP. In this case the UAP stands for "unidentified aerial phenomena." There are also those who are trying to start a movement for UFO to signify "unconventional flying object," in an apparent attempt to sound more middle ground and remove themselves from the tendency people have to associate UFO with alien. Most unconventional flying objects would then be theorized to be that of advanced technology from as of yet unknown origins to the general public. This may also speak to the current climate of pilots and aeronautic professionals of all types not reporting UFO sightings to any source with their names attached, if at all. When a brave heart stands up and shares his or her unusual experience related to a UFO, UAP, or whatever at this point, ufologists do have some protocols and procedures they can follow. I cover some of these generally accepted procedures with greater detail in my following UFO book. Of course if a UFO becomes identified at some point during the sighting or proceeding investigation, then it can become an IFO or "identified flying object." So what happens when the UFO gets too close and there is a whole new level of interaction going on? We get another system of categorization.

A close encounter of the first, second, and third kind are some of the well known categories for UFO experiences. From the research and investigation performed by ufologists came the need for some form of categorization of the many sightings. Before Steven Spielberg made the film Close Encounters of the Third Kind there were ufologists hard at work creating terms to help explain their research. Ufologist Dr. J. Allen Hynek brought forward this idea in his 1972 book, The UFO Experience: A Scientific Inquiry that categorizes a UFO witness's experience. Let's concisely give relation to just some of the different classifications. A close encounter of the "first" kind can be any distant sighting of an unidentified flying object, where that is the complete extent of the interaction between witness and UFO. A close encounter of the "second" kind involves evidence left behind such as, crop circles—circular shapes seemingly pressed or weaved into vegetation such as crops growing in a farmer's field. Another physical or trace evidence could be radiation burns, historically found on persons who have gotten within close proximity of a UFO. A close encounter of the "third" kind is when the witness views an apparent being in direct relation with the UFO. If you're looking for some added challenge with this book, when reading through the reports starting in the next chapter, keep those three in the back of your mind and see if you can't sort the reports into the appropriate categories. There are however two main systems of categorization in the field and with them come dozens of sub-categories for any set of variables. Ufologists can use these categories to efficiently move through the increasing wealth of data in the field, including searching for connecting theories drawn from categorized experiences.

One of these categories of experiences, a close encounter of the third kind, can lead to what is called an abduction. An abduction comes when a person is taken from their normal Earthly environment by what they believe to be an alien race. Said person then becomes an experiencer or abductee reportedly aboard a UFO.

Seventy-four thousand Wisconsinites consider themselves to have been abducted by aliens, how well is your memory! Got your attention? In a recent Roper Poll 3,700,000 Americans claimed to have been abducted by aliens. That statistic in itself may be startling to say the least. I did some simple math (took a dozen tries) in my head (with five different calculators) and ended up just dividing the Roper Poll results with the number of states in America, 50 (I double checked, still 50). So in reality that number could be much higher or lower since it is quite unlikely the abduction experience is evenly distributed throughout 50 geographical states or that every experience is reported. Let's not cruise over that number, as potentially 74,000 Wisconsin residents believe that they have been abducted by aliens. Really, I'm a ufologist, and have been studying this stuff for around two decades and it still surprises me how large that reported number is. Now I know that number was not too precisely arrived at, but let's move forward with it as an approximation for the sake of time and for the fact that there are no better-finished statistics, in my opinion, of this real-life example. So let's bring this number into your own backyard. With 54,310 total square miles in Wisconsin, divided by our abductees, we get 1.363 persons per square mile (almost 1 out of every 68 people) in Wisconsin who believe they have been abducted. How many people live in your neighborhood, your city, go to your school or get paid to be in your work place? If you're bored sometime, try opening up the conversation to UFOs and see who comes forward with a story. What of our Canadian neighbors to the North? If we are seeing things here in Wisconsin what are they seeing across the Lake? Approximately 3 million Canadians claim to have seen UFOs, maybe on their way to abduct the 3.7 million Americans. While many of these abduction experiences shown in the popular media are of people being levitated from their night-time slumber and pulled through an open window, many other abduction scenarios have been reported right here in Wisconsin. Whether driving down a road, canoeing on a lake with friends, or walking through the woods, people have reported abduction experiences during all these activities. After the abduction takes place then what and why? We'll avoid the why for now but the what has been reported as anything from harmless trips to far-off planets, not so harmless medical experimentation, too that of coupling with strangers aboard the UFO. Whatever the particular experience not all of these persons remember the abduction experience immediately following it. Some merely observe missing time, only to have the full experience gradually slip into their consciousness over days or even years.

What is this missing time, sometimes called time loss? There are those UFO witnesses who seem to notice a period of time they cannot account for. Time loss is believed by some researchers to be directly caused by the alien beings manipulation of the experiencers' perception via erasing their abduction experience. Such was the case in a similar report from Travis Walton on November 25, 1975. As six coworkers looked on, Mr. Walton was seemingly struck dead by a beam of light that emanated from an unidentified flying object in the Arizona mountains. His friends, fearing for their own lives, sped away from the scene only to have a massive manhunt begin for their then-lost friend. Mr. Walton phoned his friends to pick him up over 30 miles from where anyone had last seen him. To Mr. Walton, only hours had seemed to pass. He had missing time, an entire five days worth. His fantastic story touches on some of his recovered memories and was later made into a book and a movie by the same name, Fire in the Sky.

During a time loss experience, abductees who recall undergoing surgical-like experiments sometimes report the placement of implants into their bodies. These implants have later been removed by human medical doctors. Of these procedures that are monitored by ufologists, the video documentation remain in the researchers archives. There is still much unknown about the implants themselves however some ufologists report radio frequency signals being temporarily broadcast from some.

Hypnosis, as defined by the American Heritage Dictionary, is "an artificially induced altered state of consciousness, characterized by heightened suggestibility and receptivity to direction." James Braid coined the word "hypnotism" in his 1843 published Neurypnology several years after working out the idea following a "mesmerism" demonstration popular during that time. There was then, and is now, a perceptible controversy surrounding the actualities of hypnosis and any potential uses. In ufology there is a movement for hypnotherapy regression or repressed memory therapy to be used. The idea is, by using hypnosis a practitioner may help a person recall fuller the events that may now be clouded or hidden from recallable memory. Such is the apparent case with missing time. This method may be used for extracting memories of supposed alien encounters out of the hiding place that either the human psyche has placed them in for the mind's own protection, or from where they have been hidden by a malevolent entity. In an effort to keep my readers as informed as space allows, it should be stated here that currently the American Psychological Association and the American Medical Association both caution against using hypnosis when dealing with such matters as suspected childhood disturbances. These alien abduction occurrences may have happened at an older age, thus removing a major sensitive variable in hypno-regression however, this word of caution from some leading mental health organizations shows they feel that, without subsequent and outside supportive evidence, it is difficult at best to distinguish the truth of the memories brought forward. That being said, many abduction experiencers have found this method to be effective for bringing to light what they feel was their true full experience during abduction scenarios.

Some in the UFO field might consider a theory that does include hypnosis but excludes any actual alien entities. A bit more on this thought shortly. A supporting factor in this theory does put the past actions of our own government onto the table of possibility. Certain United States Code lists restrictions on use of human subjects for testing of chemical or biological agents. You can view this code yourself by referencing Title 50 War and National Defense, Chapter 32 Chemical and Biological Warfare Program, Section 1520a Restrictions on use of human subjects for testing of chemical or biological agents. To me, on the surface it seems to address the situation of outlawing the act of our government performing secret experiments against its own civilian population.

```
(a) Prohibited activities
The Secretary of Defense may not conduct
(directly or by contract)—
(1) any test or experiment involving the use
of a chemical agent or biological agent on a
civilian population; or
(2) any other testing of a chemical agent or
biological agent on human subjects.
```

A reproduction of section 1520a showing "Prohibited Activities." Reproduction by Noah Voss

However there are three wide exemptions included in this code that seems to restrict, not outlaw the act. Indeed portion of the codes title, "Section 1520a" reads "Restrictions" implying that there are something's quite acceptable.

```
(b) Exceptions
Subject to subsections (c), (d), and (e) of
this section, the prohibition in subsection
(a) of this section does not apply to a test
or experiment carried out for any of the fol-
lowing purposes:
(1) Any peaceful purpose that is related to
a medical, therapeutic, pharmaceutical, agri-
cultural, industrial, or research activity.
(2) Any purpose that is directly related to
protection against toxic chemicals or biolog-
ical weapons and agents.
(3) Any law enforcement purpose, including
any purpose related to riot control.
```

A reproduction of section 1520a showing "Exceptions." Reproduction by Noah Voss

I am not attempting to prove anything in particular other than to introduce, what is for some, a very unrecognizable reality. There are entire books that reference page after page of documented near outright atrocities perpetrated by the American government on its own civilian population. In this reality lies the theory that under these exemptions some experimentations have been carried out on the American public. Even though it seems some sections of this code may have been altered in recent years under certain repeals, the "exceptions" stood for more years than not. Another thought out there, or maybe out-there-thought, is one including governmental conspiracies and hypnosis. With our new potential perspective on reality let's take a deeper look into this missing time, abduction theory that has our own nameless government organizations included in the twisted web.

Perhaps not surprising, there are as many theories on UFO phenomena as there are people researching it. If subscribing to any one of these theories, then one might say the government is aware and able to utilize this hypno-regression on people who witnessed top secret military technology. After all, what are people other than biological entities who are moving thanks to chemical processes constantly happening inside them?

For instance, say you find yourself all alone driving down a long and lonely country road, when all of a sudden a craft of unbelievable proportions and motion appears in the sky ahead of you. Impossible to miss, your next thought is impossible to forget—for now. You then find yourself sitting in your car, still in the driver's seat but now, pulled off to the side of the road, engine off, and the UFO gone. Whether an alien craft or advanced terrestrial technology, this theory would have the powers that be simply covering the memory of the sighting with an experience of alien interaction. This would not always allow the witness to fair well with the inputted alien experience, but does keep the top secret information unknown. The government, concerned you might tell the wrong person about your sighting, such as an enemy of the state, forces them to create an unbelievable scenario for you to tell instead. This could also be spun in the direction for your own safety. Said government might hide the sensitive material now in your head, as it could be extracted by not-so-nice means, should the wrong people find out what you might have witnessed. Some abduction reports have additionally odd characteristics such as experiencers finding their clothing on inside out immediately following time loss. This could be an attempt to feed fuel to debunkers about these reports by a manipulative government procedure, showing that aliens could traverse great distances with their advanced technologies, but cannot figure out how to re-dress an abductee. Of course, please take note that this theory for many does not exclude the existence of UFOs or extraterrestrial races of beings. Quite the contrary for most who can find at least some logic in this idea.

Using the same example as before, that governmental craft that you witnessed while driving down that lonely road might be piloted by a human however, might not be completely terrestrial technology. Those following this theory hold that the alien technology was indeed either: stolen, recovered, or exchanged from said alien race. Maybe even exchanged for uninter-rupted experiments with the next person to drive down the wrong lonely road. Though perhaps not quite yet a theory as much as it is literally an idea allowing some circumstantial data to flow together, and in this context the governmental related points thus far, are indeed closer by definition to a story. Even if an intriguing one, worthy of further investigation, I have not and will not in this book scrutinize every angle, cite multiple credible sources in order to strive for an irrefutable end product, aimed at convincing the most stringent of skeptics. I am, however, motivated to inform the most casual reader in the UFO phenomena of some wide spread theories. Regardless of the theory or entities involved, if there is a secret being kept what would the cost be?

Looking at only one area of the U.S. government where such a secret project could potentially be, OpenTheGovernment.org finds a 2005 acquisition budget of $315.5 billion for the Department of Defense or D.O.D. The D.O.D. earmarks 17% or $53.6 billion for secret or classified operations. Regardless of the costs for creating new secrets, the estimated expense for keeping old ones runs around $8 billion a year according to the "Information Security Oversight Office," compiled by OpenTheGovernment.org. Throwing around these large numbers proves nothing in itself other than perhaps potential. How much would it cost to keep you quiet? How much would it take for you to keep someone else quiet? Obviously this is speculation based upon half-visible facts. We can also look back through our own history for other indicators, which on the surface at least show the climate of acceptance or standing of the UFO field. What that standing reveals is of course, open to interpretation. In 1979, Wisconsin State Senator William Proxmire was in such disapproval of a pro-posed appropriations bill that he awarded it his infamous "Golden Fleece" award. The appropriations bill if passed would go on to budget the new NASA program under the direction of SETI or Search for Extra-Terrestrial Inelegance. The program would utilize several approaches in an experiment, to monitor for communications of intelligent life off of planet Earth. Proxmire's, "Golden Fleece" award was personally handed out to those who he felt were wastefully spending the taxpayer's monies. The funds for SETI were dutifully removed from the bill. NASA was still able to budget some finances for the SETI cause through other means until the 1980s when Proxmire again was made aware of this. He spoke up on the matter and had the funds terminated without argument. The discussion would eventually come in the form of numerous scientific world leaders that included seven Nobel laureates. The following petition and an open dialogue between the Senator and Dr. Carl Sagan allowed for an informed decision and the funds to eventually resume. The federal resources were again removed from the

SETI programs, ultimately leaving it to operate as a privately funded organization.

For now, that is enough picking on our government with arguable accusations of half-explained theories. Perhaps we will find someday they are not all completely baseless, or precisely just that. To conclude our discussion here on hypnosis in the UFO field, it is if nothing else a very intriguing area of study with much more to learn before we can fully understand the scope of the human mind. Clear cut data in the UFO field is a rare and appreciated occurrence. One such clear data pool does come from when and where UFOs are reported.

A "UFO wave" sometimes mentioned as a "UFO flap" in UFO literature refers to any period of time where the reported UFO accounts are greater than the normal running average. There are several UFO waves many researchers frequently speak of, including the 1896–1897 Airship Mystery that had not only dozens of sightings right here in Wisconsin but in at least 18 other states. 1947 came with a crash in Roswell, New Mexico, and an infamous sighting in the North Cascade Mountain Range of Washington State from where the term "flying saucer" may have been coined. The year 1952 arguably has the highest number of UFO reports, including one with film footage of unidentified flying objects appearing above the White House. July the same year the sightings taking place above our nation's capitol were reported by multiple airport radar stations, passengers and crew of commuter airlines, along with F-94 fighter jets scrambled continuously to intercept this interpreted threat. A press conference directed by Major General John A. Samford stated the official explanation for the UFOs to be temperature inversions. The press at the time seemed to accept wholeheartedly the explanation, and it was left for a few to carry on asking pointed questions for the data that didn't fit the temperature inversion "explanation." It was later noted in Project Blue Book that these sightings were labeled as "unknown," even when other reports in the project's findings were labeled as temperature inversions. An interesting contradiction maybe? Wisconsin was no stranger to the 1952 wave, with our very own F-89 interceptor jet from Madison's Truax Air Field that disappeared over Lake Superior while racing to investigate a UFO. Jumping ahead to 1997, Phoenix Arizona. It is perhaps conservatively estimated that more than 10,000 people witnessed a UFO pass directly over the city. I was on the scene within weeks and can personally attest to the wide spread sighting. These sightings were only some of many UFO reported during waves documented throughout America. What follows are more than 120 reports from Wisconsin, some had while the country was in the middle of a UFO wave and some, when there were no other reports at all.

"RIINNNGG!"

The bell rings one final time as school is finished for now. With Alice Cooper shouting "schooooool is out foooor ever!" through your head, the ufology 1-0-whatever is now behind us. Much as with life, and whether you saw the prior analogy as high school or college, you have graduated into a world of equal uncertainty. As with your own very real and sometimes very unavoidable life situations, the learning hopefully did not stop there. Quite the contrary as some would argue (especially those still in school) that they could learn more by doing something else. If to become learned is accomplished through education, to become wise is reached through living. Let us then live vicariously and hopefully become wiser together from the following persons brave and bold enough to share their very real life experiences.

Top 5 UFO Hot Spots!

A Look Into Wisconsin' UFO Hot Spots

"After success has been reached in anything, the necessary
things seem obvious enough to all.
The discovery of the obvious is a slow and costly process."

Inventor A.E. Dolbear
Professor of Physics, Astronomy and Natural Sciences

Why choose these for the "Top Five"?

I searched my archived databases with certain criteria in mind when I sat down to write this section. I wanted to find areas that had concentrated numbers of reported UFO sightings or unexplained "alien-type" experiences. Narrowing down those results, I remained intent to find the all-too-often unobtainable uniqueness. Detailed reports of the experiences, including a thorough synopsis of events and object descriptions, helped raise an area to contention. I searched for reports that had locations people can still visit and interact with today. For example, at least three locations on this list still have active festivals that celebrate its connection to UFOs. Include all of these criteria, stretch them over a period of time, and you have got your current "Top Five Hot Spots!"

I've been searching through UFOwisconsin.com archives for years with this project in mind, along with the files of Project Blue Book for a lifetime, days on end in each Project Grudge, Project Sign, and Project Twinkle. I've spent half a lifetime roaming the state, personally visiting as many locations with UFO sightings or legends as resources allow. With on those trips was the life work of many ufologists before me. These five locations have several things in common with each other that have made them unique and especially worth documenting. It wasn't an easy choice, though since this is a personal list, my opinion is what mattered in the end. What meant most to me after weighing all the above variables was for there to be some sort of ongoing UFO community. Something there for people, who, with this book in hand, can still visit and interact with on some level. What follows in the next five locations is an overview of as many cases that had enough relevant documentation to include and space allow. I hope this helps illustrate to the reader the vast quantity of sightings coming out of Wisconsin and what that potentially means to the average citizen's perception of reality on finite and infinite terms.

I will only interject my thoughts where absolutely necessary to help make clear any apparent or perceived connection between multiple sightings, developing patterns, possible known explanation and or relation of experiences to those that were had outside of the state. In my subsequent book I have been afforded the opportunity to reach deep into each experience in the Top Five UFO Experiences. Due to the greater documentation and detailed research I am able to pull out of those five experiences, profoundly fantastic UFO experiences from right here in Wisconsin. I take that opening to share expanded thoughts and additionally exhaustive possibilities on the points in the experiences as they become clear.

Without further ado and no longer any more delay, let us get to the top five locals as I now see them...

#5 Milwaukee, Wisconsin

Currently weighing in with more than 60 UFO reports online at UFOwisconsin.com, Milwaukee covers a lot of land. It also holds a fair amount of people and along with it perhaps the greater opportunity for reports to be made. Milwaukee brings an additionally unique perspective to our Top Five list, with the introduction of a large body of water, Lake Michigan. This adds several variables, such as people who gather to enjoy a panoramic view of an unobstructed horizon. Looking at our reports outlined in this section it would seem while having the normal development, countryside and roadways for sightings to be made from, we would have to include shipping lanes and flight paths provided by Lake Michigan. Starting from the beginning, chronologically speaking, here are some of the peoples' experiences had there.

The Wisconsin State Journal reported on November 17, 1870, that several University students in Milwaukee were witness to a "Spiral Meteor." Thanks to researchers like Chad Lewis and his book Hidden Headlines of Wisconsin we have multiple stories of such known occurrences. The reporting on the event is quite detailed, including, "It fell from near the zenith toward the south-east, and one peculiarity of its descent was that it came down spirally." While not exactly what we might consider a UFO, I do feel this helps show there were still rational accounts of unusual phenomena in the Wisconsin sky. Even with the arguably limited knowledge on the cosmos during the 1800s, we still find these non sensationalized reports. This could lend some perspective to those reports we do find that are a bit more unique in nature. Some 26 years later there were new reports of things in our skies that weren't as easily accounted for.

Starting around November 1896 a great wave of mysterious airship sightings swept across the country. Any commonality among reports seemed to describe a balloon or early dirigible. Descriptions ranged from cigar shaped, to huge balls of fire, even an egg on its side. Reading the documents of the time one would find that witnesses included Wisconsin Judges, good church going folk, and those not predisposed to drink whisky. Some had estimated the speeds at more than 100 mph and going against the wind. From the Pacific to the Atlantic, and most points in between, at least 18 states had documented reports of unknown flying machines in its skies. Wisconsin was not the exception and even the Ringling Brothers in Baraboo were thought to be the source at one point.

The Madison Democrat, Tuesday morning edition April 13, 1897. Article in the upper most right corner titled "AIRSHIP EXPLAINED."

As the image above shows, the "AIRSHIP EXPLAINED" article was front page news at the time. The article goes on to site "Railroad men..." as the most specific source for insinuating the circus be the culprit of the great airship wave of sightings. Reportedly there were sightings of it hovering "Suspiciously Long Over the Winter Quarters at Baraboo," of those "RINGLING RAZZLEDAZZLERS." It is a colorful read to say the least, but not full of what I would consider factual proof. There were unexplained sightings all across central and southern Wisconsin. In David Michael Jacobs book The UFO Controversy in America he documented witness testimony from Milwaukee. It was reported that possibly thousands of persons watched "the machine, or whatever it was," as it hovered over the city hall "as if signaling to the earth." By May of 1897 there had been too many reports of sightings to count, rides purportedly given to onlookers, conversations had from airship to ground, and even letters dropped from Wisconsin's skies to the Earth below. Those letters implicated Thomas Edison in the great mystery and were documented in the Milwaukee Sentinal. Even though over one hundred years have passed, an agreed upon explanation for the airship mystery remains elusive.

One sighting we have early on from the Milwaukee area may better be called an experience. In 1947 it was documented by newspapers as far away as Texas.

The San Antonio Express ran the headline above regarding the Grafton, Wisconsin 1947 mysterious object.

Father Joseph Brasky was pictured in one of the papers reportedly holding the crashed UFO. The FBI was contacted and the story instantly became layered with possibility. The Father in Grafton, located just north of Milwaukee, was the firsthand witness. Reports from the time say he "heard a whirring noise" external his parish. It was followed by a "thump" that drew him outside to investigate. Some accounts of the story detail how the UFO hit the lightning rod on top of the church as it crashed to the ground. This entire event has been placed by history as a hoax due to the UFO in this case being later identified as a circular saw blade. From the available accounts of that day it is unclear to me whether this best fits in a "hoax" category or rather was merely misidentified by an inquisitive but less than strict scientific observer. Perhaps the reason this story got as much attention as it did was the fact that only days later another little UFO sighting was reported from the sleepy town of Roswell. The Roswell, New Mexico, crash story gained worldwide attention with the official July 8, United States Air Force press release from the Roswell area stating the capture of a flying saucer. This was changed the following day with another official release, detailing a different reality on the situation. No saw blade in that experience, though a weather balloon seems to have been added.

From saw blades and weather balloons to flying dumbbells, the next sighting in 1966 nearly produced photographic proof of the experience. Bruce W., now a grown man, recounted the experience to UFOwisconsin.com that happened to him many years earlier. He and his friend were at a park on East Linus Street in Milwaukee. Stargazing with a pair of binoculars was a good way to pass the time and to normally stay out of trouble. The park has now made way to new development, but the memory of the night has always stayed with Bruce. It was around 9 pm and a clear night, perfect for watching the sky. They noticed from the north an object "with a green light on one end and a red light on the other." Immediately the story screams a nighttime sighting of a most conventional airplane. However as they continued to watch the object, two more blurry lights became visible. When viewed through the binoculars "you could see they were connected with a black bar." He remembers thinking how it looked like "the old dumbbells weight lifters used to use." The UFO continued on to the south, flying along "totally silent." The event was so startling they ran across the street and got Bruce's brother to witness the object with them. They returned, camera in hand, with just enough time for everyone to watch for about another "10 seconds" then the object "shot straight up and was gone!!" Of course they all couldn't believe their eyes and knew that this was anything but conventional. The brother was able to click off a few quick photos before the object snapped from sight. When the photographs were developed, they revealed less detail than was available watching the UFO that night with their unaided eye. Unfortunately I was unable to obtain any of the photographs and it is unlikely they even still exist.

Re-creation provided by witness of 1974 Pewaukee sighting for her report submitted to www.UFOwisconsin.com.

No photographs for this 1974 sighting, however the next best thing was available, artist renderings. The report came in from a western Milwaukee suburb called Pewaukee. Lori M. recounted to UFOwisconsin.com an event that happened when she was around 12 years old. While at her home, she first recalls a "blue light flooding in the doors" that drew her outside searching for the source. In her yard just above "the top of a tree" she found it.
Lori recounted, "I couldn't believe my eyes, there was a round saucer shaped UFO." It was just "hovering above the tree." Lori was quick to point out that at the age of 12 she doubted very much that she had any concept of what a UFO was. The "round saucer shaped" object had "round different colored lights going around the perimeter of the ship." The lights blinked "alternating on and off" and reminded her of "Christmas tree lights." To the best of her recollection the lights were "red, yellow, blue and green." Upon seeing this craft she yelled to her "little brother and cousin to come outside." The three of them were able to watch the object for approximately "ten minutes with our mouths hanging open not saying a word." As Lori and her family members continued to watch the object she had the feeling "it seemed to be

watching us too." With that the UFO "slowly started to float away from us, made a 90 degree turn and shot off extremely fast and disappeared." Looking through her memory she clearly recalled that the UFO "made no sound" and it was around 9 or 10 in the evening when they first witnessed the craft. The adults returned home shortly after, and the kids enthusiastically attempted to recount the strange events. The parents, assuredly tired after their own full day, hurried them to bed seemingly not interested.

It was the summer of 1975 and our next witness was again a younger one. At nine years old she was a professed tomboy and curious by nature. She and her friends would regularly play football in a field in their hometown of Milwaukee. She remembers seeing this "thing" hovering nearby seemingly watching them. It would change shapes and fade in and out of sight, she reported. Similar to the sighting a year earlier this witness also felt as if there was some connection or communication between her and this "thing." All the other kids had chosen dinner over football by this time yet, she remained, continuing to watch until it zoomed out of view. She remembers seeing it on and off growing up in that neighborhood, sometimes seeing "windows" going around the body of the craft. She speaks of many different colors that were indefinable and had an almost crystal deflection of light affect by the body of the craft. Our reporting experiencer recalls only recently, "I have had the pleasure to see them up close checking me out in my sleep." When reportedly awaken she found "a connect the dots kind of starman bending over me." The being was not alone but with a "smaller one walking towards him, touching his arm telling him it was time to go now." With that they left, leaving our witness confused and openly unsure on if "this was real" or not. She went on to share, "There is no history of anything weird in my family on both sides" and that she can no longer talk to her friends about such an odd "occurrence." For further discussion and greater scope please see Appendix A.

Southwestern Milwaukee is home to the suburb of Muskego. On August 7th in 1980 the Wisconsin Voice Journal ran a short story titled "UFOs Reported." The witness was a sophisticated six-year-old girl by the name of Tiffany. She was at first simply thought to have a healthy active imagination according to her mother Shirley G. Then Shirley was not as sure it was just her daughter's imagination after Tiffany "drew detailed pictures of the round object." After some time her mother, most likely a little scared her daughter was being visited by UFOs or at least more certain something "real" was going on, contacted the police. Shirley was disappointed with the response she got from the local police department, but was not through reaching out for help. She went on to contact General Mitchell Air Field of Milwaukee.

Of course the official response of the airport was "no comment." This could be an easy sighting to nearly dismiss out of hand. In fact several other organizations had done so, figuring it was no more than an active imagination of a healthy youngster. That is until August 4. This was less than a day after the original sighting had been made and the news had not yet spread. The second report eventually made its way to UFOwisconsin.com and spoke of a pedestrian sighting something similar and in the same town as the first sighting.

As the person on foot made their way up Lincoln Avenue, they watched as "from over one of the buildings a great orange orange-yellow fireball slowly crossed over the street." The witness didn't report anything audible even though, "it did not look to be very high up." It was a self-proclaimed "awesome" experience for the witness and a crucial piece to our puzzle. Is there a connection to be made between the two sightings? Unfortunately, too little is known about specifics in either case that would otherwise allow us to reach a strong conclusion.

August 25, 1985, brought about a very similar sighting. It was reported in the Wisconsin Advisor Press on the 29th of August. The publication had been receiving inquiries about a "UFO flying about 20 feet over the treetops." The time of the sighting was around 6:15 pm as the object was "revolving and making all sorts of reflections" according to witnesses. This was in a southeastern Milwaukee suburb called Cudahy that runs right next to Muskego. One witness was a gentleman who while again on the local sidewalks, saw something worth noting. He wasn't the only witness to this sighting either as, "there was a fellow in the next block who saw it, too." Unfortunately this other witness has yet to come forward, however, "he followed it as it turned the corner about a block away." Hopefully this inquisitive stranger's curiosity will bring him to UFOwisconsin.com so we may all know more of the story.

We don't have to go far for the next sighting. It is March 18, 1989, at 8:45 pm we find ourselves still in the small suburb of Cudahy. A sole witness reported watching a "gray cigar-shaped object" almost directly overhead. It was "surrounded by a shimmering lite" and approximately 1,000 feet in the air as the witness continued to watch. It was a short-lived sighting, maybe 10 seconds total. The cigar-shaped UFO "went into a vertical climb" and was gone within moments. Many UFO sightings seem to be plagued with brief viewings, and at times leaving the witness only enough time to realize what the object wasn't. These cigar-shaped sightings have recently been made the focus of much scrutiny. Photographs and video footage showing similarly shaped objects are regularly shown to be insects or birds after extensive and expensive investigation. This is not always the case of course, and when the sighting takes place with the unaided eye, the likely hood of an insect or bird being the cause is reduced greatly. For further discussion and greater scope please see Appendix B.

Meteor showers are something that the meteorologist on the five o'clock news seem to mention every year. Jeff C. was leaving a friend's house in Milwaukee around 10 o'clock on the evening of October 2, 1994. He shared with UFOwisconsin.com that he remembered hearing there was going to be meteor shower that night, and that the newscaster had said the best part of the sky to view the shower would be the north. He admitted to being a bit turned around finding himself in a different part of the city. Jeff searched for the North Star in the dark sky. Thinking that it would be one of the few stars visible against the city lights, he gazed upward quickly noticing one "star" shining over the rest. Jeff watched as it "started getting brighter." It also seemed to be moving. As it "got closer, no sound was being made" and he went on to say it "was moving slow." It got so close it became apparent that it was indeed not a star, but a craft of some sort. Jeff described the mistaken North Star as having "a white light in the center and 3 red lights making a triangle" surrounding that. From the UFO's movement he assumed "they were all one object." The lights all stayed in "perfect formation" with no discernable change in distance between any of them. As soon as his wits returned to him, he called to his friend who he had just left, "to get him out here to see." But just as he yelled, the object disappeared, "gone in an instant." This triangular shaped craft may not have ever visited Jeff again, but as you'll read, similar crafts are reported throughout the state.

Just six days later in Milwaukee, Douglas K. had his own sighting. He told UFOwisconsin.com that he was getting into his car after church when something caught his eye. Something, above the horizon but not far up in the sky. His first thought was "a low flying plane that was on fire." It was around 8 o'clock in the evening and fairly dark out. As he continued to watch, it looked as though it was "heading straight toward" him. Douglas thought maybe it wasn't on fire but just had "a bright light going." He recounted, "as it got closer it didn't make a sound and seemed to have the lights dim down." The lights were not as intense as when he first noticed it but "it had a huge, circular white light in the center." He thought the craft size was "huge" and it wasn't too high in the air at this point. The large white light in the center was "surrounded by 3 smaller red lights." The lights formed a "triangle around the white one," he remembered. As it went overhead Douglas thought that it may have momentarily stopped. He pulled his gaze from the

UFO and "looked around to see if anyone else saw this." There was no one else in the parking lot at this time and when he returned his eyes to the skies "the object was gone without a trace." This makes two quite similar sightings within days, in the same city area and nearly the same time of night.

Still October, still 1994, and a new sighting comes in from a boy scout waiting for his dad to pick him up after a meeting. Three sightings now—I believe we officially have ourselves a small UFO wave. It was again around 9 pm when our reporting witness first noticed what he assumed to be a bright airplane in the sky. Our witness thought it was strange that a very low-flying plane "didn't make a sound." He continued to watch as it moved overhead. Again we have a description of "a huge white, circular light in the center, and 3 smaller red, circular lights." All three witnesses have gone out of their way to describe how the smaller red lights made a "triangle shape around the white light." This scout had also mentioned that he thought the UFO may have paused in the sky as it moved over him. This witness, like the others, started to look for a collaborating observer. One can almost see his excitement turn to confusion as he looked at others in the parking lot all going about their business as usual. Trying to quickly come to terms with how no one else was noticing the craft, he then looked back in the sky and "it was gone." It is worth noting that it seems these last two witnesses could have been in the same parking lot at the same time watching the same object. Unfortunately due to the documentation offered, it is impossible to tell, though I know it is not unheard of Boy Scout meetings to take place in churches. When bringing up possibilities there are always many. I'm sure it's not the case here nonetheless one could, with some ease, send in two reports to lend collaborating evidence to their case. The reasoning still complete speculation but for any number of reasons from dissuading any ridicule received in the personal life of the reportee, to simply really trying to sell a hoax. It is these variables that ufologists can hope to minimize by conducting face-to-face interviews with reportees.

October 10, 1995, we join our next reporting witness as he drives down the road. Highway 43 is in actuality also an Interstate in the southwestern part of Wisconsin. As it reaches into the Milwaukee area, the gentleman reported seeing a "large, bright blue light." It streaked by his car as he continued driving, then began to descend. As it lowered in the sky he watched in amazement as it turned and continued on crossing the road just ahead of him. Before he lost sight of the UFO, he thought it flashed brightly. His final thought on the whole experience: "Bizarre!" The face value of the report seems to tell of a meteorite's final moments, however, the reported trajectory of the object would prove difficult if not outright impossible for known meteorite behaviors. This could be possibly explained by the continued motion of the car resulting in there only being a perceived movement in the course of the light. Also the meteorite could have fallen apart allowing for some odd trajectory patterns. Without further investigation and research we can only speculate as to this witness's experience and thank him for sharing it.

Business owner, computer artist, amateur astronomer, and avid sky watcher on June 1, 1997, also became witness to a UFO. It was only two in the afternoon when our witness and his roommate "noticed a very large object north of" their apartment. The next thing observed was a "reddish hue, and was moving fairly slow." It kept on the same eastward path while they watched "two smaller objects circling around it." Grabbing a nearby 4-1/2-inch telescope they "managed to see one of the objects." It was difficult to keep it in the telescope's narrow field of view but "it appeared to be somewhat like an airplane, but more like 'ship' shaped." The estimated size of the UFO was "1/2 to 1 mile long." Not something that should be easily missed, but as the witness went on to say that it was unusually slim. Estimating that the edge was "probably 40-50 feet" thin. Needless to say, our witness was shocked at the size of the UFO. He included a plea in his communication to UFOwisconsin.com, "I would like to know if anyone else in the area reported anything." We're still waiting for someone to answer the request.

The next sighting on September 25, 1998, was not the first time a bluish UFO was spotted. Our next witness is a cargo pilot, a job with notorious regularity. For the pilot, flying between Milwaukee and Eau Claire nightly has created familiarity to the route. Pilot and copilot both first noticed "a very intense light." They described it to be "a light blue in color" as it moved "directly overhead" their plane. The glowing blue UFO continued on "north bound over the northern horizon." This was of course a wider view of the horizon, than most are accustomed to, at 12:40 am and 6,000 feet above the ground. The pilot found it interesting that, "there was absolutely no tail associated with this craft." The report lists the pilot as saying "the size was that of a pea" and I can only assume he is using the tried and true method of comparing an object relative to something else held at arm's length. Basically if you held a pea, in this example, at arm's length it would have been approximately the same size of the object in the sky, relative to your position. The speed was given as "slower than a...meteor, but faster than a satellite." Indeed the odd bluish orb-like UFO is reported at least ten other times on www.UFOwisconsin.com alone: summer 1974, October 20 1999, November 16 1999, March 19 2001, March 31 2001, June 9 2001, May 1 2003, December 1 2003, February 11 2004, and November 13 2004. From the little data we have it is difficult at best to postulate with any level of accuracy what this truly means. Perhaps those witnesses who report seeing blue lights on UFOs that they have watched at closer distances grow brighter at higher altitudes, or their blue light is simply more easily seen at far distances. Again, without further data we are not able to formulate a more complete theory. For further discussion and greater scope please see Appendix C.

I received a very detailed report from the night of October 15, 1998, at UFOwisconsin.com. While there was some blue light recounted, it was only the beginning in our next report from "I'm a real skeptic." Our forty-some-thing-year-old female witness was outside with the family's dog for the last time that night. This was like any other night around 10:30, with her spouse already in bed she stood waiting for her dog to finish outside, while enjoying the stars. The sky was clear and she was facing a "northeasterly direction" when "an enormous flying craft appeared." Our witness stressed the just appeared part in her extensive report, continuing to say "almost as if it had been 'Star Wars-like uncloaked'." She observed and remembered several things right away like its "seeming closeness to the earth" the "relative silence" and the "almost COMICAL display of two huge single-row banks of lights."

Artist rendering by the witness's husband for the October 1998 sighting in their report submitted to www.UFOwisconsin.com. Witness noted that the color should probably be black not silver.

The craft itself was described as triangle in shape. The side of the craft our witness could see "looked almost exactly like a row of lights on police cars." She said the colors were quite clearly "red, clear and blue." She continued watching from her yard in Port Washington. Thinking how odd it was that she was allowed to see this, assuming it was some top secret government project of the United States, "they sure want to be seen!" She hesitated, thinking a witness for collaboration on this strange sight would be crucial, but felt as if the UFO was going to be gone at any moment. Wanting to get everything she could from this "once-in-a-lifetime experience" she stayed and watched from the shadows of her house. She had jumped there out of instinct when the craft first appeared in the sky. It was close enough to her that at one point she wondered if she could wave or signal the craft somehow. Feeling that a response back would validate this real experience somehow, she then hesitated, maybe making her experience too real. She resisted, her mind was racing, searching for all the observations possible before the craft disappeared. She went on to say that not possessing the "advanced physics/mathematical skills to measure items based upon horizon/angle, etc." she did her best comparing the object to other things in her line of sight.

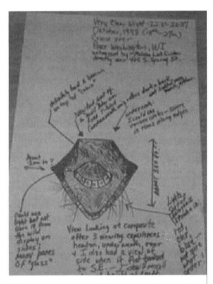

Illustration created by the witness' husband after the October 1998 Port Washington sighting for their report submitted to www.UFOwisconsin.com.

She thought the object's width was "150-200 feet" and "front-to-rear, perhaps 200-250 ft." She thought at first impression it was "a triangle" but when seen from the perspective of "directly underneath it," maybe more of a "pentagon with a flair" and finally her "last impression" was of a "pentagon with enough of a flair to be considered an arrowhead." She also observed what she took to be "either windows or perhaps black reflective surfaces." The craft performed a "flat bank" and headed out to Lake Michigan. Even though it banked right over head there was still never any "exhaust/exhaust noise—only a low humming." She put the noise level another way, if a "helicopter's noise being a '10', then this craft, many times the helicopter's size, was barely a '1 to 2' in noise level." As it moved off toward Lake Michigan she again made a great observation "the rear section of 'arrowhead' had a luminous red 'grill'." Some time had passed when I received an update from the witness. She spoke of a "bare patch of lawn" that for "several years" was "totally barren." It was approximately "10-12 feet from where" the witness was standing when she watched the craft that night. Admittedly she didn't know if this was at all connected to the sighting. There was one thing for certain, there was a motivated individual behind this nearly 2,000 word report that included numerous reproductions of the UFO. Indeed I have had several communications with her over the years now and whatever experience caused the motivations, clearly she was extremely compelled by the incident. One connection many witnesses immediately make to their sighting is potential government involvement. Patterns in UFOlogy can be fleeting so even those that focus on the witnesses more than the UFO still deserve scrutiny.

From Port Washington down the road to Greendale. About five minutes into the witness's drive home from work they noticed "a diamond or an arrow head" shaped object in the dark sky. 2:35 in the morning normally allows for a relaxing drive home. This evening it instantly turns terribly frightening, so much so our witness "had to pull over to the side of the road." The UFO was flying very low and was as dark as the sky behind it. The outline was noticeable due to a "dim blue type outline." It moved very quickly "toward Lake Michigan" and out of sight. Our witness was so moved by the experience, they brought it up to the clerk working at the gas station just down the road. With a full tank of gas our witness went on to drive by the local airport, hoping to see something there that would help shed some additional information on the sighting. Finding nothing there but the usual planes, our witness returned home feeling somewhat defeated. Their mind continued to race the rest of the night. Weighing what had just happened, and wondering "who do I tell and who don't I tell" fearing being placed "in a rubber room" after witnessing what they did back on March 11, 1999. On the Internet they found the National UFO Reporting Center (NUFORC) and thankfully shared their experience. It is perhaps worth noting the similar shape described down to the comparative object as the same triangle or "arrow head." This witness was quite careful in sharing the experience not giving there name or even identifying if they were male or female. For further discussion and greater scope please see Appendix D.

In Glendale, a suburb of Milwaukee, our next witness is no stranger to things flying in the air. April 8, 1999, he witnessed a triangle-shaped object that was orange in color, pass directly overhead. Having spent 15 years in various branches of the government, including the United States Air Force, he was familiar with aircraft carriers and knew to watch for "gas emission," "jet blast," and "sound." With this craft, nothing other than the color, great speed and "3 lights on each corner" were noticeable. He estimated the speed at "500mph" as it quickly moved across the sky in front of him and his coworker at 1:45 am.

As kids will do, they have done. Loitering about as I recall doing for hours on end during some of my younger years. It was the early morning of August 23 in 1999, when two friends were watching the stars, their backs on picnic tables. It was an average park for the suburb of Oak Creek, on Milwaukee's south side. A few picnic tables in the green space skirted nearby with train track. Chelsea and her friend were calmly watching the stars and time drift by when their solitude was broken with the clanging of train track bells and flashing lights at the road crossing. They both "jumped up to see the train" only to not have it arrive. They barely had any time to think on this oddity as they "heard a sound like a airplane but not as loud." This hard-to-discern noise drew their attention back to the skies and in her words "we freaked out." Because "there in the sky was something moving rather low and rather slowly with only 3 lights." Chelsea went on to share with UFOwisconsin.com that the lights were "spaced out like a triangle." She was attempting to recall every detail; however, the years had made her too uncertain of their color to say. The craft continued moving through the sky as the bells and lights at the train crossing flashed and rang. As the craft move off into the distance the girls ran fairly frightened all the way home. Chelsea did make an astute observation on the arrival of the UFO and the train crossing activation with no train in sight or within earshot. She further noted, "the arms that come down when a train comes, never came down." Chelsea shared that she would have come forward sooner with her story "but I didn't know who to tell." The experience is something that she told us "still haunts" her to this day. For anything Chelsea's report may be lacking in specific details can certainly be understood with years between experiencing and reporting it. The fact she openly shared that her memory was too unclear as to the color of lights lends great credibility to the rest of her report. The apparent interaction between terrestrial objects such as the train crossing and the timely appearance of the UFO are of utmost interest for the modern day ufologist. The more times such interactions are documented, the greater the chance of discovering patterns and with it perhaps a deeper understanding of the UFO phenomena.

June 4, 2000, may not stand out in history for most; however, for Vaughn and his girlfriend Liz it will never be forgotten. Around two in the morning they were hanging out in a park. Liz was first to point out a bright light in the sky and said, "Is that a UFO?" As they gazed upward just above this bright light they could make out a "dome like shape." It reminded Vaughn of the local baseball stadium, though this was flying through the air. He went on to say, "the lights were very wide across" and as they watched "the craft turned sharply to the right." It "hovered about a mile away," and it was at this point they ran for their car. Liz looked back and exclaimed "The craft was landing!" She described its movement as though it was "almost like it was going down stairs." The two jumped in their car and drove towards it. But only for a short time as the UFO then seemed to change course and be "coming towards" the pair. This caused them to rethink their original plan. The two high school students turned and sped away from the craft; Vaughn used his rearview mirror to look back. It was no use as no more had they turned around than had the craft disappeared. The witnesses went on to share some of their characteristics to help give scope to their credibility. They both cited there high school attendance, "high grades," and that they do not partake in drugs.

In the home office of a Milwaukee resident was a distracted entrepreneur on March 13, 2001. Around eleven o'clock that evening he took a break and recalled watching "a little Jay Leno." After he "got ready to go downstairs" to his office, there was a "rumbling noise that made" him curious, but with "lots of computer work to do" he didn't investigate further. As most home office employees learn, working with headphones on can noticeably increase your productivity. As he listened to his music he was "vaguely aware that the rumbling noise was louder." He shared that it slowly began to actually vibrate the house. He reported that his wife was upstairs working with their son on his homework when the noise began. She wasn't able to figure out the cause for the commotion and called her husband saying that he "should come up and figure out what was making noise." As the he came up the stairs the "noise suddenly stopped." He was met by his 15-year-old daughter who had just turned in for the night when the noise started. It became so loud that she rose to look out the window. From her vantage point she watched what she thought might have been a meteor. She went onto describe "a light as big as a basket ball twice the height of trees flash across the sky." Her father remembers that her daughter actually exclaimed "holy shit!" first, and then went on to describe what she witnessed. The daughter said that as soon as she made it to the window the light and "the noise stopped abruptly." His wife recounted having the "sensation that it was passing slowly over" the house "from a SW to NE direction." She also said her "ears were hurting because of the loud noise." Curiosity and perhaps a bit of annoyance got the better of him. He called Mitchell International Airport, located in Milwaukee and inquired about the noise that night. The person on the phone shared "they were testing engines at about that time." Our reporting witness wasn't satisfied with the information he received. He felt it didn't answer all the questions, adding that he can "hear them testing engines all the time." Normally he recalls it doesn't go for nearly as long and the fact that he lives "3 miles away the sound never is very loud." The wife's observations of the object passing over the house and the daughter watching as the sound stopped and light disappeared also seem to reduce the engine testing explanation.

Our reporting witness said he spoke with several neighbors the following day. Everyone he spoke with "reported hearing the loud sound." One remembered looking out the door due to the "deafening" noise, but didn't see anything. The same neighbor became frightened as the "whole house" was "shaking" as the noise passed. A different neighbor had also heard the noise and "went all the way out to her drive way and looked up in the sky" on the clear evening. She reported seeing "no lights but couldn't figure out what was making such a loud noise." She compared it to "a squadron of jumbo jets." Our witness was clearly moved by the event as two weeks after he mentioned it to a friend living, "about 5 miles SW" of his house and home office. That friend and his wife both remembered hearing "something just like" he described the same evening. After speaking with several of his neighbors they had come to the conclusion it might have been an earthquake as their homes shook so much. For further discussion and greater scope please see Appendix E.

The next witness contacted UFOwisconsin.com hoping others had seen the same and maybe more. It was a rainy September in 2001, when our first witness was hanging up the phone. She "looked out the front door" and "noticed a light gray triangular shape object against the dark gray clouds." The triangle was off to the northeast where a low cloud cover had moved in. Right away the witness thought the object didn't look anything like a plane saying its movements were "side to side at first then it started doing loops." Then the loops started getting "bigger" and "it would disappear into the clouds and come back out and move side ways again and do more loops." While watching this triangular object dart about "all of a sudden" a second object appeared. The witness and her friend both now watching the objects, reported that it looked just like the first one and seemed "as if they were playing with each other." Realizing what they may be watching they snapped out of their amazement and ran for the "camcorder." As they "returned both objects disappeared." It was a late Sunday afternoon on the 23rd maybe around 4 pm. The witness shared that the objects "seemed to be out over Lake Michigan just off the shore from Oak Creek" and was hoping somebody else had noticed "the two objects." The witnesses were able to watch them long enough before running for the camera to rule out any "airplane, bird, or kite." At this time no one else has come forward in connection with this sighting.

The November 2006 sighting at Chicago O'Hare International airport made headlines around the nation, but this wasn't the first or only airport that has had visitation from unidentified crafts. December 22, 2002, two friends were parked near Milwaukee's General Mitchell International Airport. They enjoyed hanging out, watching the planes and time go by. Thanks to the National UFO Reporting Center (NUFORC) we have this report that shows first the friend "saw a triangle shaped craft." It was only "a few hundred feet off the runway" and they both stated it "seemed to be rising at a high speed." It lifted further and "disappeared into the sky." The friends both reported that even though it "wasn't that far away" the craft "made no sound at all." There are many triangle-shaped sightings in Wisconsin and indeed around the world. It is difficult at best to determine whether these types of sightings are of known stealth technologies that are flown by United States Air Force pilots or are something else. The more information given by each witness in his or her respective reports, the easier it is to take the experience on a case-by-case basis.

For further discussion and greater scope please see Appendix F for an entire sighting not included here.

An anonymous report came in to UFOwisconsin on January 17, 2003, from the Milwaukee area. The reporting witness was visiting her neighbor during the time of the sighting. She and her neighbor sat in front of a large "picture window," catching up on each others past week. The guest first noticed "two silver type objects in the sky" that late afternoon around 4:40. The two crafts appeared the same, however, one "seemed to be motionless" at first. The other silver object "was traveling in a westerly direction." Using "a pine tree and electric wire as a visual guide of its movement" the witness was able to note, both objects were moving. The first object "hovered for a bit and then went higher." There it "hovered, again" then, "moved southward." This action repeated and "within a few seconds after this, it disappeared." The objects were "extremely bright white color" and "seemed to have a, slightly, curved top." In addition to the witnesses at that location, they found another lady friend "that lives across from the lake saw two objects in the sky too." To me, reports that come in with the witness documenting some of his or her own research into their experience are great. Our witness has her neighbor as a collaborating observer, and she openly questions other people in her neighborhood and what's better, actually finding someone who purportedly saw the same thing. The fact that she wanted to remain anonymous, once may have been a good indicator of a hoax. But feeling compelled enough from your experience to contact and question your neighbors, then to search out a place to share your story such as www.UFOwisconsin.com shows me that the experience made a big impression with the witness.

One month later and around 62nd Street in Milwaukee our next witness also shared his experience at www.UFOwisconsin.com. It was around nine o'clock and Michael was taking out his dog for the last time that evening. He remembers looking up to enjoy the "stars on a clear night." As soon as he looked up he "found a strange light" that, "almost looked like a falling star in the sky." He continued to watch, appreciating that he got to enjoy the sight, when "it moved very fast to one location and stayed still" for maybe five minutes. This was undoubtedly uncharacteristic of most falling stars. When the light once more moved, it did so "very slowly" to the "north" where it again stopped. With that Michael ran into the house and grabbed his camera. Returning outside he took a quick photo of it and either coincidently or as in a response to his camera's flash "the light in the sky seemed to flash back lightly." Michael assured us he is "not crazy" or "on any kind of drugs." Michael said this is the first time he has experienced anything strange like this. As he shared other details of the evening, he noted it was only about five degrees that evening with a slight wind. His photograph of the "white and yellow" light when developed unfortunately came back "just all black." Sidenote here for any budding ufologists out there: should you take photographs on your investigations, request "expose all frames" to your developer. To help keep costs down, some businesses will not develop the dark exposures, unless requested. Back to the sighting on 62nd Street. Was this a case of a shooting star gone bad? Did Michael perceive that a shooting star disappeared right where another star was in his line of sight? Then it wasn't a star where the actual shooting star faded out, which would technically be a meteorite but in reality need to be an airplane at high altitude. The appearance of stopping mid route would of course be explained by the change in heading by the pilot of the large commuter jet. That this was observed but somehow still not apparent to the witness even though the plane would then have to be coming directly at or directly away from that person for five minutes. This without giving away the fact that it was an airplane by crashing into his yard or disappearing altogether into space; either which would have most likely made the news. Then while Michael took a picture of this plane the flash from his camera actually reflected off of something else in his plane of view and just seemed like the UFO flashing back. Or perhaps the shooting star/meteorite, turned star, turned plane then gone from view, left our witness watching a satellite whose solar panels then caught some of the sun as its onboard stabilizers fired to realign right after he took the picture giving the appearance of flashing back. Of course this 'explanation' requires that a potentially equal, unbelievable set of events to have transpired. I never met Michael, but from his report he seemed to be a completely level-headed, and detailed-focused witness, not out looking for UFOs but simply an inquisitive person going through his normal daily motions who happened to encounter something not-so-normal.

Just south of Milwaukee on February 8, 2003, our next report comes from a family driving on Interstate 43. At first the passenger "noticed a round shaped light in the southern sky" around 5:30 in the morning. At first she just thought it was "unusual" and kept an eye on it as they drove. The light "gradually became larger and started paralleling" them as they drove east. It grew near enough at this point for our witness to make out "a saucer shaped object." At this time she also noticed "light showers" emanating from the saucer object. After seeing this she quickly pointed the object out to her husband who was driving and her daughter in the back seat. The mother and daughter stared intently at the UFO while the husband watched when he could. Continuing down the interstate, the "light showers" became more noticeable from the "top and bottom" of the object. The showers didn't seem to "project a great distance" from the object and were "red, green, and purple" in color. As time and miles passed they could make out what "looked like an oblong saucer shape with a lighted dome above it." The "light showers" continued and the craft would jump ahead of their position and then jump behind them for some time. They were able to watch the craft for "over an hour" allowing them a good look at its details. At some points the craft was "out-lined completely as red and green lights lit up across the saucershape, blinking on and off as they came across the saucer." As dawn advanced the sky lightened which allowed them to notice an airplane in the same area of the UFO. They watched as the saucer "began to climb rapidly southeastward at a 70-degree angle until it was once again just a small dot in the sky." It continued until it "disappeared into a bank of dark clouds." The family was not sure of what they saw, but together ruled out "a plane" or "helicopter." I know what you're thinking, "they didn't rule out a blimp." Well, as I discuss later in greater detail it is a pretty hardened rule that blimps don't fly in the winter months of Wisconsin. To say the whole experience can be ruled out by the rebel dirigible pilot, would be to ignore other observations made such as a 70 degree climb while disappearing from view would require speeds not known to conventional blimps.

January 11, 2004, was like most every other day in more ways than one. Trisha N. reported to UFOwisconsin.com that after letting her "dogs outside" she watched from the "kitchen window." Standing there she noticed presumably an "airplane flying from the south, with too many lights." It was "flying really fast" and "all the sudden it stopped in mid-air and disappeared." With this she became fairly certain she was no longer watching simple airplanes and called to her boyfriend. The two of them looked out the window together as "another object from the south" came into view, again assuming it was an airplane "until it also stopped in mid air." This time it however did not disappear. They watched as the object "did a zig-zag shape flying up towards space" until it disappeared from site.

Trisha and her boyfriend were "astonished" at what they had just witnessed, so much so that she stepped away from the window to make a call. As she rang her friend that had "a telescope" her boyfriend "saw a bright flash of light that did a sort of M shape" then again disappeared. The events seemed to end around nine o'clock that evening.

Their report becomes difficult to quickly dismiss when we look at some similar reports. April 7, 2001, over the skies of Milwaukee came a report that first appeared to be a meteorite by the observer. It "made a pronounced streak as it entered the atmosphere" within moments the witness heard a "high frequency" sound that stopped as the object "moved in a zig-zag like fashion across the sky directly overhead to the western horizon and then disappeared." On the 3rd of the following month we have another report from the Milwaukee area when the anonymous witness saw a "can shaped object...glowing" in the sky. The witness turned off a nearby light to remove any "glare from the window." As the light went off the object "moved really fast going left to right about 3 feet at a time." There was a "low-pitched noise that made the stereo shake like a bass amp was in the room." The noise stopped suddenly as another "smaller" object "appeared from the bottom" of the first. On February 12, 2002, our next witness reported to UFOwisconsin.com they were shooting some hoops in their backyard. It was around 8 am when "the UFO appeared out of the west." The witness didn't initially think too much about the unusual, but not amazing sight, "until it made a series of darts across the sky." It was present for several minutes then "darted off east." On November 13, 2004, Diana reported watching an object performing "acrobatics around the sky." It was "Danceing [sic] at unlikely speeds" then "stops and hovers for a minute or two." I received another report on July 5, 2005, witnessed from a window at the Pfister Hotel in Milwaukee. The witnesses were watching the sky over Lake Michigan when a "bright white light" that came from a "long object" was seen. It "swooped in one direction, then slowly lost velocity until it came to a halt, then swooped in the opposite direction." It was reported as continuing this pattern a few times until it "disappeared into the night." Lastly, or firstly chronologically speaking, on June 14, 1997, a couple was sitting outside in the afternoon when they "spotted something strange in the sky over Lake Michigan." They recalled the "bright yellow/orange light" was doing "crazy spirals" until it "dropped out of the sky." The couple shared the report hoping more people might come forward who witnessed what they saw. There's not much one can intelligently say about mysteriously appearing, behaving, and disappearing lights in the nighttime sky. At first glance some of these reports may appear to be military flares, which can be ruled out on some cases due to color, length of time observed and location especially when cross-referenced with released military flight paths and known training schedules. For natural options not as easy to explain away, we find ourselves again looking at ball lightning or plasma balls. In my opinion I hold both of these phenomena in almost equally high regards of interest. The scientific community still holds more theories on these possible events than it does answers. Learning more about those natural but rare occurrences might hold the answers to related questions of technology and a greater understanding of the global environment and as a result potentially could shed light onto our UFO phenomena, whether it be terrestrial or extraterrestrial.

Scott shared an interesting sighting that he and his brother-in-law had on an early morning walk. It was February 5, 2004, and as many night owls do they were enjoying the clear and star-filled sky above them. They soon noticed "4 red" spheres, one "in the south west sky," the other two in the south east and "north east sky." They stopped their walk to watch more closely as the red objects moved "back and forth in the sky but never broke formation." They all stayed in a "box" like formation the whole time and appeared to be gathering over Scott's home. The pair watched the objects for about 15 minutes then continued on their walk. However, the objects seemed to follow them as they moved on. They walked for another "15 minutes" until the uneasiness became too much causing them to turn for home. Upon returning home the red spheres were again positioning themselves above the house. The lights seem to dim and brighten "every second." Scott made his way to bed, shrugging off the odd lights for now. He awoke several hours later to a loud "hummm." He "rolled over" and saw that it was 5 am. The hum continued as he rolled the other way to wake his "future wife." The next thing he recounted to UFOwisconsin.com was rolling back over to the clock and seeing that it was now 6:30 in the morning. With this, Scott "ran down stairs" and asked his mother-in-law if "she heard anything last night," yes, she replied. The hair stood up on his neck and Scott went to clear his thoughts in the hot water provided by the shower. In the steam filled bathroom he recalls noticing a "scoop mark on my left calf one forth of an inch" in size and in a "perfectly round circle." Scott said it looked "like a very small crator [sic] on my leg." Further examination showed another similar mark above Scott's "right shoulder blade." Scott didn't share any other notes on the night or anything that he may have recalled other than it "was the last time we seen [sic] the round red spheres." An intriguing report and one that sounds like it may have some related physical data to study in the form of scoop marks and testimony perhaps forgotten in the hour and a half lost that morning. As odd as it may or may not sound to you the reader, and if an unofficial study can hold anything classic it would be scoop marks to the UFO field. They have been reported by many persons over many years and have been theorized as anything from a scar unnoticed until the odd event in life caused further self-physical examination to that of alien or governmental genetic studies. It is this type of report that ufologist's hope to have enough resources for further investigation when they are reported.

As odd as this experience may seem, it is not unique to Scott. Similar red UFO reports are on record from the Milwaukee area for June 1 1997, February 6 2001, March 19 2001, June 2001, March 10 2002, April 24 2002, December 1 2003, March 12 2004, and November 13 2004.

For now, October 3, 2006, brings our next-to-last witness in the Milwaukee chapter. Enjoying the night sky he noticed an object that had a belt of lights. He thought the object was "a gunmetal color with lights of some kind all around their middles." There were three objects all sort of stacked on top of each other vertically. The witness was surprised no-one else had reported them as they were "so easily visible." He and his girlfriend had both seen the objects and on more than one occasion.

May 21, 2007, brought another pet lover to their nightly duty. While on a walk with his dog in the Milwaukee suburb of Shorewood, Brennon noticed how clear the sky was. The Moon was so bright, "the only thing in the sky was the Moon and one other star." Brennon went on to say while enjoying the clear view of the Moon he noticed "small flashes aroung [sic] the surface." He went on to say "the flashes kept moving away from the moon [sic] as if they were blasting off from it." This went on, "a few flashes every couple of seconds," for "3 or 4 minutes." It was just after 9 pm when everything stopped and nothing else out of the ordinary was noticed. Beyond the possible migraine visual hallucinations that are arguably the only good thing from a bad headache, what are some other possible explanations for this sighting?

Peculiarities with our own Moon have been noted for, well, many moons. Perhaps it is that our Moon is so prevalent in our sky that it has naturally brought about additional scrutiny ever since people were around to bask in its glow. Some might have you believe that it wasn't always around to share its glowing light. A civilization called the Proselenes declared the lands of Greece to be its own because it was granted to them "before there was a moon in the heavens." Much of the collected works outlining different cultural materials referencing a potential time when no Moon shown in the sky comes from Immanuel Velikovsky. He was many things including a published psychiatrist and practicing medical doctor, debated against by Dr. Carl Sagan and correspondent with Albert Einstein. His works are to say the least interesting to a mind inquisitive of ancient history and controversial to many accepted main stream ideas of it. None the less his works are cited and if you are able to read the language of the original texts, you can determine for yourself if his and other's interpretations are accurate. According to Velikovsky and other researchers of similar alternative ancient history theories Aristotle, Greek philosopher 384 B.C; Plutarch, Greek historian 46; Ovidius, Roman poet 43 B.C; Apollonius director of the Library of Alexandria, 290B.C; the book of Job and Psalm all make alluring mention of a time before the moon. Perhaps only literary license taken by an author of one time, and then rewritten as fact by a later researcher? Could the examples of a moonless Earth be nothing more than a society lacking our current understanding of mathematics? Past societies could have been simply using an analogist approach to show great length in time and large numbers.

Alright so beyond, half speculation on ancient archeological digs and over-playing perceived statistically odd astronomical occurrences; we do have some newer anomalies associated with the Moon. In 1953 an amateur astronomer by the name of Leon Stuart reported capturing a bright flash that appeared on the darkened area of the Moon. It wasn't until the 1990s offered new photographs of the Moon, that scientists verified a newly formed crater, establishing that Stuart may have indeed captured a meteor strike. This was vindication for Stuart because up to that point, his observations along with others who witnessed similar anomalies were criticized and doubted. What can this all mean on the grand scale of things; my hopes are that time will reveal most but always leave some for the adventurous individual and the curious mind. Perhaps we will learn more in the year 2020. In 2004 then President George W. Bush announced, "manned missions to the Moon" including construction of proposed permanent structures. The interest in the Moon is also found in the People's Republic of China, India, Japan, and Russia all having announced their own manned and unmanned desired missions. We can only hope that some answers will be uncovered with the international endeavors to the Moon. For further discussion and greater scope please see Appendix G.

From possible kites to satellites, ball lightning to weather balloons. Mix in a top secret but earthly based advanced technology, beautiful lakeshore views, the more terrestrial Brewers baseball to beer brewers in general or yes even the truly unexplainable, inexplicable, and unbelievable but true experiences, the Milwaukee area touches on it all. You just have to know where to look to find some of the less publicized places of 'interest'. With this book in hand, you are on your way.

One way to visit: Milwaukee is located on the western shores of Lake Michigan and is about an hour east of Madison, Wisconsin, on Interstate 94. Head north from Chicago on Interstate 94 for about an hour and you're there. Taking most of the major arteries of the city will lead you past some great views of Lake Michigan.

#4 Madison, Wisconsin

At 40-plus reports on www.UFOwisconsin.com, Madison has it all: wooded hills, open prairies, large lakes, small ponds, and swamps, with plenty of cement and urban development to round it out. As mentioned earlier, it is difficult at this time to scientifically determine if larger populated areas are going to naturally allow for more sightings or do just the opposite in Wisconsin. If sightings are not increased, it would seem logical that the loss of horizon from development of the land and additional light sources that dull a person's natural night vision capability are greater factors than simply more eyes. The added population also brings increased distractions from peaceful star gazing such as traffic on the ground and in the sky, flashing advertisements and the constant hum of people going about their own busy day. Of course, more people equal more eyes for UFOs to be spotted with. For now, let's enjoy some of the numerous sightings that have occurred in and around Wisconsin's capital.

October 1938, the night before Halloween. Wisconsin-born Orson Welles was to become an accomplished film and radio producer whose newest radio program was to premier that evening. It had begun as many other programs from "The Mercury Theatre on the Air" had, orchestra playing behind a narrator giving introduction. What the majority of listeners didn't hear or fully understand that evening was the program, as stated in the beginning "…the

War of the Worlds by H.G. Wells" was indeed based on a fictional book from 1898. The confusion could be forgiven as everything else about the show was made to seem to the listening audience as a mundane radio program that was continually interrupted by fake news broadcasts as the fictional events unfolded. This was the programs real intent.

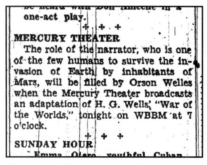

The Capital Times listing of that evening's radio shows, October 30, 1938.

Despite how things developed, the program was not a complete secret ahead of time. In 1938 the radio schedule for each evening and several days to follow were carried in the newspapers much as today's television programs are listed. The image from *The Capital Times* even explained the show and when it would air, "...role of the narrator, who is of the few humans to survive the invasion of Earth by inhabitants of Mars, will be filled by Orson Welles...." It goes on to share "...an adaptation of H.G. Wells', "War of the Worlds," tonight on WBBM at 7 o'clock."

For those listening that evening, the first sign this was not going to be a normal program came suddenly. Only several moments into the show the host seemingly interrupts to make a startling announcement: explosions were visible on Mars, citing a professor in Illinois. Cutting in and out over the next hour the story line continued with faux experts and onsite reporters speaking of crashed flying saucers and alien beings reeking havoc across the country side and indeed around the world. The shock waves of this live radio program were felt instantly by the country. "The Crosby Service" estimated that over 32 million people tuned in to listen to the program that infamous evening. Some studies of the time showed over 1 million persons thought it to be a broadcast of true events. The New York Times reported on October 31, 1938; front page and above the fold "Radio Listeners in Panic, Taking War Dramas Fact." The sub title directly underneath read, "Many Flee Homes to Escape 'Gas Raid From Mars'—Phone Calls Swamp Police at Broadcast of Welles Fantasy."

The article goes on to cite locations mentioned in the radio broadcast were the most affected. Some "...apartment houses in New York were emptied hurriedly by frantic listeners...," "...newspaper offices and police stations everywhere were swamped with calls from terrified people, many of them weeping.," even so far as a nameless "…woman in Pittsburgh tried suicide, saying 'I'd rather die this way than like that.'"

The Capital Times, Monday October 31, 1938.

The fallout in Madison was reported as nothing too horrific.

As a former Madison resident myself, sure we would like to claim that it was just our better senses prevailing. When it was more likely attributed to the popular Charlie McCarthy's radio program that ran a similar time slot on a different station. In fact it was speculated that Orson Welles timed the most sensational segments of his broadcast to coincide with breaks of other popular radio programs running at the same time. As a result of this broadcast there were numerous probes and general grandstanding by American Senators, the CBS (Columbia Broadcasting System) network and the FCC (Federal Communications Commission). Adaptations of this program were re-broadcasted around the world over the years with some meeting even more tragic and deathly results.

The Capital Times, Monday Afternoon edition, October 31, 1938. The first line reads "'Madison residents are either too wise or too loyal to Charlie McCarthy to be excited by invasions from Mars."

In 1952, Project Blue Book, purportedly under the immediate control of the United States Air Force held open records on an investigation that brought them to Madison, Wisconsin. As you can read in some of the following documents, this was stamped with an explanation that the witnesses may not have been in full agreement with. Section "12." covers "CONCLUSIONS" and as you may be able to make out (upper right hand corner of following image) it is marked by "XXX Possibly Aircraft."

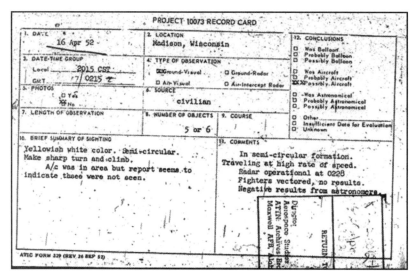

Official Project Blue Book record on declassified case from April 16, 1952, in Madison, Wisconsin.

This time the call came in from a Mr. Dino of Lake Street in Madison. It was 8:15 pm when he watched "5 or 6 objects in the sky" almost directly overhead. Describing them as "semi-circular in shape and formation" also that they were "glowing with a yellowish - white light." He thought it was odd that no "sound nor exhaust was noted." Mr. Arthur observed the sighting with his friend Mr. Dino. They watched on as "the object(s) made a sharp left turn in a North NW direction and gained altitude rapidly." The lights almost "seemed to fuse or come together" as they disappeared into the distance. Our observer Mr. Dino was vigilant.

He called the 176th Fighter Squadron Operations stationed at the Truax Air Field in Madison. They in turn contacted Captain R. Cambell at the radar station. That was to no avail, as the radar station was "off temporarily due to preventative maintenance." Three minutes later the Captain had it operational showing no unknown aircraft or radar returns. Captain Cambell redirected "some F-80 type" aircraft into the area to investigate which yielded "no results." Not to be outdone, he "then took a flight of F-86 type aircraft at 30,000 ft over the area, sighted nothing." The weather was listed as "clear and better than 15 Miles visibility" and a check with the local airlines revealed no "flights in the vicinity." The notes had also recorded the attempts in finding an answer by contacting the two area astronomical observatories including the one at the University of Madison. Those findings were recorded in the page below as "there was nothing unusual recorded."

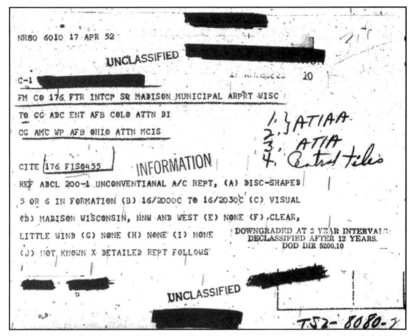

Redacted or edited official Project Blue Book record regarding the April 16, 1952, Madison, Wisconsin report.

These areas of quick research were accomplished by letter or phone and were the usual methods used by researchers in Project Blue Book. As would historically happen by the end of the project, when these avenues turned up no conclusive evidence for the natural explanation of the events they turned to the people reporting them.

The official conclusion of Project Blue Book was that the witnesses "…possibly observed jet aircraft in area and the apparent high speed and rate of climb was an illusion." I'm left to only speculate from the hundreds of pages of documents referencing Project Blue Book that I've read over my brief lifetime. I am forced to step off the few succinct pages referencing vague data accumulated by federal agents openly searching for one thing while other information reveals how they may have been ordered to find another. This experience that happened over fifty years ago is interesting and intriguing to some, but I think we can learn something from then, for today. These experiences continually happen, to your neighbors, to your doctor, to your police officers and maybe even to you someday; assuming it hasn't already. Should we continually share our experiences, creating an opportunity for research and investigation while the events are still current, will be a much shorter route to any answers than should we not. This documentation could help uncover the necessary clues aiding the development of better theories and dare I say even an answer or two. If we step back and look at the bigger picture at least to the American audience, one might mention a 1997 CNN & Time Magazine Poll resulted with 80% of Americans believing the government is concealing knowledge of the existence of Extraterrestrial life forms or we could lean on some data shown in the documentary "Dan Aykroyd Unplugged on UFOs," saying 3.7 million Americans believe themselves to have been abducted by aliens. With all the uncertainty in the field, one thing seems to be certain; if we turn a distracted ear and an uninterested eye to the phenomena today, we will know nothing new tomorrow. That might also mean not just experiences lost to time and knowledge never gained but something more. Even if there is nothing more to the UFO phenomena than misunderstood subjective experiences had by the witnesses, there still remains a mystery in that stance itself to be unraveled. Something only time will fully reveal.

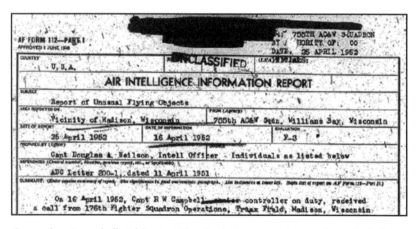

Cropped portion of official Project Blue Book document giving a chronological synopsis of reported events on April 16, 1952, Madison, Wisconsin.

Stepping off of the philosophical and foreshadowing soap box; our next report we have is also documented in Project Blue Book.

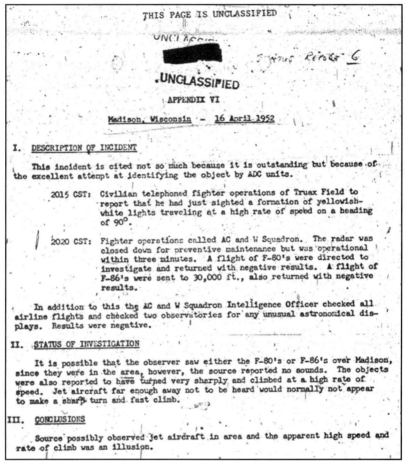

THIS PAGE IS UNCLASSIFIED

UNCLASS...

UNCLASSIFIED

APPENDIX VI

Madison, Wisconsin - 16 April 1952

I. DESCRIPTION OF INCIDENT

    This incident is cited not so much because it is outstanding but because of the excellent attempt at identifying the object by ADC units.

        2015 CST: Civilian telephoned fighter operations of Truax Field to report that he had just sighted a formation of yellowish-white lights traveling at a high rate of speed on a heading of 90°.

        2020 CST: Fighter operations called AC and W Squadron. The radar was closed down for preventive maintenance but was operational within three minutes. A flight of F-80's were directed to investigate and returned with negative results. A flight of F-86's were sent to 30,000 ft., also returned with negative results.

    In addition to this the AC and W Squadron Intelligence Officer checked all airline flights and checked two observatories for any unusual astronomical displays. Results were negative.

II. STATUS OF INVESTIGATION

    It is possible that the observer saw either the F-80's or F-86's over Madison, since they were in the area, however, the source reported no sounds. The objects were also reported to have turned very sharply and climbed at a high rate of speed. Jet aircraft far enough away not to be heard would normally not appear to make a sharp turn and fast climb.

III. CONCLUSIONS

    Source possibly observed jet aircraft in area and the apparent high speed and rate of climb was an illusion.

Official Project Blue Book document showing in part "III." the "CONCLUSIONS" of the investigation into the April 16, 1952, sighting.

The following report is of another Madison-area sighting. Investigators for Project Blue Book were following leads after a pilot observed bright objects flying in formation at 400 mph. The sighting was given case number 2267 for Project Blue Book and starts just 10 miles south of Madison. United States Air Force (USAF) Captain Bridges and his First Lieutenant Johneon were conducting jet training flights in a T-33 jet. It was 5:45 in the evening when they viewed, "four bright lights, in diamond formation." The pilots noted the objects to be heading 130° or southwest. They gave chase in their T-33 at 8,000 feet and 450 miles per hour. The two over took the formation of lights five minutes later, and now just 10 miles northeast of Janesville, Wisconsin. A request for a radar confirmation yielded no positive results. The radar scopes only showed the T-33, which now was on an eastward heading and running low on fuel. Whatever it was they were chasing was not showing up on the very same radar that tracked them. Another five minutes and now just west of Racine, Wisconsin they streaked across the southern part of the state heading east toward Milwaukee. It was December 9, and with Milwaukee Wisconsin visible in the distance the crew made one final observation: there was no "silhouette visible even when objects seen against Milwaukee city lights." This wasn't proof of anything in-itself, but certainly an intriguing observation. It does show that the pilots were looking for any additional information regarding their quarry that evening. The chase may have continued however, by 5:55 pm the T-33 was too low on fuel to continue. They turned and headed back to the Madison base. The investigation of the two USAF pilots however was to continue.

In 1952 this experience warranted the attention of those working with Project Blue Book. It is still part of the now declassified archives of the program, officially listed as an "Unknown." What does one think when reading such a classification? Well, coming from the United States Government, following an investigation that included a physical visit of investigators to Madison, it could on the surface carry some weight. The project had several categories to place the cases into based upon the findings of any investigations. During the active period of Project Blue Book the classification of "Unknown" was given to at least 15 reports in Wisconsin. However some new research by Brad Sparks may reveal up to 26 Wisconsin cases that were listed as unknowns. Why the discrepancies? Simply said, the Air Force had multiple reviews of acquired data by Project Blue Book. There are official and non-official findings made during, immediately following, and some more present, after supposed review of the collected data. Each of the different studies, committees or reports undertaken had different criteria of controls, definitions of language, and agendas known or not, for scrutinizing the data. For the projects intentions "Unknown" cases are typically defined as one would expect: defying explanation. We'll look at this idea of unknowns again in the Mystery over Monticello case, in my following book.

Another "UNIDENTIFIED" or unknown sighting came in south west of Madison. A quick glance at the documentation found in the below Project Blue Book page could make the sighting seem lackluster. At 9:11 in the

evening, Miss Marsh watched as "One light with faded edges seemed to follow" her in the car "…for 5-6 minutes." Lackluster indeed; Venus maybe, a
plane sure, all plausible with the few details we have. Her location a notable
distance from Madison, is only foreshadowing our next sighting.

*Project Blue Book documents cropped to show the listing of Stoughton, Wisconsin in
the February 16, 1967, incident.*

Fast forward barely a year later, within miles of the previous sighting, and
only a two hour time difference. The scenario as reported is not all that different: a UFO gives chase to yet another woman in a car. Jay Rath in his
book The W-Files records a chronological set of events including names of
additional witnesses from the sheriff's department. It is researchers like Jay
and ufologists such as Timothy Good that we can thank for having such
detailed accounts of the following events.

On January 21, 1968, Shirley was driving home with a car full of girls after
a dance recital in a nearby town. Just a few miles from Madison Shirley and
her friend Mrs. Knipfer were passing time in the front seat. The only girl
awake in the back noticed the "large, round, dark-gray object" in the sky.
Shirley remembers having to pull the car over as the girl became "very
scared." Then the object "…appeared to drop sparks and flaming debris" as
it moved about in the dark sky. The UFO drew ever closer to the car as the
seconds passed. The occupants now screaming in fear helped Shirley quickly decide they had better keep driving. They compared the size of the object
to that of a "hot-air balloon" and that it was at a distance of "the top of a
barn" away. Shirley recalled how she "could almost see the bottom of it" but
with the "sparks" coming out, it was difficult to get a super-clear view. Mrs.
Knipfer's home was the first stop and she recalled as they pulled into her
driveway that the UFO followed. The object then continued on as they lost
sight of it to the east. The UFO ended up at the Berge farm. Already there
was Sheriff's Deputy Shaffer along with three "neighboring youths." The
Sheriff was apparently contacted earlier about the strange sightings, then
became a witness himself watching the object "disappear from view." The
Sheriff was reportedly looking for other eyewitnesses to the events that
evening, but it is not recorded if he found any. There were reports of similar objects being sighted just a few months earlier and a bit south west of this
location. Those sightings were had by local police officers and sheriff
deputies, along with motorists and "25 patients and staff" at an area hospital.
Shirley had continued in her report from January that she remembered

"someone went to the Berge farm and did see something on the ground there."

If Wisconsin has its very own version of the Roswell crash site, the following story has yet to break with as much attention. Nonetheless there were rumors that something was found, whether it was a smaller part of a big crash or merely something smaller that was seen breaking off the UFO as it sparked by. It is thought that this sighting may have yielded just such an object. Eventually this purported piece of UFO craft found its way into the hands of investigative journalist, Mr. S. Perhaps tracking down the lead offered by the involvement of the Sheriff's department in the previous report from the 1960s, Mr. S. ended up in Madison.

Using a local Holiday Inn as his headquarters he met with a local farmer, perhaps even the Berge's. Apparently the farmer had "recovered a piece of metal," presumably "from the UFO" and gave it to Mr. S. Upon arriving back at the Inn Mr. S. received a phone call from the farmer. He mentioned, "a fertilizer salesman had been out" to see him and was, "asking a lot about the UFO and the metal but not working too hard to sell fertilizer." The farmer wanted to see Mr. S. again, and he now did not feel comfortable being out and about with this mysterious metal object that had seemed to increase in value over the afternoon. Mr. S. carefully took apart the television set in his room, tied the piece of metal to the inside and replaced the back cover. He then shared, "I asked the maids and hotel maintenance man to watch my room during my absence." No sooner had Mr. S. left his room to meet with the farmer did two men approach his room. They reportedly used a key to let themselves in. An observant maid saw this unfold and followed shortly behind into the room. She watched the two men, "going through S****'s suitcase." She acted as if she was none-the-wiser and was simply checking the room per her job. A few miles southeast, Mr. S. arrived at the farm. At this time the farmer is now convinced that he needed to return the metal as it is "national security, a danger to the world, and the government's desire." Apparently after his personal meeting with government representatives he had a new outlook on his current reality. Mr. S., most likely disappointed that his guardianship of the mysterious metal object was short-lived returns to the Inn.

Upon entering his room in Madison, he found the two men waiting for him. One of the men was casually sitting at his desk and the other comfortably laying on the bed. Assuredly this was an uncomfortable and immediately confusing situation for Mr. S. They reportedly exchanged some "small talk" before one of the two men asked without pause for rebuttal, "You have something we want. A farmer gave you a piece of metal the other day. Our job is to pick it up." Mr. S. was determined to not be completely intimidated, and asked to see their identification. To which one of them unflinchingly replied "Name the agency and we'll produce it." As if that wouldn't be disconcerting enough in that situation, the other man added, "Would you like Air Force, FBI, or maybe NORAD?" Mr. S. remembered thinking that even as uncomfortable as this situation was ever growing; the mysterious metal was not actually his to give.

Asking if the two might answer some questions before he handed over what they wanted, earned him a trip to the "hotel coffee shop." Yup, no typo there or skip in the story line. That is how the researchers have documented the situation progressing. While to me it seems quite foreign for a situation to go from threatening or at least domineering and insincere to sipping drinks in a relaxing coffee house. Perhaps it was how Mr. S. asked, or maybe demanded giving himself a temporary level of power while still silently wielding the exact whereabouts of the mysterious object. However, these two visitors could have been very aware of the power they could inevitably bring forth at any point and just found themselves in a mood to humor Mr. S. After all, who would believe such a story that Mr. S. so far could tell. In real life the 'bad guy' has more of a life than the occasional fight scene with the hero. These perceived government officials most likely had cover positions, something that whoever was signing their paychecks could offer to accounting as a job title. That is to assume that there duties don't fall into perhaps a dark project such as the budget mentioned in UFOlogy 101, where transparency and oversight remain hindered at times. Think about it for just a moment if you care to. These two people who found their unwelcome way into Mr. S's room may have had quite mundane occupations as far as everyone around them was concerned. These two men may have went home every night to a run down apartment, neon lights buzzing outside their window as they drank themselves to sleep. Or since this isn't the movies they most likely had fairly distinguished and skilled backgrounds to be hired to handle any situation encountered when working that particular line of interest for the government. They probably weren't going to hire some sleazy slouch that would mess things up worse. Most likely a family man, going home every night to a white picket fence, 2.5 kids and a loving if not only half aware wife. These were peoples fathers, uncles, brothers, grandfathers and if you can't get past Hollywood's interpretations, as least the loner in your class growing up and someone's child. Someone with something to loose, is someone that can be controlled they might argue. So what's the point right? Well as unlikely as most people might reflex think it to be, just take a step back and see how it could be possible. I know a brother, father, grandfather, uncle and so on. I know all sorts of other people who are not immediately related to myself and could easily have hidden something from even me, a self professed paranoid. Who do you know, really? We all get tied up in our own problems, interests, work, and life in general.

Another thought could be one of disinformation. Maybe the two traveler's entire mission was not to secure this metal object, but rather create an atmosphere of disinformation about the object or direction that Mr. S's investigations were taking him or to even reach a colleague and their endeavors. Of course if there is any one point I should like to drive home, it is possibility. Even the one where this story has been recorded incorrectly over time, completely made up to begin with or anything else in-between. So to continue the story we left off with our main characters heading into a nearby coffee shop. Mr. S. was told "UFOs involve more than you or any civilian can realize. They're the most important thing and perhaps the greatest hazard that mankind has ever faced." Fairly heavy conversation for a coffee shop to be sure. Mr. S. was not feeling comfortable enough to keep them from their quarry any longer. He returned to his room, handed the mystery metal over and watched as they drove away in a car wearing Illinois license plates. Being an investigative journalist, Mr. S. did just that. He contacted Mr. Brad Steiger who was well known at the time for his research and investigation into just such phenomena. Mr. S also traced the plate numbers he had recorded. Mr. Steiger had been interviewed and asked about the phone call from Mr. S. and remembered how he sounded "genuinely frightened." Mr. S.'s search into the plate's owners led him to a man residing in Chicago with "CIA links." Mr. S. soon after this incident seemed to fall off the map a bit. He was not found by myself or others before me looking for clarification on the events above.

West Madison 1973, a family with a short history of unexplained sightings, had their attention now drawn to another object in the sky due to its bright lights. They were on a highway heading into Madison to run some errands. It was a cool October. In Wisconsin this meant that the colorful leaves of September had exchanged the confines of branches for the freedom of air, showing which way the wind went each time it blew. The family first assumed the lights were that of a low flying plane.

The bright lights as seen in the previous photograph can be a perplexing experience for most first time witnesses. These forward shinning lights called aircraft landing lights are normally used during take off and landings. In the original photograph of the previous image you can faintly make out the port side red anti collision light. A clear silhouette of the entire object is difficult. The overlaid and enhanced image reveals additional detail not afforded by the original unaltered photograph. The witnesses in this case reported that they thought it was a plane, until the object stopped directly over Highway 12 in front of them and silently hovered. They figured it must have been around 6:30 in the evening as they had a 7:00 appointment at Sears. They reported that the object's shape or size was difficult to discern. Their vision was obscured due to four large white lights that were in an even row with "one red light that stayed on all the time" located in the center. They reported seeing other cars on the road that also had to drive under the object, but noted no one stopped, including themselves. For further discussion and greater scope please see Appendix H.

A plane shortly after takeoff from Dane County Regional Airport, Madison, Wisconsin. Photograph and enhancement by Noah Voss.

From a group of apparently busy, frightened, or oblivious passerby's to the next sighting; where pilots, fire department personnel, civilians and radar operators became involved.

Wisconsin offers tangibly hot and humid summers paired perfectly with bitter cold, blizzard filled winters. Most of us don't get to close to UFOs in the Wisconsin sky with the elevation topping out at 1,952ft above sea level. One of the most grippingly documented UFO events happening in the Madison area took place 18,000 feet off the ground. For that reported UFO sighting we must go back to June 24th, 1978. The following witnesses were interviewed by Allan Hendry of the International UFO Reporter (IUR) and the Center for UFO Studies (CUFOS). The IUR is a publication of CUFOS founded by the late Dr. J. Allen Hynek a renowned ufologist with over 40 years experience, including time spent working with Project Blue Book. Philip J. Klass is sometimes referred to as the most outspoken 'debunker' of the entire UFO phenomena. He spoke of Allan Hendry's work in "The UFO Handbook" as "one of the most significant and useful books on the subject ever published." Thanks to Allan Hendry's investigation, documentation found in IUR and continued by Francis Ridge along with two particular witness's perseverance in reporting their experiences I have been afforded the opportunity to share their reworked report here.

This sighting starts with a call from a Wisconsin "citizen" to the Madison Fire Department who reported a light doing circles in the sky. They in turn contacted the Madison Airport Tower and spoke with controller Joan. Madison control went on to contact another airport where they were attempting to find the cause of the lights and determine whether they were a "threat" to the air traffic at the time. Their communication starts at 10:45 pm. The following is a transcript of the conversation between a Madison Control Tower at the airport "MAD" (Madison) and the Aurora Airport Controllers "AUR" (Aurora):

MAD: You don't have anything over Madison anywhere do you, doing circles?
AUR: No, we don't have anything over Madison, doing circles.
MAD: Well, I tell you --
AUR: We've got some weather out there that's doing circles.
MAD: Ohh...would you believe I've got a UFO?
AUR: Well . . .
MAD: -- that I can see?
AUR: Let's take a look at him. Where's he at?
MAD: He's just south of the field and he is—uh—he's doing circles very fast in a small . . . looking out one window. I can't see "him," I see this light.
AUR: OK, just a second, let us flatten out the other radar a second. You say he's how far south of the field?
MAD: Well, he looks like he's over the marker, but . . . you know, it's just a light doing a circle.
AUR: Probably just a bunch of little greenies out there, eh?

The Madison control tower had been able to get a visual presumably on the reported object. They went on to say, "it looked like a spotlight searching the sky, only weaker, and located just in the cloud layer." It was now 10:48 pm and a "multi-engine" aircraft traveling over "200 m.p.h." located just south of Madison on a northwest heading was contacted. The pilot (PIL) speaks with the control, we join the radio transmission already in progress:

AUR: have you got your landing lights on?
PIL: Negative.
AUR: Do you see any kind of unusual lights ahead of you?
PIL: Yes, sir, I've got a bright light right at my 10:30, 11 o'clock position that just seems to be hovering out there.
AUR: Any idea of the altitude?
PIL: Yes, sir, the same altitude I am.
AUR: OK, I've got a VFR (Visual Flight Rules) target at 2 o'clock at about 6 miles westbound squawking (a radar return) 1200 which would indicate a lower altitude.

Certain regulations dictate how pilots may operate their aircraft. The visual flight rules mentioned above regulate that the pilot is able to "see and avoid" any potential collision hazards during reasonable visibility. This gets complicated quickly but suffice it to say the one other main regulation or category of aircraft operation is IFR or instrument flight rules. The air traffic control has a greater responsibility to aircraft operating under IFR, ensuring they do not enter into a course with undue risk of collision. Basically the pilot operating under VFR has accepted the responsibility not to collide with anything, where as a pilot operating under IFR is handing more responsibility to the air traffic control to keep them out of harms way. One could speculate that VFR pilots should have more UFO sightings than IFR operating pilots who might otherwise be more focused on instruments while at the same time relying on air traffic control to keep the heading clear.

PIL: Uh, this isn't at 2 o'clock; this is between 10:30 and 11:00.
AUR: OK, we just had a call from Madison tower; they're a little concerned about lights out there. They're obviously seeing what you are. Any idea what it is?
PIL: No, but you're starting to worry me. I hope this isn't one of those—uh—UFOs.

At this time a "possible stationary target was found at the plane's 10:30 position three miles distant." The weather in the general area of the plane "left the controllers uncertain" as some natural conditions such as thermal inversions can cause "false returns" and confuse the data from the radar equipment. The pilot quite accurately estimated that the "bright light" was maybe "two miles" from his position. He was 32 years old with "8500 flight hours" and a "first class medical certificate" holder "with no waivers." It was now 10:49 pm and the pilot shared an additional observation with ground controllers regarding the lights in the west-northwest:

> PIL: I have some lights racing around on top of the clouds down here (according to the interviewers from that time, "there are no clouds blocking his view of the other light"). I saw them below me and I have a light that is making a circle   . . . It's doing a 360° circle about once every 5 or 6 seconds.
> AUR: Could that possibly be a searchlight on the ground showing up through the clouds?
> PIL: That is a distinct possibility, yes, sir. The stationary target is now moving closer to me.

The first light observed behaved in a rhythmic pattern. This light was all but dismissed as most likely a "searchlight" by this time. The observation of the light to the west-northwest however, kept a parallel course to the plane for ten miles and as result gained the pilot's full attention. The pilot had undergone a United Airlines physical one year prior and was later reported by investigators as being "good-natured, earthly self-presentation and professed no previous interest in UFOs."

It is now 10:53 pm as their conversation continues on the west-northwestern light:

> PIL: You mean to tell me that you got nothing on radar down there at all?
> AUR: We're getting a lot of temperature inversion in that area. We are painting no targets whatsoever. There are no airplanes in that area.
> PIL: Tell you what, this ain't [sic] no-o-o weather inversion?
> AUR: OK, could it possibly be a weather balloon?
> PIL: Not unless a weather balloon lights up like a 10,000-candle light.
> AUR: OK, you're sure it is an object and not a light reflecting off a cloud or anything?
> PIL: Affirmative.
> AUR: Have you tried moving your position in the cockpit to see if that changes the position of the target? Perhaps you're getting a

reflection of some type in the cockpit.

PIL: Sir, I'll try it. I just woke my passenger up and he sees the object, too, and it is not a reflection.

Now 10:56 pm. It is documented that the passenger awoke to see the "light out of a rear window." The passenger was a 36-year-old "extremely wealthy business man from Phoenix" and a paying customer to the pilot's charter flight business. The pilot shared with investigators at the time, the passenger was "upset by the experience." The object moved about the plane as they continued their steady course and to follow in their terminology it helps to visualize an analog clock in your mind, one with only the hour hand. Moving from the pilots "ten-thirty position at an estimated 15 miles" away to as close as two miles from the plane. Now considerably closer to the plane, it then "dropped back to the 9 o'clock position" and again moved out to a 15 mile distance. When the pilot estimated the distance of the light to be "15 miles" there was still no radar confirmation made. This may have been due to the "large area of temperature returns" in the immediate vicinity. It was recorded that the plane in question here can only "be seen on radar...because he is equipped with a transponder." A transponder communicates information about the aircraft to reduce dangerous and uncontrolled variables for air travel. Assuming the pilot's estimates are correct, all that distance was traveled in approximately just one minute. This wasn't to be the most startling show yet that night. Then the object loss an estimated "500 feet" of altitude while moving to their "11 o'clock position." With this the ground controller responded:

AUR: Any chance that it's an aircraft with lights?

PIL: Negative, sir, negative—uh . . . uh—it's a white light and it's changing to—it, it's a weird color. It's alternating colors so I would have to say it's not an aircraft, negative.

AUR: I take you don't want to make any guesses as to what it is.

PIL: I may be dumb but I'm not stupid.

AUR: (Laughter in background) uh, roger. Does it pose any possible threat to you?

PIL: I would say—uh—no, sir. I'm getting some turbulence right now. The object has faded now down into five distinct lights . . .uh, it's a white light with five red ones around it now.

Around 11:01 pm the ground controller contacted the pilot informing him that the radar scope should again fully function as they cleared "fifteen miles northwest of Wisconsin Dells." This means the temperature obscuration anomaly would be less or completely gone so the plane and presumably the object still following in the "ten-thirty position" would show up on radar. The pilot reported that the sky was "quite clear: every star was seen in the sky." Seemingly on queue the object responded to the new, news:

AUR: Do you still have the target?
PIL: It went—uh—from my 10 o'clock over to my 2 o'clock and it's now hovering over there...when that baby took off, it took off.

With the same speed the object's next move was to return to the original side of the plane it was sighted on. Of course it must be stated, "the plane was holding straight northwesterly course on autopilot." For these effects to be explained from watching a stationary object in a moving plane, the pilot and passenger would have had to be 'jostled' 120 degrees. For those of us who haven't studied our compass lately that would mean they would have had to turn nearly all the way around facing the opposite direction, then, back all without falling from the sky. This was a small to midsized plane, able to seat "two up front and eight in the back." Not that a stationary object viewed from a moving airplane is the only explanation in this sighting by any means. Only moments later as the plane came out of the radar distorted area, the plot thickened again.

Ground control had radar confirmation on "some type of non-transponding target." Remember that the plane had a transponder that can be simply thought of as a device in the plane that communicated its position back to the radar stations it passed by. The ground controller at Aurora recorded, "every 6-second sweep" of the radar that the object "jumped" from "the left side of the pilot's position to his right and back again." A radar "sweep" can be thought of as the time it takes for the radar to refresh one full cycle, revealing an updated interpretation of the sky to the radar operator.

The object reportedly appeared in similar positions to the pilot and the radar controller at the same time as it moved about the sky that evening. It is worth mentioning that the object appeared in nearly five consecutive sweeps of the radar except for the second sweep. This means that the UFO was picked up on radar for 24–30 seconds while at the same time being observed visually by the pilot and passenger making the large movements. That equates to some really interesting large space traveled in a relatively short period of time. Why the UFO did not appear in the second sweep of the radar, but did appear in the first, third, fourth and fifth remains unclear. The radar controller was recorded as saying he had "never seen it 'appear' and 'disappear' so fast before." With the new developments the pilot and radar controller run through some additional ideas:

PIL: You know if that is an illusion, I can see how somebody could be easily fooled by it.

AUR: Could you possibly turn off all your dash lights and external lights for a few moments to see if that does anything?

PIL: Sir, we already did that.

AUR: OK, so it's definitely not a reflection of any type off you—uh—off your aircraft?

PIL: Definitely not, sir.

AUR: Do you have the Moon in sight?

PIL: Stand by. No sir, no Moon in sight.

AUR: Roger. Madison tower said that she could see you visually but—uh—she could still see you on radar, but she also picked up no targets on radar around you!

PIL: How thrilling! (According to the transcriber, this was said in a "sarcastic" tone).

With that the object "shot up in altitude to approximately 45 degrees above him." CUFOS report went on to show that it was now 11:05 pm and the target moved from a twelve o'clock position in front of the pilot to an estimated "six or seven thousand feet higher than him." The pilot conceded the difficulty in estimating distances, making the "degrees" or angular position of the object to himself important as they can more accurately be ascertained in that situation.

It was now 11:09 pm:

AUR: OK, I've got a very possible target right over the Volk Airport.

PIL: Is that cotton-picker keeping pace with me at the same speed?

AUR: No sir, it appears to be stationary over Volk Field right at this time. I'll put him at 12 o'clock at seven miles.

PIL: Target's moving closer.

AUR: Roger, the target I have is stationary, you're heading right for it . . . possibly, maybe, 10 degrees off to the right of you—dead on course.

PIL: Target's coming in closer.

AUR: That target is definitely growing -- uh—I don't know exactly what would cause that unless it was a change in relative position. It's almost the same size as your aircraft. It would now be about one o'clock at three miles.

The investigators at the time determined that the target "growing" was noticed on radar and confirmed with the pilots following observations:

> PIL: Yes, sir, it's getting very bright and turbulence here. ("The pilot would later tell IUR that he was getting 'white caps on his coffee'").
> AUR: Would you like to change course?
> PIL: Uhhhh. I think it's just the weather. Let's go and find this thing out.
> AUR: OK, down to about one-thirty and two miles.
> PIL: Yes, sir. Still got it at my 12 o'clock position at about that. I'm not painting any weather in this area, and I'm in clear air, but I'm getting moderate to—uh, um—lightly—um—you know, about moderate turbulence.
> AUR: Roger, we—we've—uh—been having—uh—turbulence reports from that area all day long from North Central jets at 20 to 24,000.
> PIL: Good. (Again, according to the transcriber, this was said in a "sarcastic" tone).
> AUR: OK, you should be at about 2 o'clock at two miles.
> PIL: Whatever it is, it's lit up like a Christmas tree.

As the pilot neared the object he was forced to remove autopilot and fly manually to "hold trim." The radar showed the UFO and transponding aircraft to convene on each other then:

> AUR: I now show you having passed the target I was painting (showing up on radar).

The pilot was too focused on his developing situation to reply. It was 11:11 pm now and the plane had just passed "directly under" the object. Thanks to the investigators we have the pilot's description of the object as he flew underneath. The pilot reported "small red lights held their positions on the surface" of the "oval-shaped form." From the most distant view of the object he reported it being the size of a "large star" to that of "half the full moon's [sic] diameter." There was no sound reported as being heard from the object, even at its closest proximity. All the staff located in the control room at the time reported their "hearts were beating" quicker than normal, as they awaited a response from the pilot. With that they called again:

> AUR: Where is the target now, sir?
> Just as the airplane passed beyond the object the pilot reported:
> PIL: Well, right now, I'm in extremely smooth air and—nothing.

Nowhere.
AUR: OK, you've lost the target now?
PIL: Completely.

The airplane corrected its heading "by 20 degrees" after changing course to investigate the UFO:

PIL: I'm glad you finally got something on radar, I thought I was losing my mind.
AUR: Well, sir, in this area, I picked it up . . . I'm now also picking some other things that could be temperature inversion; however, that one was pretty steady and it did certainly correspond to your position.
PIL: Where's the Air Force when you need em? [sic]
AUR: That was right over their base.
PIL: Ah, ha! The "secret weapon"!
AUR: Yep, may be. The only problem being, if that was—uh—possibly a military type aircraft that was out flitting around and—uh—was messing around in VFR conditions, I would have been picking up reflected radar signals from it and it would have been moving along with you; however, when I was calling the target out to you, it appeared to be stationary.
PIL: That's the way it appeared to me, too, and I kept moving in close on it and I would get up there and the lights would become very distinctive and it would start to depict this shape and it was a coincidence, I'm sure, and my imagination, but every time we got close to it, we picked up turbulence.
AUR: Roger.
PIL: Believe me, I'm going to talk myself out of this yet!
AUR: No need to do that, you saw what you saw, that's all there is.
Jumping ahead slightly to the end of the communication:
AUR: Do you plan on making a report of this to any type of agency?
PIL: Well! I don't know about that . . . do you?
AUR: Well, I reported it to my supervisor and—uh—that's all I'm required to do. I didn't see it so I wouldn't be of much value to anybody who would care to investigate a situation like this. However, if you'd like corroboration as far as radar reports and stuff—uh—that could probably be arranged.
PIL: Well, I'll think about it.

Allan Hendry's investigation recorded the radar controller Glen, age 32 had been working as such for "eight years." He was stationed at the Aurora "Air Route Traffic Control Center" just west of Chicago Illinois during the above sighting. He and Wayne both witnessed the events unfold and reported them to their supervisor. Their supervisor was noted in the original report as taking no further action with the information:

> AUR: If you do make a report to anybody, and they want to know what was seen on radar, they just have to make an inquiry to the Chicago Air Traffic Center and mention the time and date and they'll be able to find out what patrol I was working.
> PIL: OK, just given the time of day and I don't have to give them your name?
> AUR: (chuckling) Oh, they'll find that out easy enough. (The flight number is removed from the transcription by someone here), now direct all clear on course. Contact Minneapolis Center on 125.3 -- good night, and have a good trip.
> PIL: 125.3, good night now.

Good night and good bye for them, but not all was over for the radar controllers in Aurora. Only moment's later North Central passenger "Flight 577" contacted Aurora controllers "in conversation about the incident." It's unclear as to how flight 577 heard about the incident but most likely they were simply able to monitor the surrounding radio communications. Many others probably listening on that night found themselves on the edge of their seats, especially those that had their flight path taking them through the same air space. In response to a controller asking "if the pilot had ever seen an 'illusion like that' they replied:

> PIL: Uh, could be, years and years ago, that I had this happen. Are we going to be flying in that area where we saw this? We'll be apparently northeast of it, is that right?
> AUR: Yeah, you'll be northeast of it. The last place that we saw it was right over Volk Airport.

The controllers were still painting the UFO on their scopes, now in a motionless position. In true adventurer form, the radar controllers at Aurora offered a new itinerary that would take flight 577 to the UFO and then continue them onto their original destination. They were professional enough of course to inform the new pilots of the "turbulence" reported by the last pilot through the area:

> PIL: We—uh—we don't want to take any chances like that, but—

uh—maybe we can pick it up. Sometimes we can pick up other aircraft on our 50-mile scope so we'll see if we can pick it up on our
scope, too.
AUR: Roger, the area that I had the target in I'm getting temperature inversion off the southeast of it; however, the target that I called
out for him that corresponded to the position is still within a mile of
the same relative spot right over Volk Airport.
PIL: Very interesting.

The evening reportedly proceeded without further incident until 11:31 pm.
Flight 577 was at its closest position to the UFO at that point, "27.5 miles."
Unfortunately it does not appear that any of the passengers were made aware
of the memorable events unfolding just outside their windows. The flight
crew strained their eyes in the direction of the object:

PIL: I'm almost sure I can see a light over there.
He reported that the faint light was "at the plane's 9 o'clock position" and "seemed to be changing different colors."

The radar controller still had the UFO on the radar screen, holding its position over Volk Field that put it within a mile of its original position. At 11:50
pm the object "faded" away and no further reports came in. Nothing more
is available in the current documentation on the events, even after
researchers of the time checked with the Tomah Journal, Monitor Herald and
the county sheriff's office.

Thankfully the two radar controllers Glen and Wayne called CUFOS on its
hotline and reported their experience. This allowed Allan Hendry the opportunity to document the above experience by interviewing both radar controllers and the pilot of the charter flight business.

CUFOS report included that the normal checks with nearby military and
civilian air fields turned up no additional information. The McCoy Army Air
Force Base and the Army National Guard training site were "contacted to see
if any of their operators could have accounted for the sighting."

Additional notes from investigators show that the weather was not terribly
unusual. The only potentially intriguing note may be "high-altitude planes
in that area," had been reporting "air turbulence" all day. There was a cloud
cover that had a ceiling of 15,000 feet; however it was clear skies for anyone
above that, such were our eyewitnesses. This well documented experience
is an extremely exhilarating string of events for the average ufologist. These

fantastic reports have a double edge to them for most ufologists. Intriguing and terribly frustrating due to the amount of variables needed to be recognized, categorized, and measure against each other. This creates the all too often problem of too many variables, for the average under-funded ufologist to make sense of. By documenting these events as they happen we do continue to build an archive of experiences that perhaps someday we.

In August 1985, Wisconsin played its part in a small UFO wave that by the end stretched over six states. It was nearly 10 in the evening and local school teacher Mr. K. was walking the family dog before going to bed. He lived in a small town just a few miles to the west of Madison and he was the first to come forward to the papers with his sighting. Mr. K. watched to the south as a glowing object moved through the sky: "my first impression was that it was a plane" however he shared with the reporters that he watches the sky regularly on his walks and had seen thousands of planes and helicopters but this just didn't compare. Mr. K. went on to say, "I'm a kidder, so I was a little itsy bitsy nervous about telling anybody," "but really I'm a rationalist...I look for reasons for things." Struggling to find any for this one, he gauged the bright ball of light to be "ten times brighter than anything I'd seen in the sky. This was unusual." With his arm outstretched Mr. K. remembers it to be the size of his thumbnail. The zigzagging movements the UFO made were further confused by a bright searchlight-type beam coming from it. Mr. K. thought as if it were looking for something on the ground. He estimated that the UFO moved from an approximate height of 75° in the sky, down to around 30°. He hurried home, hoping to show his wife the unusual light in the sky. By the time he was able to get her awake and outside the object was gone. The object wouldn't stay around all night in Wisconsin as NUFORC showed 14 similar reports before the UFO wave was through. These reports not only came from the same night, but also within close time proximity of each other from Ohio, Indiana, Illinois, Iowa, and finally, Minnesota. By the end of this reported wave more than a dozen people came forward in Wisconsin and nearly two dozen witnesses from the five other states. These witnesses all seem to report a large and bright object in the sky; with a searchlight beam projecting from the object as it seemingly scanned the ground below. For further discussion and greater scope please see Appendix I.

The Wisconsin State Journal and *The Capital Times* newspapers reported in November 1985 that residents to the north of Madison were witnessing flying triangles. Our first reporting witness, John was driving just north of Madison on Highway CV. John first noticed "three white lights" hovering approximately "...30 feet above" an area farmhouse. Like many other witnesses, their first reaction to a UFO sighting is: "at first I thought it was an airplane, then I thought it was a helicopter." Searching for logical, average explanations he finally "realized I didn't know what it was." He did know however, that he wanted a better look. After stopping his car and stepping out he noticed a "roughly triangular" shape with the "bottom sloped into contours." There was no noise as he stepped out of his car or as it disappeared soon after. He shared his personal thoughts on the experience, "I'm a little reticent to talk about it - I haven't even told my wife...It sounds so crazy." Reticent, apparently John was no stranger to a dictionary. As you may tell from the context it means reserved, restrained, and silent: and yes I double checked in a thesaurus. There were other sightings added to this articulate witness's experience published in the same two papers on the 22nd of the same month. The next sighting would seem to echo the previous, but as we will read the first reported was not the first experienced.

'Sober' witness describes UFO

A 29-year-old Madison woman, who

Re-creation of a headline that appeared in The Capital Times on November 21, 1985 that gave a brief report of this same sighting. Re-creation by Noah Voss.

The Madison Police Department was involved in taking a statement from this observer who actually was witness to the UFO three days prior the last sighting. Joe Durkin, a spokesman for the police department, shared that the officers he's encountered don't always go the extra step and fill out an official police report regarding UFO sightings. Joe said "but this woman sounded normal" and "we don't see to many reports like this."

The woman police took so seriously was driving down Milwaukee Street on the East side of Madison when she first noticed the object. She recalled the time was after 11 in the evening when "three lights above a row of trees," moved over the local Baptist church. She initially assumes them to be from a helicopter.

Remembering as the "craft" descended "towards a house on the north side of the street" it lowered to just "10 feet above the road." Fearing that the object may actually "crash into the house," she pulls the car "over to the curb." Our witness is so amazed by the situation that she pulled over: "never taking my eyes off the lights." Thankfully for those perhaps in the house, the UFO "makes a sharp and graceful 90-degree turn just short of the curb." With the new trajectory the object now moves towards our stunned witness. She con-

tinues to watch on as it, "rises slightly in the middle of the block…ascending straight up, several feet in front of my car, the craft avoids hitting the power lines." This affords our brave witness the opportunity to get a better look at the object from a streetlight. "The craft is triangular, about 12 feet in length and black. A light shines from the narrow nose." She notes that the body of the craft does widen from the tip, however, still "too trim for a person to be comfortably seated" she speculates. "A wide silver streak extends from the nose to the tail"

Three lights as reported by witnesses as floating above the tree line and homes around Madison, Wisconsin. Artist recreation by Jennifer V.

and it is conspicuously missing "wings, propellers or visible engines" not only that but "the craft moves in complete silence." Moving north the triangular craft "hovers 12 to 15 feet above a house." She feels that the rear of the craft now faces her and is "about half the width of the roof." Taking note of the lights she remembers "two white lights flank the rear and a small red light is near the light on the right."

On the top there are "rectangular white lights" that "flash on" and blink in "rapid succession." The lights move in a "circular motion." and the bottom appeared to be "slightly convex." The shape and movement of the lights "give it a 'flying saucer' appearance" she noted at that time. As the moments passed, she became quite frightened of the experience and continued on her way. After reaching her destination she contacted the Madison Police Department and gave a description of the object. The police officer on the phone "mentioned he had seen something similar about 12 years ago" and witness shared she was asked "to draw what I had seen." The newspapers documented the officer on the phone that night as Sergeant Ray Warner, who was quoted as calling himself a "born skeptic." He shared with reporters his thoughts on the witness, "she was real rational…she definitely saw something, I don't know what, but she saw something." The reporters working for the Wisconsin State Journal wrote, "neither the tower at the Dane County Regional Airport nor an Air National Guard spokesman reported any unusual flying objects." Our witness also shared, "a check was made to see if anything had been picked up by radar at the Dane County Airport. Radar was not in operation at the time of the sighting." The police were again involved in a sighting not long after and this sighting location was just northwest of Madison in "The Only Waunakee in the World."

It was July 1987 when our next sighting is reported. Waunakee, Wisconsin and as the sign on the way into town proclaims, it's the only Waunakee in the world. This particular July they were also boasting or at least it might seem hosting UFOs. Two Waunakee Police Officers, Plendl and McElroy, had responded to a call just before 2 am. When the officers arrived to the address on Division Street they were told by the caller "she had watched the lights for about an hour before notifying authorities." Admittedly the officers were thinking this would be a quick but unusual call. As the woman started to explain what she had been watching Officer Plendl reported, "it went from not being there" one moment and the next "popped into" the sky. He compared the object to "one-half to one-quarter moon shaped" that had "red and blue lights." Officer Plendl noted that it seemed to almost slowly pulsate, "very bright at times, but periodically dulled." Over all it was very bright, "four or five times brighter than the northern star." The light moved at this point from the north to the south. He and his partner watched the object for 15-20 minutes before driving to a better vantage point nearby. They drove to River Road just east of Waunakee where Officer Plendl now viewed the object through a pair of binoculars. He then "saw something come flying off it. It went at a tremendous speed." The speed was too much to keep the object in field of view with the binoculars.

During follow up interviews with The Capital Times, Officer Plendl was quoted as saying he felt "surprised and speechless…I don't know if there is a logical explanation for it or not, but we didn't have one." Since I worked for some time in Waunakee and still live not far from its city limits, I can personally attest that the talk sometimes turns back to that UFO sighting. The people who were around back then, if pushed enough, seem to all have an opinion on the matter. As one might expect, the opinions vary on what was exactly sighted. To the witnesses credit however, everyone in town spoke for the good character of the people involved with the sighting.

John shared with UFOwisconsin.com that in 1988 while leaning out of a window, he experienced a barely discernable object in the sky. It was "not quite about the size of a dime on its side at arms length." The sun was bright that early afternoon and the "bluish gray" object was "nearly invisible to my naked eye." John was wearing a pair of sunglasses at the time, insert overtones of "They Live." He thought the object wouldn't have been even noticed had he not been wearing them. Actually at first John "thought it was one of the small scratch marks in the lenses," but "after a couple of movements" of both the glasses and his head, "this was not the case." The object was witnessed for about 15 seconds, making zigzagging movements until it darted across the sky and out of sight. It left possibly behind a vapor type trail "about a yard long at arms length" in the sky and all the hairs on his body "went rigid." Barring any magical sunglasses left over from the 1988 B-list movie, this sighting allows us to ponder another point of UFO sightings.

Most of the time and for most people, we move about in a schedule of events very similar to the day before. You wake, brush your teeth, hair, dress, eat, lots of coffee if you're like me, and leave home for work. A repetition of events day after day is what gets some people through life and is what makes others hate every day of it. Whatever repetitive situations you find yourself in, your mind is probably in what is called an Alpha state. Your brain is an organ that produces electrical current. These charges generate different frequency, emanating from your noggin like your own private radio station. The Alpha state or frequency is common during tasks that allow you to mentally disassociate from them, such as brushing your teeth. If you can think about it, without thinking about it, the next time you brush your teeth, are you thinking: up-down, left-right, back-forth? More likely you may be thinking about what you should have for breakfast, what you should wear, what you have to do at work, and how does the person in the mirror look so much older than you feel. Basically you are doing something while thinking in general or specific terms about something else. Walking down the sidewalk to your office, or driving down the road are activities that you may have caught yourself wondering how you got where you are suddenly or if trying to think back on every step of your walk just moments ago, drawing a blank. No worries, this doesn't necessarily mean you have missing time and have been abducted, just that you were somewhere else, mentally speaking. Bringing this full circle, would something flying overhead that appears only the size of an airplane or smaller in the sky really catch your attention? Maybe — maybe not. The brain has several states and if you have noticed a UFO and are trying to figure out what it is you are seeing, that feeling in your head is a high Beta state. This is a wave of extreme concentration and after such an experience you'll be lucky to reach the Delta state, a wave associated with deep sleep, anytime soon.

State capitol, Madison Wisconsin

Barely any green space lies between Madison and Sun Prairie now. On January 13, 1989, there was a bit more between the state capital and my current home town. The Mutual UFO Network (MUFON) holds records of multiple witnesses watching as a "triangular shaped object" moved over a local Sun Prairie roadway. It was approximately "1,000 feet in altitude" and within view for roughly "...45 seconds." There was no sound heard from the object but "six bright lights in front" were seen. The triangle was estimated to be one-and-a-half "football fields wide" by the witnesses. I know what you might be thinking when you read these triangle-shaped UFO sightings because I'm probably thinking the same thing.

By now most of us are familiar with stealth technology. Those who aren't were not watching the first Gulf War. Flights of these black colored, triangular shaped United States Air Force stealth crafts, was a regular sight on television and in print during that time. It fits as a probable bill for some of the sightings, especially those where exacting details are left out of the report due to the untrained or perhaps unmotivated reportee. For further discussion and greater scope please see Appendix J.

A year later another object was reported, this time described as bluish green in color and oval shaped. A husband and wife watched in amazement as they sat at a traffic light. The husband exclaimed, "what's that?" As the wife looked on she saw the "oval shaped object traveling low and fast towards the west." They thought it similar to that of an egg on its side if held at an arm's length. As the stoplight changed and they continued on their way, they could just barely see the UFO in the distance. They both remembered how surprised they were to see the "bluish green sparkling light" while just waiting for the traffic light to change. All right, so are you waiting for me to reach for another less exciting and more earthly explanation? On the surface it does resonate similar to sighting a blimp. Since the witnesses didn't acknowledge in their report that it specifically wasn't a blimp, it is still a possibility that they are not familiar with that technology or at the very least have never witnessed one in flight before. It is just as possible that they felt no need in casting doubt on perhaps an easy explanation, since they took the time to find their way to an UFO website to share their experience. Assuming that this act in itself would show that they had weighed and discarded all conventional explanations for what they witnessed, including a blimp. The other issue I would take with a blimp explanation is the perceived size. The analogy they used with an egg at arms length, if accurate would lend data that the object was extremely large and or extremely close. If it was simply close, then it further lends weight to the fact that the witnesses should have been able to easily identify for example a blimp. Further more if the "sparkling light" reported were advertisements of some sort they would have been easily able to read them. As a result, we would have no sighting reported since this is not BlimpWisconsin.com but rather UFOwisconsin.com. For further discussion and greater scope please see Appendix K.

A pair of roommates were passing time in a farmhouse they were renting just west of Madison. It was an evening in August 1994 when they first "noticed lights, similar to police or ambulance lights" from the second-story window. Moving to get a better look they noticed that the lights seemed to be located at "the top of the hill, across the field from" their house. Their confusion grew with the new observation as "there is no road on the top of that particular hill." The lights then began to move. The pair moved onto their "balcony to watch it." The craft "moved from the hill top down into the field where it hovered, pretty much silently." They described the object now with a better view as "black in color, triangular in shape and had red and white flashing lights on it." They were most unnerved by the "silent hovering...there was no increase in wind or motion." They noticed how much lower the craft was than any conventional aircraft they had seen before or since. The roommates were able to watch the triangular craft for maybe half an hour before it "motored away." They also added, "I have met one other person from that area who saw a similar craft around the same time frame." It is always great to have collaborating witnesses however we have not yet heard from anyone else on this sighting.

NUFORC recorded another oval shaped flying object that was sighted in Madison on October 14, 1995. A family of four was so moved by their experience they contacted the county emergency dispatcher to report the sighting. Dispatch recorded the object's description as a "pointed, oval object" that emitted a very bright light. As the light from the object lessened, the family noticed "spikes sticking out." No other witnesses have come forward at this time.

The year 1997 brought the second well-reported sighting out of Sun Prairie. It was March 27 when the second report of mysteriously flying objects came from this growing community. A mother and son were playing in the park when she "noticed a glint of sunlight off an object, which appeared to be high in the sky." It was a clear day and only 4 o'clock in the afternoon. The shiny object was "moving from the SE to NW" and looked "very small." The woman was an "amateur bird watcher" and maybe as a result "thought it might be a bird, but she could see no flapping." The object moved silently through the sky in a straight line and left no visible contrail. The mother watched as "the object began to turn, executing a 180 reversal of course in 5-10 seconds." As she walked, a tree came between her and the object, causing her to momentarily lose sight of the UFO. Wanting to share this experience she "called it to the attention of other people in the park, who saw it as well." The object never came closer, as it "reversed direction, and suddenly began to climb." She went on to say, "it accelerated, and disappeared in approximately 3 seconds, or so."

Madison is cut up with several large lakes around its center. Assuming the capital is center, just to the southeast lays Lake Monona. In September 1999 our next witness was riding their bicycle to work when they noticed a "bright red light." It was "hovering over" the lake and he remembers that it was "bright enough to reflect off the water." Once stopped, he noticed the illumination was "elongated and dived [sic] into two lights." The "one light changed to a white color just as bright as the first" and with that they immediately "began to spin around each other." They "merged together to form one pink light" hovering above the lake. All of a sudden the "light then shot straight up at a high rate of speed." It was gone, and our witness had no further sightings the rest of his ride to work. A very similar report was to come in to www.UFOwisconsin.com less than two years later. Unfortunately without further details I am only left to speculate as to what could have been sighted.

For one terrestrial explanation we could look at the railroad tracks cutting through Madison. There is at least one occurrence where the tracks cut across a bay on a dedicated train causeway. Unfortunately I was not able to ascertain the exact location of the lights or our witness in order to determine if they might have been near this train bridge. The possibility for railroad crossing lights and moving arms to be mistaken on an early morning bike ride to work would be forgivable in my mind. This possibility could be more likely especially if a train never made it to the crossing or the observer was out of the area before the train appeared.

Once a year crispness returns to Wisconsin air as colors fall from the trees. Autumn brings many things to the Madison area. Not the least of which are meteor showers. Our next witness had all but made up his mind that he had simply seen the most spectacular meteorite ever — until. The witness shared with NUFORC that it was almost 6 pm as he stepped outside to walk the dog. Enjoying the clear star-filled sky he "looked up straight up and saw this massive fireball with a long trail behind it." His initial thoughts were "it was some sort of a jet plane going down." In an instant it made sense to him. The "airport was 5-7 miles away" and the "plane" would have been on a perfect trajectory from encountering "problems" after takeoff. He estimated the height at "maybe 4000 feet" and as it moved "towards the horizon" and "went over the trees" he braced himself for an explosion. It didn't come. He contemplated running next door and getting the neighbor to discuss what he had seen. However his dog needed to be tended to and besides what exactly would he say to his neighbor after the fact. That was that for our witness, he had talked himself out of investigating it further.

Upon returning from his walk, and inside, he ran to turn on the news. He just couldn't shake how odd the sighting was. He was full of anticipation, curious to find anything out about what he had watched. As the TV clicked on, the weatherman from a local Madison channel was right in the middle of explaining that there was a meteor shower. The man on TV directly replied to numerous people who had apparently been contacting the news station with what they had seen in the sky. Our witness admitted that he knew of the upcoming meteor shower, but the object he saw "was so huge" he didn't think they got that big and "thought the meteor shower was going to be in the middle of the night." With the news cast fresh in his mind he said "that did it - I just assumed I saw a meteor." That was until the next evening when he was listening to a little late night radio show hosted by a gentleman named Art Bell. He had a guest representing NUFORC that has a toll free number for reporting current UFO sightings. The guest played a recording of a woman who had reported what sounded to be the exact same object our dog walker watched. She watched from northern Michigan and reported, "it was moving slow enough to pull over and get out of a car." It was an incredible sighting for the both of them. Our witness here in Wisconsin shared, "although open to the idea of UFOs and such, I have never seen anything which I would describe as unidentifiable until last night."

March 3, 2001, brought more lights over a downtown Madison lake. It was 9:15 pm when people exiting a building after a lecture first spotted "four light objects." The lights were "hovering silently" in a "staggered formation for a few moments." As more people filled out from the lecture including the lecturer who ironically points out that he had mentioned in his talk how he feels like an alien sometimes dealing with the topic of his presentation. He went on to share that one of the four lights "winked out abruptly, and just as abruptly reappeared with the other three again." The lights moved so they were hovering over a large "apartment building next to" where the people watching were. Now as all four objects were visible, they "pulsated, changed colors, and alternately grew dimmer and brighter" as the crowd had now grown to 20 strong in the parking lot. It is interesting to note here what seems to commonly happen in larger groups of witnesses. The dichotomy of various peoples allows for many reactions including "noisily making jokes about them." Other than those few, the lecturer reported that they were "all pretty amazed, albeit somewhat skeptical, and thoroughly curious." The lights then "eventually, one by one…grew very dim and disappeared from our view." The lights were watched for approximately 10 minutes before disappearing at a distance estimated at maybe a quarter of a mile. The lecturer left us with "I do not know what the lights were or what they might have meant." Less than a month later the lights were to return over Madison.

Only 27 days later to be exact, unexplained "hovering lights" were again noticed. A group of four people were also exiting a building in downtown Madison when they noticed "an apparent group of 3 hovering red lights in the sky." The reporting eyewitness recalled that the lights formed a triangle shape and that "they just hovered and occasionally one would blink bright white." This behavior continued "a total of 2 or three times and then another would almost appear to answer." The group watched the lights in the sky aimlessly blinking about, not far from the capitol building in the middle of metropolitan Madison. They watched the lights for some time but needed to continue on with their planned evening. The lights were still visible in the sky as they got into their car and drove off, "I hope others who saw this will write their accounts as well." The gentleman seemed to half wonder "could this be some kind of lazer [sic] light show hoax? Maybe but highly unlikely!" Again we could find some underlying similarities to a misidentified train crossing. This train crossing speculation helps illustrate the importance of details given in reports. If we had some additional notes on the height of the "red lights in the sky" it might then help rule out the train crossing possibility. For example if the lights were seen at great altitude, say 80 degrees then it would certainly remove the likelihood of train signal crossing misidentification. For further discussion and greater scope please see Appendix L.

Just days before Halloween, 2001, our next witness watches an almost cloaked triangular craft float through the sky south of Madison. Taking in a star filled night our witness was "looking straight up in the sky" when they "noticed that the sky appeared to be moving." Straining their eyes they, "looked closer, and noticed a triangular object that appeared to be transparent, and outlined in lights." The lights were not noticeably bright as with some sightings, but rather only "1/2-1/4 the light of the nearest stars." The reporting witness watched the craft as it moved steadily 45 degrees over the sky until "disappearing" as "it became to hard to see." Adding some detail to his report he said the "body of the craft fluctuated, acting as if it were floating atop the waves in the ocean." The "lights all appeared to be fixed to the craft, and moved in unison with the body." The witness made a comparison that the craft "appeared to be bigger than a full moon in size." A specific clue to the experience may be in the final words of the report, "what was interesting, is that it seemed like you could look through the body of the craft, and see the sky behind it." Invisibility technology has been around to certain extents for years. Could this have been some advanced invisibility technology already in use? For further discussion and greater scope please see Appendix M.

From invisible crafts to visible beings? Thomas E. was "driving west on Old Sauk Road" on the west side of Madison in 2003. Februarys in Wisconsin can be cold and blustery, with crisp clear views of the starry sky. The fourth day this February was no different until Thomas noticed what he "thought was a plane." Continuing on with his drive he kept a watchful eye on the possible plane. As he neared the object he noted "it appeared to be shaped roughly like a boat." After only a moment he found himself driving "under it." This gave Thomas a clear perspective as the object seemed to be "stationary." Thomas estimated "it to have been about 30-40 feet in length, maybe 10-15 feet wide." It was "hovering" above the ground maybe "200-300 feet" up as he passed underneath. Additionally spectacular was the lack of running lights but the presence of "lights or windows running along each of the sides" in which "there appeared to be people at the windows." He went on further to qualify his statement saying "at least black circles in the 'windows' which" Thomas "interpreted to be occupants." As he looked up at the UFO "there seemed to be about 10 'occupants' on either side of the craft." Thomas thought perhaps it "was possibly a helicopter" however was puzzled that it "didn't have any blinking lights and made no sound." He closed the report to UFOwisconsin.com by saying, "not sure what I saw but was puzzled enough about it to file this report." Well I'm puzzled too, Thomas. A dirigible of some sort might also be described as Thomas noted in his report above, however, there are still some observations not fitting that explanation, such as operating collision lights and the time of year was not ideal for blimps. There are some large helicopters out there that could fit most of what he saw but the absences of flashing collision lights, and the usual loud propeller noises or even prop wash from that altitude all being absents start to cast doubt on that explanation. I like when the witness points out the most obvious accepted explanation but has still taken the time to report it. To me it gives great credibility that they are a sane and sound person capable of applying logical trouble solving skills to their specific situation and still not certain that the normal is what happened.

David H. and three of his family members were heading south from Madison in July of 2003. On their travels down Highway 51 toward Illinois, David motioned to a section of the sky "up over the trees" for his wife to look. They were looking at what he described as a "silver thin disk." He shared that he was "doing 70," in maybe a 65, but your secret is safe with us. Due to the "hill full of trees" and his faster than limit speed they quickly lost their line of sight on the object. When their view returned "only one minute" passed. Even with the relatively short time their new view was a fairly wide one "able to see 4 miles but it was nowhere to be seen." David now filled with disbelief went on to say that even though they couldn't see anything "there's no way but it was not there." Summer of 2004 brought about several general sightings of "chromed" crafts. Though there were multiple witnesses and multiple sightings the reports still remain vague and brief.

Our next witness shared that she is a middle-aged woman, a teacher, and had "never seen a 'UFO' before." That is before August 2, 2006. She was on the far west side of Madison in the vicinity of Middleton when she noticed "three lights in a row: white, white, blue." Her first reaction: it "was an airplane, but the object circled in a way that an airplane cannot." If she was forced to make a comparison to something else in the sky she could identify, perhaps it "moved more like a kite than a plane or helicopter." However she said "the lights were large enough that I doubt a kite could have held them at that altitude." She didn't hear any "sound" and "after about five minutes it disappeared behind the tree line, and I did not see it again."

Much of what is now developed Madison land was once marshy swamps. As I conclude this section, I'll mention the whole swamp gas, will-o'-the-wisp light phenomena as a descent potential for this land. That is a potential once upon a time, before most of the marshes were filled in for development. The non-paranormal cyclical nature of a swamp or marshland ecosystem by default causes certain gasses to form. It is in this formation where circumstances are right for the gas to gather into concentrated and larger quantities.

When this happens eventually it is released into the air above the swamp, sometimes igniting or passing by an unsuspecting person on the surface. Depending on the variables surrounding the situation such as the type of gas released, the density, and the presence of an ignition source all play a roll on how the gas is noticed, if at all. Perhaps altering the person's perception on reality such as mind altering drugs do or giving a mysterious and fleeting visual display if ignited. It should also be mentioned that there is still much of a debate on whether those explanations are ever fitting explanations for UFO sightings. The naturally released gas from swamps is similar to the venting and sometimes controlled burning of gasses from city dumps. You will first notice perhaps that you are driving by such a facility due to the scent. The next time that you are, look for the tall pipe that is protruding from the ground. It will be easy to spot if in use, as it may have a tall flame emanating from the top.

So what do the sightings in the book up till now show us? The Madison area has the same large population as Milwaukee variable and with it the still uncertain increased chance for UFOs to be sighted. Baring a wide spread, non-pattern forming, and as of yet detected swamp gas/UFO connection specific to the Madison area, it seems that the additional eyes might just play a role of slightly increased reports. There are of course more than just the two variables in this equation. For now Madison has afforded us a very wide demographic of persons and their personal experiences with unexplained phenomena in the sky above them.

One way to visit: Madison is the state capitol of Wisconsin and is located approximately an hour west of Milwaukee. To navigate Madison it helps to know that Highway 12/18 traverses the city to the south and west. Everyone local seems to refer to it as "the beltline" just in case you're getting directions from the third shift worker at a gas station. Interstate 90 comes up from the south and passes by Madison to the east. If you're heading north around Madison, you'll most likely run into Highway 19. Downtown, most roads lead to the capitol at the center of the city with East Washington Avenue/Highway 151 connecting the capitol to the Interstate.

#3 Belleville, Wisconsin

Winter of 1987 may have changed Belleville, Wisconsin forever. Belleville holds its own UFO festival every October, borne directly out of incidences the city had in 1987. It was between January and April that year when dozens of UFO sightings in and around the small town were reported. It seemed like everyone was witnessing UFOs in a town with a population that's less than 2,000. Parents, pilots, and police are on record sharing their experiences of witnessing the UFOs. Even area doctors have anonymously reported that they saw patients displaying unusual affects from their sightings. Within days of the January 1987 sighting, the national spotlight fell on Belleville.

The UFO phenomena's connection to this area does not start in 1987, but rather 1964.

April 3rd to be exact. This was reported to me 39 years later in 2003 and seems to be connected to an experience officially investigated by Project Blue Book in the 1960s. Fred was a senior at Monroe High School, my old alma mater, in 1964 and remembers the unique events from that evening to this day. He and his friend were returning home from New Glarus, just three miles from Belleville. Highway 69 is the main thoroughfare connecting the two smaller towns. Heading "south from New Glarus" takes you immediately by the "New Glarus Woods."

Fred recounted, "this object appeared suspended over the highway." It was only "about a mile ahead" of them and "had red and yellow lights." He couldn't "recall the exact number" of lights, only that "there were several of each color." It didn't take long after Fred saw this object to notice "it was out of the ordinary." Only moments later "it took off at a high rate of speed, "heading southeasterly." That heading takes you to where the next sighting took place as noted by investigators from the United States Air Force in Project Blue Book. Fred remembers how he and his friend "looked at each other with amazement, and discussed" what they had just "seen." Clearly Fred was moved by his sighting sharing it so many years later with me, but at the time he vigilantly "checked the local media for several days, and did not hear of any other report of the object." With that Fred and his friend "decided to not say anything."

Photograph by Noah Voss of sign on the edge of Belleville, 2006.

But then when "quite by accident" he stumbled upon my website www.UFOwisconsin.com that lists the Project Blue Book sighting from the same area, and the same time. Fred didn't recall the time exactly but "the night was very clear, with stars, but no moon." There is a vast amount of documentation on the sightings that took place just after Fred's the same evening. So much more that it makes the list of "Top Five UFO Experiences" of Wisconsin, which will be detailed in my following UFO book. Investigators from Project Blue Book were looking for additional witnesses to the events that night. They didn't have this report then, however the new information allows me to further scrutinize and feature events from that infamous evening in my proceeding book.

Highway 69 and the New Glarus Woods (woods to the right of the highway) in 2007, looking south as Fred and his friend would have been driving more than 40 years earlier. Photograph by Zachery Allen Boynton.

We have to jump ahead to January 1987, for the next reported Belleville area sighting. The UFO wave of sightings was researched and investigated by many organizations and individuals including CUFOS. Much of what we can now learn of the experiences had, comes from the heavily covered events in the newspapers and the work of ufologists such as Don Schmitt and others at CUFOS. Mr. Schmitt reported that his efforts turned up a close encounter of the first kind had by an "unnamed couple" that had sought guidance from their minister. The couple was hoping for some clarity after seeing a circular object with a "row of lights" that appeared to be rising up into the air less than 500 feet away from them. They reportedly had this experience on January 13 and hadn't shared anything about it with anyone else. Only two days later the entire area was abuzz with the reports that follow.

Reproductions of headlines, top to bottom: Jefferson County Union January 27 1987, Monroe Evening Times February 1987, Unlisted Paper 1987, Unlisted Paper 1987, Wisconsin State Journal January 27 1987, Capital Times January 19 1987, Chicago Tribune July 9 1987. Reproductions by Noah Voss.

Local newspapers the Monroe Evening Times and the Monticello Messenger quickly picked up the unique stories as word began to spread worldwide on the area's newly publicized activity. Wisconsin ufologists descended on the area in true form and added to the well-documented sightings.

The evening of January 15, 1987, started as many others had for Officer Kazmar of the Belleville Police Department. At 8:15 that evening however, he noticed something out of the ordinary in the sky. Officer Kazmar "kind of disregarded" the first sighting "at the time." He was used to seeing planes in that area of the sky knowing "it's a plane route." After awhile he thought it was odd that the object was "not moving." Just less than six hours later Officer Kazmar had his next sighting. With him at the time was a ride-along from a program the police department offered in attempts to empower and educate the civilian community, through first hand observation. Officer Kazmar's ride-along was his neighbor Jeff. That Friday morning around 2:50 they recalled, it was a "clear night" as they headed west on Highway 69.

Photograph by Noah Voss of 2007, of population sign on the edge of Belleville, Wisconsin, showing 1,908.

They remembered watching a "close-knit cluster of red, blue and white lights" in the sky to the southwest. The two drove to the best vantage point they could think of, which was up a nearby hill on Quarry Road. From their new vista they watched for approximately 15 minutes before Officer Kazmar contacted the Dane County Sheriff's Department. The object appeared to have a line of "bright red, blue and white lights, with the blue light in the middle shining brighter than the others." As he spoke with the dispatcher the two discovered that no one else had reported the object — yet. Attempting to verify the appearance of no motion, the pair "lined it up with a telephone pole; and it didn't move whatsoever." The Dane County dispatcher had contacted O'Hare International Airport in Chicago, Illinois as no one at the Madison airport was reached. To their surprise O'Hare reported that they were indeed monitoring an unknown object in the area. As time passed, the number of onlookers would increase at Quarry Road.

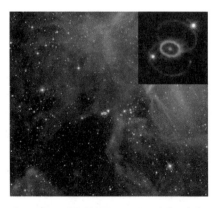

The first two witnesses were joined by a Dane County Sheriff's Deputy out of Verona. He had been watching the "same sight" and was followed by a Green County Sheriff's Deputy. Of the four men who watched the object that evening there was only one discrepancy. The Sheriff's Deputy from Green County who was last to arrive and had initially a differ-

Supernova SN 1987A, center of the above image and magnified in the upper right. Image credit: the National Aeronautics and Space Administration (NASA), and the European Space Agency (ESA)

ent theory. He shared his opinion that the object might have been "a nova." Novae or supernovae can be thought of as a different stage in the life of a star. When stars enter this stage of life they typically and temporarily grow in size and light magnitude. Throughout history we have records of these nova events being observed in the sky. Novae are sometimes so bright they even become visible during daylight hours.

Launched in 2004, BESS-Polar is pictured in the above image with the balloon in the background and instrumentation in the foreground. Image credit: NASA

The above image from the Hubble Space Telescope (HST) was taken in 1994. The image shows supernova SN 1987A that first became visible here on Earth in January 1987. Now before we get too excited that this may be a viable explanation for our UFO wave in Belleville, it must be stated that it wasn't actually discovered until February of the same year. The optical discovery date aside, when it was finally documented by astronomers, it was only visible to the southern hemisphere due to its location in the sky. This supernova does hold some unique characteristics however, such as the closest supernova to the Earth since the invention of the telescope. In my subsequent research I did not find any novae or supernovae documented for the 1987 timeframe that could have been misidentified as a UFO. Also, historical observations of novae and supernovae do not seem to fit with the descriptions being given by most of the witnesses in Belleville. Those observations of UFOs that include large movements, distinctly separate lights, and structures behind the light sources do not fit with novae events that normally appear in the night sky as a bright star.

The other observers that evening were indeed "awe-struck" with the event. Jeff thought at the moment of the sighting, that perhaps the "most likely explanation" was "a weather balloon."

This theory was dismissed in the newspapers by most researchers and investigators in the following days.

Even Jeff himself reportedly contacted the National Weather Service which replied, "a weather balloon would not have lights." The previous picture shows a balloon that is larger than a ball field, with a large reflective payload carried underneath. Officer Kazmar shared with reporters at the time that he became "more prone to scanning the night sky" and even "went out the next night" but didn't witness anything. Ufologists investigating the case, later received confirmation from the Federal Aviation Administration (FAA) that there was a radar target that night. We can't call ourselves thorough investigators and ignore the difference in observations that come from eyewitnesses standing right next to each other during a UFO sighting.

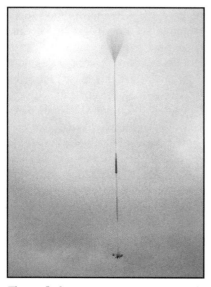

This in-flight experiment using a scientific balloon pictured in the top used an instrument called InFOCuS (International Focusing Optics Collaboration for u-Crab Sensitivity) that is seen tethered below and is approximately 26 feet in length. Image credit: NASA/Nagoya University

My experience with any perceived observational discrepancies found between eyewitnesses are not necessarily due to ignorant people who are watching next to smarter ones. Two of the largest variables I've experienced are: have you thought about this potential moment before it happened, and where your head is at when it does happen. To help clarify those two variables let's use an example. Say the UFO is right in front of you, are you full of fear, saying to yourself "run, hide, I hope it doesn't come this way, oh-no" or do you remind yourself once "notice everything" and proceed to do so. Perhaps we can reasonably expect the "notice everything" response from someone who has visualized the possible experience ahead of time. As a result, this practiced witness may remain calmer and be prone to focus their attention on the details of the UFO. To elaborate on "where your head is at" we can look to my own experience discussed later, however, simply said the mental state and or emotional mood of the witness does play an important role in how the sighting is interpreted. This becomes quite apparent as you will read later from my own first hand experience in the Long Lake area. The historically short duration of most UFO sightings causes people who haven't imagined the possibility before that moment, to still be muttering to themselves, grasping at reality even long after the sighting is over. The person who has for example, read this book, while not ensured a great report, I feel has a better chance at remembering important information for investigators later on. Practicing anything, most always makes you better at it. Whether you are learning to drive a car, break a board in Karate class or preparing for the off chance you witness a UFO. Visualizing yourself in the moment and how you could react gives you an added edge when you are actually in the moment, should that time ever come.

Larry was not with the crowd on Quarry Road during their sighting, however, was in the Wisconsin Recorder on January 29, 1987, sharing his experience of what was believed to be the same evening. His initial reaction to seeing this certain something in the sky: "It was like a Goodyear blimp." Working a night shift in Madison for Larry required nearly nightly drives up Highway 69. Larry was returning home to New Glarus early in the morning and as a result was made witness to an unusual sight. That morning nearing town he "watched a strange, flashing object hovering in the night sky." The Wisconsin Recorder and New Glarus Post reported that Larry said the craft "slowly cruised over New Glarus at a very low altitude, going northwest." On that trajectory it would need to change course for it to go over Belleville, however, if the UFO had stayed on a north western course from New Glarus it could possibly have been visible from atop Quarry Road.

UFO sightings in area continue to be reported
by Michael Burke

Re-created headline that ran in the New Glarus Post first published January 28, 1987, that recounted several sightings in the Belleville area. Re-creation by Noah Voss.

He went on to describe the object further "It was like a big cigar. It was about as long as a DC-10 or longer, but it had no wings." The normal aircraft navigation lights were not observed as Larry noted "one red on both the front and rear of the craft." International conventions have dictated that aircraft including manned spacecraft use a red light on their port or left side and a green on the starboard or right side. He "didn't think much of it" at the time however, considered the connection to the other reports he first heard about "the next day on the radio." There was substantial research done into the blimp possibility with this sighting.

It seems the paper had contacted the Dane County Airport located to the north, only to be informed they don't monitor blimp traffic in the area. The researchers went on to contact Goodyear and spoke with a public representative by the name of Dick S. He informed the paper, "There's no chance whatsoever that craft was a Goodyear blimp." His strong stance is understood as this was January in Wisconsin and normally full of wintry weather. Blimps are traditionally quite susceptible to the winter elements and are normally hangered or migrated for the season. Dick went on in the article to also explain that "they're supposed to be flying at least 1,000 feet over any populated area." Larry's report indicated the object he watched was "at a very low altitude." It is difficult for us to determine what a witness might consider "very low" in any case, let alone several decades later.

When interviewing a witness to anything, it takes a skilled investigator using pointed questions minimize subjective and unqualified answers. It is not an ufologist's way to demand a specific altitude or any qualitative data that is not easily observed during the sighting or recalled after. I feel, however, it is the ufologist's duty to strive for clarity in such situations, and utilize analogies so the witness can attempt mental visualizations. For example: Was it bigger than a plane, the size of your closed fist at arm's length, if you remember where you were when you saw it, or how far above the horizon or tree tops was it? These types of pointed questions can be used to potentially yield clearer information. This, of course, should not be a forced interview as a pushed witness can quickly become coerced and simply unhappy. An unhappy witness in my experience is an uncooperative one. Where as a coerced witness no longer has any information on their experience that can be entirely trusted.

The Monroe Evening Times reported that Don Schmitt of CUFOS had some intriguing data from one sighting where photos were taken. The article later went on to explain that a witness by the name of Funseth had taken 11 pictures of an object he best could describe as a cigar or submarine type craft floating through the air. Cigar shaped was also a common comparative for the airship sightings that swept over the entire state and beyond in 1896 and 1897.

When he had the roll of film developed however, the 11 photographs exposed blank white. To add to this mystery the pictures on the same roll before and after were reportedly normal. For further discussion and greater scope please see Appendix N.

Another sighting coming in from the area and also printed in the Monroe Evening Times had several objects hid behind white lights and later verified by radar in the very busy winter for Belleville in 1987.

The sightings continued later that same year.

Friday morning on the 23rd of January our next witness requested to remain anonymous. She was reported as a 26-year-old woman in the Wisconsin Messenger who had watched "three lights, all flashing" in the sky around 6 am. She was driving on Highway 81 about 10 miles south of Belleville when she noticed the lights all "in a horizontal pattern, white next to blue next to red." She thought "it wasn't a plane" then suddenly "it went straight up and then veered to the right a bit." Thankfully her car had a sunroof that allowed her to continue watching the object as she drove under it. The last time she got to see the object was after she reached the top of a nearby hill. Looking back she recalled how "it seemed pretty high" and shared that this was her first and only UFO sighting.

It was around 7:15 in the evening on the 6th of February, 1987. A family driving on County Highway PB sighted several craft. As reported in the Wisconsin Messenger on March 11, "one of her sons told her he saw something odd in the" sky. The mother pulled the vehicle over to the side of the road and looked at "a red light in the sky with lights moving around it." She "remembered clearly, there was a red one with vehicles darting around it in the sky." The family was able to rule out from their observations saying "they weren't stars, and they weren't planes." The mother went on to say that one of the objects "streaked through the sky unlike any aircraft" the family was familiar with. She shared how one of the objects "looked like it had white lights in the center and red ones around it." The family was reportedly very moved by their experience but still decided to keep things anonymous. Upon returning home she reported that one of her sons went on the roof to watch the skies and possibly saw another craft. Though no additional details were given on the possible second sighting, I do appreciate what was shared and hope that someone else may yet come forward with more to the story.

Another sighting that appeared in the Wisconsin Messenger told of two men who saw something in the sky that was later reported by as many as a dozen people. March 6, 1987 fell on a Friday. While I was only 15 miles away probably watching the latest rerun of In Search Of or taking EVP (electronic voice phenomena) recordings at one of my friends "haunted" home at the tender age of nine, Harvey F. and Fred G. were just north of Belleville and poised to see something they would not soon forget. As they drove down Highway 69 they first noticed something "unusual" in the western part of the sky. Harvey shared with the newspaper it was "four objects, one above the other." He thought it maybe could be "a long kite." Not satisfied with their distant observation the pair turned on the next road toward the object. Finding an open field they stopped to get a better look and to take some pictures. Harvey said "the sun was in the way" and unfortunately didn't create a setting for useable pictures. From their new perspective they described the four objects as "cigar-shaped, in a vertical position, and unmoving." At first they thought them to be "grey" but as one object "came closer, it looked like a light blue color." At this point the two estimated that the "four objects were about 1/8 mile away" and only a "couple thousand feet in the air." As the "uppermost craft" moved from the rest it allowed "another chance to take photographs, away from the sun." As this object moved off to the right of their position "it emitted flames from its end." Harvey shared, "a vapor trail started coming out of the back of it." It "picked up speed; in a minute it went out of sight." Looking back to the remaining three crafts they "were still about the same position, but there was some mist or steam in front of them, and they were starting to get blurry like clouds." None of these last three had any visible lights, but Harvey mentioned the first craft to leave had "flashing lights on its front end." The whole sighting lasted "about 15 to 20 minutes." Harvey contacted the Dane County Airport but "they wouldn't confirm that they saw anything on radar."

While I read over reports like this my mind goes through a series of stages. Bear with me as you are about to step into the dark and confusing confines of my standard thought process. First I think, plasma balls, that while self illuminating at night have been theorized to possibly appear silver or metallic in daylight. Then I remind myself that so little is known about ball lightning and plasma balls that investigating those occurrences still may reveal answers to great mysteries. When other details come forward just as they do in the above experience then my momentary theory falls apart and I move onto the next one, such as a kite. The witness himself thought this was a possible explanation for what he was watching, even if for only a moment. The kite theory falls further down the plausible mental scale I'm keeping as I read more details. Observations by the witness such as "flames" yeah, sure maybe shinny colored streamers that just weren't visible until the sun was out from behind clouds and reflecting off them. Of course clouds are in the previous report however they appeared to be exclusively mentioned as an analogy for how the UFOs disappeared. The "vapor trail" well, maybe a different colored streamer or even the kite-to-ground string, but again requires additional misidentification and a very unique set of circumstances to be

occurring one after the other for them to be visible at the exact times for it to
then appear as aircraft propulsion, not to mention the entire report reads like
the objects are nowhere near kite sized, though never specifically discussed.
Throw in the pile of variables that it could have been some ignition source
on rockets or fireworks attached to a kite, created by someone to perpetuate
a hoax and I get my headache. But my mind is still determined to exhaust
all possible explanations for what mystery the witness is watching. I think
next on weather balloons. Not to jump on the double-agent, government disinformation program wagon, but hey it could actually explain some of the
characteristics of the UFO being reported. I could see how any witness not
experienced with large scientific balloons could easily mistake them for
something like a kite, yet able to tell that it wasn't quite a kite. The inflated
buoyant balloon part typically has a payload tethered to it underneath. Some
larger scientific balloons as the one image showed earlier can actually have
several large payloads tethered below. However I'm not able to find any
documentation of these scientific balloons having flames, smoke, or even
vapor coming out of them as the witnesses had described. Nope I just can't
think of a perfectly acceptable explanation for the events as reportedly
observed by the eyewitnesses. It could have just as well been a craft from
some far-off space traveling society, which has its advanced technology coincidently the same shape as our Earthly kites. Though strictly speaking this
is currently quite improbable, it does remain a potential that cannot be ruled
out completely. This is one of those wild speculations of course that holds
little quantifiable ground and is best reserved for the six-pack and friends
mentioned in Appendix E. Leaving the sometimes scary and always shad-
owed thoughts of my mind, the next report comes from a person who shared
a similar thought process while having her encounter.

We can walk alongside the next witness as she logically attempts to explain
what was seen at dusk on March 6, 1987. If the date sounds familiar it
should, as it is the same day Harvey from the previous report had his experience. Lavonne of Belleville watched what she "first thought was a kite."
She lives in the northern area of Belleville and at the time of the sighting she
"called her son to look." On the map we can find some striking location similarities to Lavonne and Harvey's sightings along with the time of day during each sighting. With that information we could speculate that they
watched the same object even if not at the same exact time. Lavonne initially described the object as maybe "a kite, hanging in the air above a nearby
grove of trees." As her son joined her at the back patio door, he "attributed
the sight to geese and left again." Lavonne wasn't satisfied with either explanation and continued to watch. Doing so yielded her the extra information
she was hoping for as the object "part," and became two. It moved off to the

"north or northeast" as she continued watching now more bewildered than ever. She spoke with the Wisconsin Messenger saying "then these other things under it...after (the top one) went, there were just puffs of smoke left." Lavonne said "I thought it was so strange" and sort of put it aside until she heard of other sightings. She noted that there was no sound heard and from the time she first noticed the objects till they disappeared was only "two or three minutes." The story doesn't end there; not yet.

On the same evening of the previous sighting, Jim V. and his wife were driving down Highway 92 toward Belleville. They were on there way from their home in Mount Horeb, to dinner plans. People in Wisconsin will drive halfway across the state for a good fish fry, though they rarely have to venture that far. Highway 92 hits Belleville on the western side of town. Jim's wife first noticed something in this area off to the west. Her description as recorded in the Wisconsin Messenger said it "looked like a Chinese kite hanging vertically in the sky." She chose not to continually watch the object but did recall later, "the column had separated into four segments in the sky." Was this a simple case of a mass kite sighting? Or does the fact that those involved logically included the possibility of a kite and then still felt compelled to report their experience as a UFO, all feeling that a kite just wasn't a fitting enough explanation. This of course leads my mind to the next step of a simple hoax perpetrated with the use of a kite and additional effects. This isn't exactly acceptable if we are to include the witness's observations during the relative closeness to the object. Not just once were witnesses close to the UFO, but at several times. This along with the fading out and eventual disappearance of the objects seem to decrease the likely hood of a hoax. The fading out could perhaps have been an undetected cloud cover moving in however, the witnesses don't directly discuss this possibility, so I am left to speculate. For a hoaxer to make the kites either appear to or actually fade away adds a certain increased level of difficulty. The likelihood in both the last two reports of undetected incendiary devices used to turn the entire hoax prop into ashes, mid-air also seems unlikely, again, due to the proximity of the observers. Unfortunately we may never know for certain what was exactly being witnessed.

Some years later around 1993, four friends were walking along Highway 92 from Belleville to one of their homes in Brooklyn. It was nice enough outside for t-shirts at 2 in the morning that day. Someone noticed an airplane "at what appeared to be at least three to five miles away" and pointed it out to the group. The sky "was cloudless and it's very free of light pollution out that way" our reporting witness shared. Then two from the group mentioned its "change of course to the other two." The first two friends to notice this stopped walking to watch the object. Then the object's "altitude dropped to that of what you'd normally see an ultra light or a hot air balloon." The object continued moving through the air and as "it passed over…the others took notice and stopped walking as well." By this time the group of four was separated by "about 150 yards." They reported seeing "pretty much an equilateral triangle cruising at what couldn't have been more than 60 mph or so." They went on to share with UFOwisconsin.com that the visible lights were "red and white" with "one in the center of the triangle and one on each of the tips." The reporting witness was open enough to share with us that the "lights were nothing outrageous in brightness" however couldn't remember clearly enough what the color of each light was at each location on the object. They reported, "it was soundless until it was pretty much right there." At which point "a quiet whisper. Like we were only hearing the the [sic] sound of it moving the air it went through…not an engine." The group exchanged a few expletives of excitement with each other about the sighting. After that they "pretty much forgot about it."

There are several sightings in Wisconsin that are severely similar in witness description. The blue orb or blue light is certainly one of them. On January 23, 2001, some folks were traveling east in their car near Belleville. Through their front windshield was reported "a wide horizon" before them. This is also where they saw their UFO. It was a "single blue light" that traveled "from the far left to the far right raising in altitude." The travel time was "about 30 seconds" and noticeably "about 2-3 times faster than a commercial jet would move." It "disappeared to the far right" and "there were no other tail or running lights." They watched as "a single spherical blue light" moved across the sky. An interesting set of observations. Taking everything on face value the object would seem to fit with a classic meteorite or satellite sighting. If we look closer at the report the witnesses observation of the UFO rising in "altitude" doesn't really fit with most traditional meteorites. A satellite sighting doesn't fit perfectly either when including that they saw it through a windshield, most likely with their headlights on, near a cities ambient light pollution and for an entire "30 seconds." Though only lights in the nighttime sky, this is a true UFO by most definitions. For further discussion and greater scope please see Appendix O.

Once more in March of 2001 the Belleville area fell host to a string of UFO sightings. It was the 4th of the month and almost eight o'clock in the evening when our next witness "saw a very bright object in the shape of a star." The witness went on to describe "red and blue lights" that acted as if they were "floating side to side and up and down." The witness thought the lights were in motion but saying "the object seemed to stay in the same place." Our witness called a neighbor who then tried looking but had an obstructed view. The neighbor asked our witness in response if he "had seen the different colored lights?" The neighbor still not being able to see the object shared that his "brother in law" had "seen the same type of object earlier" and reported to him the "colored lights." The last thing the witness shared in his report to NUFORC was, "the object had 5 or 6 very long and sharp pointed arms."

The next day March 5, 2001, started with a sighting. Witnesses reported a "bank of lights," appearing to be "horizontal and wide." The sightings continued in much the same fashion through the 6th of March. Since this was sighted during a small UFO wave, in a smaller town where unique news travels quickly, let's take a moment and reflect on a hoax possibility. Now, if I were a debunker I would focus on the sightings where the object was not seen independently moving through the sky, but rather having the characteristics of swaying and bobbing. This could reflect how it was lights tethered to a kite or balloon being watched. This would lend some credibility to the hoax explanation. Since I am not a "debunker," but rather an open minded skeptic, I would say that it is certainly one explanation for a situation full of variables that we do not have enough information on to categorize accurately. I would also not be able to just dismiss the sightings where the object was noted as freely moving about as misidentifications without further data directly indicating such.

I currently hold several stances as an ufologist. I feel that simply because a subjective experience could be explained through known and accepted phenomena does not mean that it is the only possibility. Equally so, I do not hold a reported UFO experience to be extraordinary in nature just because I am not capable of explaining how it could have been hoaxed or misidentified. It is probably this stance that helps me become very passionate about those sightings that are new, include extremely articulate records of the event and ideally have trace evidence left behind. These variables occurring all around one sighting still don't necessarily create proof, but do help to develop strong indications of events, leading to a greater understanding based upon stronger data.

Several months later our next witness saw something mysterious in the night sky, even as a "former astronomy tutor at the University." It was August 30th, at an early one in the morning. Regularly watching "Mars move across the sky over the summer months," our witness and their roommate had created a close familiarity with the constellations. The witness enjoyed the fresh air and watched as "Sagittarius…was pouring her tea and Scorpio was setting in the west" all from the southward facing porch. He noticed "clusters of stars moving" through the sky "about 30 degrees above the horizon." This motivated our witness to wake up their roommate bringing him "outside to get a second opinion." They described, "several spherical lights clustered together" in the south eastern sky from their vantage point in Belleville. The pair "both agreed it was unusual and probably unlikely that so many places [sic] could be in one area of the sky at once." Noting that in the past they could recall seeing no "more than three planes" in the sky at once, but the night in question they may have seen "15 to 30 of them."

Later still in 2001, two friends collaborate each other's sightings. Our reporting witness got in touch with UFOwisconsin.com to see if anyone else had contacted us "about a strange object in the sky at sunset on the evening of October 6?" Unfortunately we only have his report at this time. The witness went on to say that he received a phone call from a friend who had seen "something." The friend was on the line as "it left his site" which was a few miles south of Belleville. While on the phone our witness said they "saw this thing too." The friend on the phone had later shared with our witness, "he and his grown son had it in site [sic] through binoculars." They said "it looked like a long oval with two spumes of fire coming out." The reporting witness shared what he had seen with his unaided eyes "a long BRIGHT cylinder moving very slowly." He estimated that the direction of travel would have taken it "towards New Glarus." After getting a decent look at the UFO he rushed off "to get a scope." By the time he had returned "it had finally disappeared from my site." Not far from this area a triangular craft was seen less than a year later in 2002.

It was December 26, when this reporting witness was working in a security capacity at a "junkyard" near Albany. Located just miles from Belleville, Albany has many classic characteristics of small a Wisconsin town. It was around 2 am when our anonymous witness "looked up into the night time sky almost directly overhead and saw the object." They reported the UFO was "very high up" and "triangular in shape." They had trouble telling "if it had any mass or not." All they were able to clearly see was "a triangle of lights four wide at the bottom, then three in the next row, two in the third, and one at the top." The security guard remained in the area for one hour before they "ended up leaving." This was a much longer sighting as the witness reported that they were able to see the UFO the entire time before having to leave. Not being for certain the witness speculated that "object appeared to be very large." The lights were pronounced as you can tell from the report. The witness was able to remember that "the lights faded from red to green to either white or blue." An interesting observation was made surrounding the lights as there "was a noticeable blurring around the object." The night was clear of clouds but presumably due to the "blurring…there were no stars" visible within a close proximity around the object. Everywhere else it was a star filled night. The witness made note that he "didn't hear any sounds and the object just seemed to hover there."

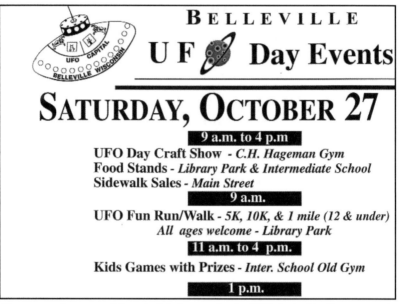

Flyer promoting some of the scheduled events for the UFO festival held every year in Belleville, Wisconsin.

Same month, different year. Troy G. recounted to UFOwisconsin.com, "around 6:00pm" on December 5, 2003, he and his girlfriend were driving south not far from New Glarus. They "noticed a really bright star in front" of them as they drove west on County Highway D. Troy related: "I have thought that I have seen strange flying objects before but as you get closer you'll notice a strobe blinking or some other sign that it is just a plane." At first the pair thought the object "didn't seem to be moving at all." To the best of their estimate it was "hovering over the town of Belleville." As they neared the town the "object was moving west/southwest in the direction of New Glarus." Afraid that they would lose sight of the object driving through town they rushed to the other side. The pair "decided to try and get a closer look and hurried toward New Glarus." As they now neared New Glarus the object "increased speed and continued SW." It continued in that direction until they "couldn't see it anymore." The two thought the object "could only have been 1000ft-2000ft in" the sky and its color was "kinda yellow orange."

Lights that are seen without the possibly attached object behind them and that also remain motionless in the nighttime sky are easily recreated. Moving lights in the nighttime sky, to make another broad generalization, can easily be misidentified known phenomena. Those that are reported to have both moved and at times remained stationary, as in the case above, make a hoax less likely while at the same time minimizing the potential for known aircraft and other scientifically accepted natural phenomena to be the source.

The following experience has no follow up at this time either. It was October 8, 2006, when a Belleville area resident found "2 circles in" his farm's "horse pasture." He measured "one approximately 12-15 feet across and the other was not quite a complete circle about 25 feet in diameter." Other oddities surrounding these circles were unfortunately never publicly documented. Though what other little information is available, the UFO connection is made in passing.

If you visit Belleville, shoot for the end of October and you might just find yourself in the midst of their very own UFO Days.

Take in a parade, local food, even a haunted trail is set up some years and be sure to ask for us by name: UFOwisconsin.com. It is in part because of the celebration being held here annually that helps place Belleville on my Top 5 list. Though it may not have as many reports of UFOs and strange phenomena or spread over as many years as other locations in our state, Belleville does still provide a very unique opportunity to visitors, by hosting one of a few UFO festivals right here in Wisconsin.

One way to visit: Take Highway 69 South out of Madison, Wisconsin until you reach Belleville, it's almost that easy. Belleville is about 35 minutes south of Madison. You can find some additional food and gas options in New Glarus just a little further down Highway 69.

#2 Elmwood, Wisconsin

Located just west of Eau Claire the self proclaimed UFO Capital of the World is falling into place at number two. Elmwood has an intriguing connection with UFOs over the last 50 years and about 430 million years of odd events starting with a 600 foot wide meteor striking just miles from where Elmwood now sits. As a result of the meteor impact gold, diamonds, and a local park can now be found in the area.

So where to start? A proposed UFO landing pad grabbed worldwide attention in 1988. Perhaps December 11, 1956, when it is reported that cars came to a stop just East of Elmwood to watch a "silent, reddish, glowing disk" with a "windowless cabin beneath" about 45 feet in length and flying an estimated 20 feet above the ground.

There are so many experiences, legends, and quite possibly outright stories surrounding the Elmwood area that this rabbit hole almost seems to only continue, twisting, and splitting with each dark turn.

As reported in such news media as the Minnesota Pioneer Press and Melrose Wisconsin Chronicle the UFO related events surrounding Elmwood Wisconsin are diverse. One of the most well known events took place with police officer George Wheeler when he had a close encounter that left him unconscious and his patrol car unable to run. For many this is where it all started, April 22, 1976.

But for me, I like to start as close to the beginning whenever possible.

Photo by Noah Voss Main Street Elmwood, Wisconsin.

That takes us back at least to the evening of March 2, 1975, and one specific family. Carol and her three children were driving the family car home when they noticed what at the time they assumed to be a very bright star. After watching the object for awhile, Carol remembered contemplating whether she should stop at a nearby home to have some validation and reassurance in an otherwise puzzling situation.

Braving through the event she continued on towards home. After the object dipped low enough to reportedly buzz the tree tops Carol changed her mind and stopped at the next house. The family was home and as a result brought into our UFO history. Roger W. was then witness to the same unidentified flying object. Now high in the sky again, they convinced themselves the object they were now looking at must be a "satellite" of some sort. Unable to explain the larger and lower object from moments earlier, Carol and her family parted ways from Roger. Back on the road again Carol was heading for what was to be the climax of her family's experience that evening. As they drove towards home, the bright star like object still in the sky lowered to the road in front of them. Carol was forced to stop the car. The extraordinary sight of this object lowering to the road in front of them was met with screams of terror from the children. Carol quickly placed the car in reverse and drove back to the home of Roger and his family, frantically beeping her cars' horn. Roger responded to the noise and rushed out of the house reportedly to see the object lifting up past the tree tops. After some time the family again tried for home. This time with Roger leading the way in his own car, followed by Carol and her family. There were no other close encounters that night but the caravan reportedly was escorted the entire way by the same bright "star", giving off an orange glow. The next sighting came just one month later.

George Wheeler was a police officer for the city of Elmwood Wisconsin in 1975. At one time he was the only police officer for the town. He brought with him over 30 years experience on police forces including time as a New York Highway Patrolman. Officer Wheeler's professional observations didn't start there as he was also a combat flyer in World War II. I have been afforded the great opportunity to hear Officer Wheeler recounting the experience in his own words of the momentous evening. I will transcribe from the audio recordings I have of him, in his own words, with his own personality, and share his experience on his first UFO encounter. It was the evening of Sunday April 6, 1975. We join Officer Wheeler during his patrol on county road PP just south of Elmwood when it began.

County road P and PP signs outside of Elmwood Wisconsin. Photograph by Noah Voss

Officer Wheeler remembers first "I was just about to make this left turn, when I noticed this large ball of flame." He goes on to explain "it was almost upon me, I, I had hardly time to think, but it looked like it was coming right straight at me." His initial reaction was that it may be a large plane heading towards the ground covered in flames. As the ball of flames moved out of his direct view to the south he gave chase, still thinking he was going to be the first responder at a plane crash. Upon meeting back up with the object he realized it was not a crashing plane or anything else he knew about for that matter. He found it now hovering about 1,500 feet above the ground estimating, "I'd say it was the size of a football field. ...looked like a cigar" and illuminated the meadows below. At this time he was able to get a clearer view of the object, "it wasn't pointed, on the ends, it was rounded on the ends." Officer Wheeler watched as the object began to move again. "...when it did move, it lurched real sharp," he noted that it took off at a "...ninety degree angle." The Officer didn't get any further chance for additional details as "when it lurched, it took off." Officer Wheeler finishes speaking of his UFO experience of 1975 with "I don't think I would have been able to snap my fingers once, and it was gone...couldn't see nothin." It did appear to me that unfortunately the audio recordings I was able to acquire were edited and seemed to have removed perhaps at least the questions from the interviewer or at worse Officer Wheeler's longer descriptions of the event.

Before the UFO left that evening for good, the James K. family may have had a visit from the very same object. Thankfully for us today, Howard Blum documented many people's sightings of the time, in his book "Out There." Our next witness, James resided at the time about 12 miles south of Elmwood and less than 15miles from where Officer Wheeler had first witnessed his object. James and his family reported they had watched a large silent UFO that was so bright it lit up the area surrounding their house and the neighbors'. At the time they had a 3 year old daughter who reportedly became very frightened. Their experience was so moving that they actually left their residence for a relative's home fearing the object may return. Sometime shortly after 11:30 pm that evening, the James's family contacted the police who were then dispatched to their residence. The police reported that there was no UFO to be found but the family's pet dogs that remained at the home seemed very anxious.

Yet another encounter that same evening happened just miles away from both earlier sightings. Nancy T. witnessed a silent "glowing UFO" and also reported it to the police department. She later contacted the police department a second time to update them on her situation. The UFO she originally reported was now accompanied by three other similar objects. The sheriff deputies who were also in the area confirmed Nancy's observations of four UFOs. Nancy T. had reported that she was frightened by her UFO experience. The police reported that she was noticeably excited when speaking with them at 12:55 am Monday morning, April 7th. If we look at this experience on the surface it seems quite remarkable. It has at least two separate families' sighting something in the immediate area of Officer Wheeler's sighting, then verified by another two police officers. To me with the descriptions we have of events and experiences it is not a large leap to logically consider them possibly connected.

The reporters looking into this case at the time found that the National Weather Service out of the nearby Twin Cities remained unable to offer an explanation of what people were witnessing. Investigators also attempting to confirm any radar returns turned up none. Sheriff Stanley Christiansen recalled that his office had received various reports of what he called "the UFO." Reports to his station came in from Elmwood, Ellsworth, and the Maiden Rock areas, all within 20 miles of Elmwood.

Officer Wheeler was reported in the media as "dieing to see it again."
He may have gotten far more from his words than he understood at the time.
For one year later nearly to the day, at again approximately 11 pm, he got his
chance.

It was the evening of April 22, 1976. We know much of what we do today
about both sightings Officer Wheeler had, thanks to the efforts of intrepid
investigators such as Bill Johnson, Robert Pratt, and Jack Bostrak. This
sighting begins when around 11 pm Officer Wheeler noticed an orange glow
emanating from the direction of Tuttle Hill.

View showing the top of Tuttle Hill and the quarry where Officer Wheeler saw the UFO in 1976. Photograph by Noah Voss.

He called it in to Gail Miley-Helmer, who was working as the police dispatch that evening and was also the police chief's wife. Officer Wheeler, thinking it was possibly a fire, drove up county road P to investigate. When he arrived atop Tuttle Hill, he radioed the dispatcher "My God, it's one of those UFOs again."

George later described in great detail what it was he saw at this point. He viewed a silvery craft approximately 500 feet from his location and about 100' above the alfalfa field. There was a limestone quarry to one side of the craft and Mr. O's. farm house to the other. Officer Wheeler estimated the size of the silver craft at maybe 250 feet wide and as he radioed the dispatcher "bigger than a two story house."

Officer Wheeler later mentioned that during his sighting, he recalled the
advice of Mr. Jack Bostrak, an original investigator of his 1975 sighting. Mr.
Bostrak had asked Officer Wheeler to notice as many details as possible
should he ever have a similar experience. This time he recalled in great
detail the craft, describing "six bluish-white lights, windows or portholes on
the side," and that he "could see shadows as if someone was moving inside."

Officer Wheeler went on to describe the side of the craft facing him as having an opening. Inside he spoke of seeing something "revolving slowly" that had "fin-like parts similar to a turbine." Officer Wheeler also spoke of what he interpreted as "legs" on the body of the craft along with a "long, black, hose like appendage on the bottom." He couldn't recall whether the hose appendage reached the ground as that part was obstructed from his vantage point by trees. The orange light that first caught Officer Wheeler's attention was originating from the top of the craft. It was so bright, he reported it couldn't be looked directly at, as it hurt his eyes. Officer Wheeler was describing this light to the dispatcher as the craft started to rise with a reported whooshing noise. A blue flash of light from the craft came next and then he remembers nothing.

Gail earnestly tried raising Officer Wheeler on the radio "George, can you hear me? Are you all right?" When dispatcher Gail didn't get a response from Officer Wheeler, she called the nearest person to his last known whereabouts. Enter Paul F. who managed the local nursing home. He lived just east of Officer Wheeler's current location on Tuttle Hill less than two miles away. Gail asked Mr. F. over the phone "maybe you can look out your window, Paul, and tell me what you see. Anything unusual out there?". Paul got out of bed and headed outside to take a look in the direction Gail asked. He returned to the phone a

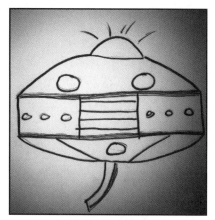

A re-creation of the UFO Officer Wheeler saw that evening and sketched shortly after his sighting. Re-creation by Noah Voss.

moment later and reported "I saw this flaming orange object in the sky." Paul recalled "It resembled a bright orange half moon. I watched it for a full ten seconds and went back to the phone. By the time I returned to the window with my wife, the object was gone." Paul mentioned in later interviews that he wasn't on the phone with the dispatcher for more than five minutes. At the same time, Officer Wheeler's wife was listening to a police scanner they kept at their home. After hearing dispatch was not able to get a response from her husband she headed out the door for Tuttle Hill.

Police Chief of Elmwood, Gene Helmer was also monitoring the communication. Chief Helmer attempted to raise Officer Wheeler on his radio after Wheeler cut-out while describing the UFO.

Back on Tuttle hill, Officer Wheeler had been helped to the radio by David M. David a 36 year old local farmer was returning home after dropping off the babysitter for the night. He had remembered seeing the patrol car parked elsewhere in town with the lights on earlier. Now he came across the police car sitting dark and in the middle of the traffic lane. Concerned he stopped to check the scene out. The driver-side door was open and he found Officer Wheeler unconscious, sprawled on the front seat. David asked, "are you alright?" to which he got no response. As David asked a second time, it roused Officer Wheeler to where he tried to sit up and right himself. He slumped back into the seat according to David and "was the shade of milk." Officer Wheeler then muttered that he had been hit, to which David responded, "by a car?" Officer Wheeler corrected him saying it was a UFO. He asked David to help him to the radio. Chief Helmer was setting out to investigate for himself when over the radio came "Get somebody up here — I've been hit."

Chief Helmer didn't have to go far and was next on the scene. The Police Chief reported in later interviews that he had worked with Officer Wheeler in a wide variety of stressful situations but had never seen him so upset. Officer Wheeler's wife arrived shortly after, she contacted their family doctor, Frank S. and took her husband directly home. Dr. Frank had been Officer Wheeler's doctor for 25 years. He examined Officer Wheeler, and gave him a shot to help him relax. Police Chief Helmer arrived at the Wheeler's home shortly after and proceeded to interview his Officer for approximately an hour and a half. After which Officer Wheeler was still too upset to sleep according to his wife. She contacted Dr. Frank over the phone who then instructed her to get him into the hospital. From what I am able to piece together, it was now after 1 in the morning on the 23rd of April when Officer Wheeler finally headed to the hospital, in the back of an ambulance no less.

Chief Helmer reported to investigators that the patrol car Officer Wheeler had been driving that night required work following the event. The patrol car had a regular checkup not long before that night however, still it needed new points, plugs, and the starter began to act up. Officer Wheeler was not fairing as well.

UFO investigators spoke with residents near the sighting area and came up with potentially collaborating data. Mr. Bostrak interviewed Mr. O., whose farm house was very near where Officer Wheeler witnessed the UFO hovering. Mr. O. couldn't recall noticing anything out of the ordinary except for having his television quit working for awhile just after 11 pm that very same night. He remembered this as he was reportedly watching *Perry Mason* which at the time came on at 11 o'clock and the TV went out just after it started. Mr. Bostrak also learned of a now additionally intriguing situation when he visited another nearby homestead.

Mrs. Miles W. reported that while watching TV on the same evening of the 22nd that it suddenly shut off. She recalled that her coocoo clock had sounded 11:00 pm not long before. She got up from bed, put her slippers on and fiddled with the televisions on-off button. She said the TV would not turn back on. She then noticed a light coming from outside. It was so bright that it illuminated the room. She went to the window to witness a large object on Tuttle Hill. She described it as a "bright orange moon-shaped" object. After watching it for a "few minutes" she then went back to bed. Her husband was at home and remained in bed during his wife's observations. He had remarked to her in the past that people in the area were just probably misidentifying the moon. The apparent television interference is very intriguing. Unfortunately the reports from the time do not address the very next question on my mind, was there any scheduled outages or other televisions in Elmwood that didn't experience anything unusual. Particularly ones a bit further away from the object and that used the same service however remained functional. I am left to assume, which I do with no great weight, that all the other televisions in the area of Elmwood that night had no issues. We are also left to assume that the television broadcasting stations also were doing nothing on their end to cause any outages. If this is the case, then it is very telling data that should be ushered to the annals of UFO data history. What this could tell us about the UFO remains yet to be fully understood. However one could at least speculate how it seemingly interacts with the technology found specifically in those two television sets. The make and model of those television sets is also not documented nor is the broadcasting technology used at the time. Some of this information could be generalized as an estimate of the television industry technology used during that decade. Let us examine this potential as a fact for a moment. The year was 1975 and barring any outside coincidental timing of localized unknown atmospheric conditions interrupting the signal or two television sets naturally malfunctioning at the same time, we can make some intelligent speculations. Such as what technologies do we know on earth to have an effect on television signal today, that may have been classified over 30 years ago? Is this technology being used or has it ever been implemented by any earthly industries that could be logically connected to perhaps advance aeronautics? If no on all fronts than we have at least moved forward towards looking for worldly explanations before jumping to other worldly ones. Where arguably the data is less and the variables more. Now moving on from the television data point in this case, it is not the only variable that is deserving of such logical scrutiny. It is however a fairly unique observation turned up by the intrepid investigators of the time. Another interesting, albeit subjective overtone to this sighting is the continual nuance of fear felt by the witnesses.

The other potential data came from another family living in the area of Officer Wheeler's sighting. The information came from the children in the house who reported that the pet dogs had acted different that evening. The dogs were reported as normally playful and begging for attention whenever family members returned home. Upon the daughter returning home the dogs did not come out to greet her or respond to her calls. They stayed distant and barked more than normal through the late evening.

Officer Wheeler had recounted the events of the evening to Chief Helmer with clarity up until the blue light. Chief Helmer thankfully recorded his testimony of the night in writing. Officer Wheeler reportedly stayed in the hospital for three days before returning home. After his first stay in the hospital he was no longer able to recount from memory his experience of only a few days earlier. He suffered serious headaches and nightmares which earned him a second visit to the hospital not long after the first. This time for a purported stay of 11 days.

Within a year of his last UFO experience, Officer George A. Wheeler passed away. According to some, his death was said to have occurred as complications from that evenings events. What may have happened during the time Officer Wheeler lost consciousness? Was his decline in health a direct result of the blue light that he remembered? Officer Wheeler had recovered from at least one heart attack before this evening, could their have been further complications? We may never fully understand completely what role that evening and the UFO played in his health, so close to his final days.

I was able to personally interview ufologist and associate professor Bill Johnson regarding Officers Wheeler's experiences. Bill was the first ufologist to interview Officer Wheeler and remembered his earnest recounting of events that we discussed in the last chapter. There was no doubt that Officer Wheeler was recounting events as he truly remembered them occurring.

From Elmwood Wisconsin to the island of Colares Brazilufos were seen. It was only one year after Officer Wheeler's encounter with the life altering light emanating from the craft that this small island a world away was inundated with similar reports. Reports of bright lights mysteriously appearing in the sky, so bright they pierced homes, and purportedly affected the inhabitants. The area medical doctor treated persons showing physical symptoms that matched their reported experiences. Dr. Carvalho is on record reporting her patients had, "low arterial pressure...low hemoglobin levels...burned skin at the light contact locations...small puncture marks inside the burns," and "permanent hair loss in contact areas." She also said some corresponding symptoms were feeling weak, not being able to walk, dizziness, and headaches that, would seem to match Officer Wheelers state upon being found in his patrol car. The events eventually drew the attention of the country's Air Force. They gave no definitive answers of their activities until the 1990s when some documents were declassified only to reveal more questions.

Over the next month many people from the Elmwood area were witnessing unexplainable things in the night sky. What follows are the experiences from those who came forward to report them. Mr. and Mrs. Don Y. were heading home from an EMT training course when they noticed something in the sky. Along with Paul F., his name sound familiar, he had also possibly been witness to Officer Wheeler's UFO after being called by the police dispatcher only weeks before. In the car behind the three, two. women, Kathy H. and Gayle B., were following their fellow classmates from the same EMT training course when they all noticed an orange glowing UFO. This intrigued them all to the point where both cars pulled off the road to stop for a better look. None of them have been reported as knowing for sure what they were watching but it seemed enough to keep their eyes to the sky as the last pair had one last experience the following week.

It was around 10:30 pm when Kathy H. and Gayle B. noticed an object pacing their vehicle from some nearby tree tops. The evening of May 20, 1976 the two ladies were returning yet again from an EMT training course along the familiar road. They were driving along State Road 29, a local county road that you cross on your way into Elmwood. However this evening they were just outside River Falls and their UFO sighting was about to get much more real than their previous one had. The pair first noticed the object moving in the same direction as them, while showing two distinct lights in the front as it silently moved along the tree tops. After a few moments curiosity got the better of the two so they pulled off the road. As they stopped the car they were no longer able to view the object. They moved their heads out of the car's window for a better look. To their surprise they noticed the object was now 80 to 100 feet directly above them silently sitting there.

Several minutes passed with the object on clear display for them to appreciate its subtleties. They were able to observe blue and red flashing lights located on the side visible to them. The object appeared absolutely round to both of the ladies that evening. Gayle was reported as saying that it didn't appear to be as large as the object Officer Wheeler had described. It seems by this time, word was out about Officer Wheeler's sighting. As the women continued their drive, the object did the same but this time in a different direction. It moved from them at a fare pace and quickly blinked out.

October 1977, Mr. Fredrickson and his son witnessed a similar UFO close up. Mr. Fredrickson remembers to the best of his knowledge that it was around the 20th of the month as he and his son drove home from work. His son was first to point out the object asking his father what it was. It was around 10:30 in the evening as they made their way over Tuttle Hill nearing their home to the east. The object was first noticed as it rose seemingly just over their house. At first Mr. Fredrickson reported that he assumed it was the moon. When he realized the object was rising too fast to be the moon he pulled his car over and placed it into park. Mr. Fredrickson and his son both exited the vehicle and watched as the large orange light moved closer. As the UFO moved directly over them Mr. Fredrickson described the portion that was visible to him as a large grey plate perhaps 100 feet in diameter. As it moved overhead a loud noise could be heard that he compared to "the roar of a waterfall." Mr. Fredrickson's boy had noticed a "blue and green beam" emanating from the side of the UFO while his dad parked the car. The object quickly faded out of view moving from East to West and at an estimated height of 500 to 1,000 feet. On the surface this report has a classic sound of an insect swarm sighting. There are as usual, variables, and observations that discredit a swarm explanation such as the colored beam of light emanating from the object. Even more still the proximity to Officer Wheeler's sighting many years earlier and similarities with blue beams of light are certainly notable.

It was almost Halloween and the leaves rolled down Grant Street in the small city of Ellsworth. Situated just west of Elmwood where several people reported seeing and this time hearing a large unidentified flying object. The noise is what drew Pat K. from putting her groceries away that evening. With noise, lights, and her son yelling about something outside Pat found herself looking out the window at stationary white lights along with red blinking ones. The size of the object could only be ascertained by the placement of the lights, as a body was not distinctly visible. The lights were just above the tree tops and the UFO reportedly sounded comparable to that of a helicopter or small plane. She was so moved by the sighting that she actually called her other sons who promptly gave chase. They reportedly lost sight of the object as it headed out of town. She also phoned the local police department around 9 o'clock that evening to report her experience. Pat also noted one large white light emanating from the front of the object.

Reverend G. recalled that during the same evening, as his wife returned home she started honking the car horn to gain his attention. Upon having his wife draw his attention upward they witnessed a wingless flying object approximately 100 yards in length. Unlike Pat, they had not noticed any noise from the object. They did however report seeing several green and red lights along the back of the object along with "three square window lights near the center."

March 7, 1988, the *Pierce County Herald* headline read "Strange lights, craft seen near Bay City Saturday night." A 17 year old girl, who had left her home in Bay City to pick up a friend to hang out for the evening, got more than she was expecting. As the two girls drove about, as teenagers do, they noticed an object in the sky. They estimated the lights to be over Elmwood. Curious and with nothing to do, the pair headed off to get a closer look. They reported the object to have "two bright white lights on one end and a flashing red light on the other." The object closed in on the pair to only 20 feet above the car. The girls didn't hear any noise coming from the object or observe any of the surrounding environment being acted upon as they assumed would be the case with a helicopter or airplane. It wasn't long before the two gave up trying to identify the UFO and instead were left speeding from it in fear. Becoming fearful of the situation, they had knowingly placed themselves in, they continued for home. After arriving home with the car, the young lady shared her experience with her mother. Knowing her daughter is not easily given to wild stories as such, she contacted the Herald to see if others had witnessed any UFOs. They hadn't had any other reports and contacted the police department to be thorough. The Pierce County Sheriff's Department hadn't had any "similar events" according to the dispatcher on duty the following Monday. The next report came in the very next month and only 10 miles to the north.

This time we find ourselves again just miles west of Elmwood in the town of Ellsworth. In 1988 around 2:30 in the morning the police received a call from Ann S. It was Friday, April 22 when she called from just east of Ellsworth. She reported seeing an object that had a "flashing white light on top, yellow and red lights along the sides." Ann was also able to describe that the object appeared to be spinning and "slightly smaller than a hot air balloon." She witnessed the object hover over the east side of Ellsworth while she waited for her friends to arrive. The two friends later stated in a police report that they didn't recall seeing anything, but remembered they "felt strange," "as if they were in slow motion." Barring any drinking jokes given the time, I feel it necessary to point out the very similar date to Officer Wheeler. It is difficult as a researcher of a greater unknown to know when you are reaching too far for possible connections. How many times removed must perceptible connections be, before it moves from useable data, to simple chance? Only 24 hours later in Elmwood another call came into the police department around 3 am.

This time, Anthony P. of Elmwood was calling about the Elmwood quarry that we are familiar with from Officer Wheeler's experience. The strange lights and "humming" sounds emanating from the quarry were noted by investigating deputies to be caused by a rock crusher "operating at the quarry." What is the reader and an investigator supposed to do with reports of this nature? Dismiss the first experience out of hand as a bar-time sighting or obvious hoax just because it would be easy to reproduce? Especially since the second sighting was so convincingly explained as an operating rock crusher. The reports don't go into great detail as to if the rock crusher was actually operating at 3 am with homes nearby. Was the quarry even contacted, if so did they speak with someone who was there that evening or do they keep accurate records of operation? Perhaps the person taking the call at the police station was merely aware of the quarry and used the rock crusher as a final answer, removing them from any additional effort. The difficulty with the documentation surrounding this report is complicated to qualify due to little information given. Are they a result of sloppy documentation by the interviewer, laziness to examine all aspects of the experience by the investigator or outright lies by the witness? I have a higher level of patience admittedly with those researching fringe areas of study backed by their personal resources than I would when it comes to police paperwork or full time journalists. I, right or wrong, feel it is reasonable to expect more documentation out of them, if not outright optimistic and wide-eyed. You may be asking me to have more patience with the authorities when dealing with such an unusual topic. There are, depending on the organization, UFO related training materials made available to many first responders including police departments. This is no conspiracy rage mind you. Used by FEMA no less, the "Fire Officer's Guide to Disaster Control," by M. Kramer, PhD and W. Bahme, J.D. could be just the training tool needed. Alan V. Brunacini shares in the foreword "This book provides the reader, and potential participant in disaster mitigation, with a basis from which to work when confronted with emergencies that are well outside of the norm." The UFO phenomenon is not simply mentioned in passing. Earning its own chapter in number 13 titled

"ENEMY ATTACK AND UFO POTENTIAL." Subsequent sections are titled: "The UFO Threat-A Fact," "Adverse Potential of UFOs," and "UFOs-Emergency Action." It has warranted enough attention in the author's eyes, made it through the editing, approval, and publishers scrutiny even then still acknowledged by the Federal Emergency Management Agency (FEMA) as a pertinent publication for the thorough training of first responders. Whatever the case may be or might have been I can only move forward with experienced gained of what to do and not to do in my own endeavors. As resources allow I make additional efforts to fully record and document my research and investigations. In the above very specific sighting, it is not unconceivable for me to accept that the answers to my questions are indeed recorded somewhere. Perhaps someone is holding onto the information in their personal archives or working with a different UFO group to ensure the records stay available to those who look hard enough for them. Regardless of what we don't have, I am in all honesty very thankful to have what we do. The next sighting came in the following week.

Still in Ellsworth. It's now Thursday evening around 9 pm on April 28, again 1988. This time we find ourselves on rural Stonehammer Road in Ellsworth. A husband and wife living on the street noticed a flashing she described as "like a strobe light" outside her home. She went for a better look at what was going on and described "it was a very bright light" the colors "white and green." There were two major points she noted that made her feel it wasn't anything normal. The first was how the lights on the craft behaved "it really wasn't consistent in the way it flickered, not like an airplane's light." She said "what caused me to question it was that it went from side to side rather than in a straight line, like an airplane." The woman who chose to remain unidentified along with her husband for the newspaper article appearing in the River Falls Wisconsin Journal, says she has five or six planes fly near her home nightly to compare this experience to. The pair was able to observe the object for approximately 20 minutes. At which time they moved from the safety of their home to see if it was making any noise. They found only silence. The couple did notify the police, who also received a second report of the UFO that same night. Unfortunately all parties this evening declined to have their names included on record. This makes it regrettably difficult for ufologists to follow up shortly after the experience with interviews of the witnesses and investigation of the site. Something returned only a month later, or if never left at least was again seen.

And then the story got even wider attention. A UFO landing pad was proposed for the top of a high bluff near the city of Elmwood. The year was 1988 and Thomas W. from Chippewa Falls was leading the efforts on the new endeavor. It was more officially named the "UFO Site Center" that was to include a quarter mile long artist interpretation of a human figure warmly shaking hands with an alien-type figure. This was to be illuminated on a two mile square landing area with hopes of putting forward a positive gesture for any potential visiting UFOs filled with aliens. Elmwood officials understandably got on board with high hopes of what the multimillion dollar UFO hub and visitor center could do for their community. The fundraising was in full swing and everyone from *CBS News'* Dan Rather to talk show's Geraldo Rivera was bidding for the residents' thoughts. The exposure was welcomed by some and feared by others in the small community of around 1,000 people, at the time. Sadly for those involved, the UFO landing pad never got off the ground and the community was forced to be content for the time being, with their annual UFO Days festival.

As reported by the Wisconsin Pierce County Herald, it was August 1988, when Charles H. found several mysterious circles in his field. If you remember from Belleville this isn't the only time something like this will be reported from Wisconsin. He first noticed the 10-12 inch circles behind his tractor as he passed over them during harvest. Smaller than the classically thought of crop circle, that usually measure in the number of feet across. He was in his field cutting hay that lay near the intersection of County D and County Road P. There was some speculation that the busy intersection may have been chosen by pranksters to fuel the UFO fire sweeping the area at the time. Charles reported a white residue similar to graphite was found covering each of the 15 to 20 circles. Thomas W. of the UFO Site Center was reported as taking samples from the crop and ground surrounding the area. The neighbor's teenage daughter had reported seeing flashing lights and something drop to the ground around the same time. No further information was able to be obtained as she became frightened and "ran into the house" after that. Similar circles formed in crops have been reported to UFOwisconsin.com from around the state, some as recently as 2004. These smaller type of circles mysteriously found in the immediate vicinity of a UFO sighting are sometimes thought to be a result of landing equipment. This data of physical evidence are sometimes referred to as trace evidence by ufologists who specialize in this area of the phenomena. Some have made the connection between smaller indentations left in the ground in lieu of UFO sightings to landing gear after having first hand testimonial of witnesses observing these crafts on the ground, held up in the air by long appendages or landing equipment. Such was the case in a well known 1980, Great Britain sighting. It would become to be known Rendlesham Forest Incident or Britain's Roswell where multiple American soldiers witnessed a silvery craft on the ground sitting on top of long landing like equipment, later viewing the craft take off and maneuver through the surrounding countryside, leaving behind small uniform circular impressions in the ground.

In June 1998, a family driving in the area between Elmwood and Ellsworth stopped their car along side the road to watch an object in the afternoon sky. The family first noticed a large "bright white ball of light just above the horizon." They watched for about 15 minutes in all as "four red balls of light" came out from the white object. The red lights began to "zig zag around it in 90 degree angles" for about 5 minutes. The red lights appeared to return to the white object and then it began to move slowly. Next, the object quite suddenly "shot straight up and disappeared." Again with this report we see a zigzag movement being reported by witnesses along with the red lights as was discussed in the Milwaukee section.

Jumping ahead to January 2003 makes available additional reports from the area. This time further west to Prescott and to the north in River Falls. This was an unusual case of which an object that was described as a helicopter moving as fast as a comet. If that wasn't unusual enough it was said to be in hot pursuit by two military fighter jets. There were two witnesses who came forward reporting that they witnessed this formation in Prescott and River Falls. Our witnesses start their report to MUFON with being awaken by a loud noise. It was almost three in morning on the 23, while moving to the second story window for a better look. They reported seeing a low flying F-type United States Air Force fighter jet. The witness admits this wasn't terribly unusual as they lived near the Minneapolis International Airport. January in this part of Wisconsin almost always meant snow on the ground. This evening was no exception, it was a clear night illuminated nicely with reflecting moonlight. Our witness goes on to report that they watched a typical jet-airliner on approach to the airport and the fighter jets making the noise were out of sight for the moment. They watched an object about a half mile from their location that they took as a helicopter, hovering above the ground with very bright lights. They dismissed it at the time assuming it was the medical evacuation helicopter from a hospital arriving at an accident scene. Our witness wasn't quite sure about that assumption, and moved right up to the window for a better look. This is when they noticed that there were no green and red running lights and it was a "triangular thing" not any helicopter they were familiar with. After watching this triangular craft for about a minute the fighter jets had started back towards the object. The triangular craft's white light got brighter and all of a sudden the object streaked across the sky leaving a con trail that was slightly illuminated for about 30 seconds after.

The fighter jets reportedly broke "formation" and flew from sight. The witness consoled himself thinking it may have been some sort of military exercise. The more the witness thought on it, they just couldn't make sense of what they had witnessed that early morning. So much so that later that day, they were talking with a friend who lives in near by River Falls. The friend actually mentioned that they had witnessed a formation of fighter jets accompanied with the strange bright light only eight miles from where the original witness above was. This motivated the original witness to contact another friend who worked at the nearby hospital. They confirmed that the medical evacuation helicopter was grounded all night. There is no further information on this report at this time. It may be significant to note that the first witness' dogs reportedly awoke after the owner. Our witness observed the dogs to wake from the noise of the jet fighters. There was also a second UFO report about 80 miles to the southeast and only three hours later. This report had a gentleman regularly sighting the same brightly colored object to the west as he returned to home to Alma Center from work. On this morning, the third in a row of watching the object, he had it come within 100 feet of his vehicle. This was reportedly 100 times closer than it had ever come before and until this time he assumed it was a plane he was watching in the distance. As a result of this sighting however, he witnessed great detail about the object. As he stepped out of his car he "saw a craft, green in color with a large frosted white dome on top of it." The object was about 20 feet off the ground and in the dome on top "very definitely something or someone" was moving about. Scared by what he saw, he got in his car and drove off at "high speed." The craft came about and moved off to the east at a "very high speed."

Several months later another report came out of River Falls. This time several men residing at the same residence watched nightly as unusual "stars moved across the sky." Warm nights provided every year by June in Wisconsin allow for people to finally get out of doors without the weight of jackets. From what the men had witnessed they felt it was safe to rule out meteors and commercial aircraft as they had actually watched several obvious aircrafts in the area during the same time they witnessed the moving stars. This report came into NUFORC on June 16, 2003. The group of men continued to watch for approximately a week in the evening hours. They reported the objects moved the length of the visible sky from north to south, and south to north. They also later reported watching similar moving stars on a west to east trajectory. The time of these sightings were around 11:30 pm. The men report that they will continue to watch the sky and contact me again if they witness more. No other reports were forthcoming at this time.

Beyond the obvious difficulties of quantifying lights in the night time sky we could speculate that some UFOs are misidentified satellites. Yes those scientific instrument filled, space prone conglomeration of instantly outdated devices floating, or rather falling above our heads. Some satellites are now implemented to work in conjunction with other satellites. Able to perform a greater task when working together they are placed in what has been termed, satellite constellations. Creating a type of antenna array in space and if all the variables work out just right perhaps something visible from the ground for a short time. I have witnessed many a satellite from Earth with my naked eye. I have however spent a fair amount of time on expeditions climbing above 13,000 feet and smack dab in the middle of a few hundred thousand acres of wilderness. These types of environments offer a unique vantage on the evening sky. The most notable factors found in those unique places are the lack of ambient light, and at higher altitudes less atmosphere.

What else can we logically examine? Perhaps junk, space waste, or sometimes called space debris has been observed with similar characteristics in the past. It is currently estimated that approximately 100 tons of space debris orbits the Earth. Everything from two cameras and a glove lost by NASA astronauts, to Chinese rocket parts. This is so much a known issue, that here in the U.S. we have established Strategic Command. They are tasked to monitor over 10,000 different space debris orbits as a potential danger to our space missions and domestic anti missile defense programs. I'm not asserting that the previous UFO was space waste or even a necessarily satellite, just one of many possibilities as usual. There are numerous endeavors monitoring and estimating the space debris issue, so many so that they deal with sub millimeter particle sizes. Those sizes are most difficult for us to mistake as a UFO while standing on the Earths surface. To Lottie W. of Tulsa Oklahoma there was something she couldn't identify in the night sky either — at first anyway.

As Lottie walked through a park in the early morning of 1997, she first noticed what could have been a meteorite to her. Moments later she was hit in the shoulder by what was later discovered to be a six inch piece of a Delta II rocket that had been launched into space the previous year. She is the first person on record, known to have been hit by space debris. Congratulations could be given on her unique record as yes, she did survive the ordeal.

On a clear September 26th evening, around 8 pm UFOwisconsin.com received the following report. It was 2005 and a gentleman on his drive home from Hudson had just passed through River Falls. This is where he first noticed a "very bright light, larger than any star." The light "seemed to be falling fairly fast" at which point he lost sight of it until Beldenville, approximately 12 miles due west of Elmwood. This time he pulled his car to the side of the road for a clearer view. He witnessed as many as "six flying in large circles" and reported that closer to the center of the circle the lights were "bright and large like the first one I say [sic]." The objects further away from the center of this moving circle had "one red light and one green light, and very fast flashing white lights." The white lights "ran across the length of" the object. He watched for a bit and decided to keep on with his travels. Farther down the road almost to Ellsworth, he again witnessed the objects and again, pulled off the road. He reported to UFOwisconsin.com, "I saw one very close this time." He described the object as "it had a distinctly plane shape" but felt it was flying to low. It moved sharply as it "banked" as he continued driving now, on Highway 10. He had his final encounter approximately 11 miles outside of Ellsworth when one of these objects flew directly overhead. He reported its shape as "very irregular" and having "the same red and green and flashing white lights." During this time he noticed a second similar object in his rearview mirror. When he arrived home a short time later he brought his father outside to witness what he had been seeing. From what his father witnessed, "Dad thinks that they are probably military planes on practice runs." The witness tended to agree with this dad but they both said of the experience "its [sic] still unlike anything either of us had ever seen before."

I'm glad this witness decided to share their experience for several reasons. From his report it does seem that the sighting was of military aircraft on night exercises. The witness notes the red and green lights that are part of a standard navigational system on aircraft as well as the anti-collision strobe lights all coupled with both witnesses' testimony of the plane possibility. This shows that there are people open to the idea of mysterious UFOs that are also capable of accepting when the experience before them reveals that the sighting is of something explainable. I feel this sighting helps illustrate that while some of the reports in this book may sound nearly mundane they still have a person at the center of the experience. The eyewitnesses, in any of the reports included in this book, have hopefully used their good senses to look for natural explanations first. Despite the varying best efforts made by the witnesses to identify the source of the UFO spotted, most all of them judged it worthy of sharing as a mystery.

There are other positives that come from reporting experiences like the previous one that seem to have a natural explanation. For example: there may have been other people who witnessed the likely airplanes reported from above, however from a different vantage point they might not have been able to determine what they were. This experience for the second group of eye-witnesses may generate a UFO report. Since our previous witness reported what he saw with a firm level of certainty it helps to clarify the other theoretical witnesses and their following theoretical report of a UFO. This same hypothetical example I just used has actually happened before as a result of the vigilant online community surrounding UFOwisconsin.com.

With the same example of independent sightings taking place of the same UFO, we could again speculate that the exact opposite could occur. One group of witnesses watching an aerial display might dismiss the phenomena with a known explanation. The second group of eyewitnesses might be closer to the objects and acquire additional data that would subjectively disprove the first explanation. Checking out www.UFOwisconsin.com could then offer several alternative observations for the same events. When visitors search my site for the similar location, date, and time then find the above report they let me know that it looked differently where they were. These benefits appear after becoming an established UFO organization through years of diligent efforts.

Our next witness was taking a break from his studies at the University of Wisconsin River Falls, watching a comedian perform at an outside venue. Those of you who have watched a professional comedian live or even a funny movie on TV may have noticed how after a really funny or relatable joke people unconsciously use the opportunity to bond, making eye contact with whomever you might be watching it with. As Josh turned to his friend after a particularly funny joke he noticed an object in the sky. Josh estimated that the object was "200-300 feet in the air traveling from east to west." He said it had an indefinable shape to it, but that it was "definitely three-dimensional." Josh was able to notice "a dark body and lines of neonish [sic] blue interspersed all down its underside." He mentioned that it was "longer than it was wide" and "didn't have wings or anything sticking out of it." An interesting observation that he did make was that it "looked like it had geometrical shapes on it" and that it was "traveling incredibly fast." He said it left a "short tail" behind it and he felt many other people in the crowd of maybe 500 could have easily seen it. When he later asked around his friend and likely most of the people in the crowd had missed the object. He came to UFOwisconsin.com, looking for answers and nothing more. Sorry I couldn't be of more help Josh.

Elmwood still hosts a UFO Days festival typically over a weekend in July. Filled with a few carnival rides, a parade, beer tents, and food, though; any serious UFO information seems conspicuously absent. The festival has lost noticeable connections with UFOs except for the occasional reminder not so subtly placed in marketing souvenirs.

I personally hope for a return to their roots and a potential historic UFO connection. Dotting the Elmwood countryside are small notations of days gone by in the form of informative signs. These are a nice addition for those visiting or passing through the Elmwood area.

Looking back on the time I recently spent in Elmwood, the proclaimed UFO Capital of the World, I am left with intrigue. It was spring of 2007 and the first thing I noticed while heading to town on the 11 mile drive from Interstate 94, was the picturesque rolling bluffs. Bluffs covered in tantalizingly touchable foliage. It was the season of color and leaves everywhere were turning each one the rainbow makes. The visible

Advertisement in the ShopperFree Press for the 28th Annual UFO Days at "The Shack" eatery in downtown Elmwood. Photo by Noah Voss

side of the canopy was almost palatable, all grown together as one breathing, living animal. The movement of the branches in the wind was eerie and relaxing in the same motion. Hypnotizing perhaps the best single word description I can offer. It made my mind wonder for just a moment, as my mind so often does. My thoughts slipped through what a sirens call must have been like to those intrepid travelers of Greece gone by, both comforting and cautioning. My co-adventurer for the trip: Kevin Nelson, a seasoned paranormal investigator. Together we missed the first exit for Elmwood and took the next available. So technically the first thing I noticed while heading towards Elmwood was the fact that we missed the actual exit for the 11 mile drive down the local highway.

This did however allow us the always appreciated extra level of adventure and possibility of what if. Our minds focused on only opportunity as we took, well, the first option we came to. The turn took us from open fielded highway to narrow country road. The kind that doesn't really open up, but rather close in around you. As the woods on both sides slowly start to encroach the pathway you drive on your senses heighten.

One of several signs placed near reported UFO sightings in the Elmwood Wisconsin area. Photograph by Noah Voss.

Neither of us had been to Elmwood before as best memory could recall, but we had read, heard, and encountered much about the town in our travels. So the actual direction of Elmwood from our lost starting point was more of a blind guess than anything else. We were up for the adventure and were off, up, down, and around the bluffs for the next 15 minutes. Kevin, technically the one sitting in the navigators seat, had spent some time living in Salem Massachusetts, which has its own legendary history. He was quick to remark how the countryside appeared very similar.

Our conversation meandered through the rest of the day as our vehicle wound around the streets of Elmwood, taking in the local atmosphere. A tractor parked in the front of a house right off Main street, to that of a larger than expected K through 12 old brick school. The usual churches dotted the town and surrounding hills only to be outnumbered by the taverns. As our gas lessened, we decided to refuel at the first saloon we noticed.

Upon entering the first of several bars in town, a scruffy biker admiring the Harley Davidson Motorcycle parked next to the pool table, greeted us with a friendly "Hello!". After taking a stool the large gentleman behind the bar asked how we were and for our order. Now it must be said that on a good day Kevin is an intrepid beer connoisseur and a bad day a beer snob. So he had the usual question that I had heard him ask once or twice before of "what do you have." After a short pause, our puzzled bartender turned to open the two cooler doors behind him, but never to finish. As he reached for the second handle while listing some local Wisconsin brews, another patron pitched her suggestion to us from five stools over. As the biker greeter took the stool next to her, he also shared his opinion on our formidable quandary. "Shceuaps" was the verdict, and who were we to disagree. Kevin promptly ordered two Shceuaps with encouragement from our two new friends at the bar. After being assured that we made a good decision and informed on how much they like the beverage, we were served to ice cold cans of Shceuaps. Both sporting a large fish of some sort, "either a trout or musky" I speculated in my mind, my can severely dented. As I reached without hesitation for mine, I nonchalantly eyed up our new friends. I half expected them to be holding in laughter at our brazen go at a less than premium beer. I decided they were not setting up the out-of-towners for a good joke, when seeing the same can in both their hands. Kevin and I politely thanked them for the recommendation and settled into our new environment. As anyone who's ever been in a bar before, the exchanging usual pleasantries with the bar tender follows. Where we were heading? "Madison area." Where we coming from? "Minnesota on business," and with that we were left to our own devices.

Both seasoned lurkers, Kevin and I didn't exchange more than 8 words till it was time to go. Our normal method of operation is to slip into town under the radar and leave the same way. We endeavor to listen and gain understanding. This time, with the pending book deadline looming, albeit self-imposed, I felt a rush of urgency with my research. As the bartender made his way past again I casually leaned in, raising my hand in thought. "Say, isn't there a UFO festival or something around here?" I coyly question. By not sharing any credentials that I may have, my hope is to lure more information out of an otherwise overwhelmed interviewee. I don't have to wait long to see if it worked, "A yeah, ahhh UFO Days" is the succinct answer to my open ended question. It seems that this suffices his curiosity on the subject matter appearing that he would be fine leaving it there. I pry further, irresolute that he must have more to share, "So does it get pretty busy here then," "well as busy as this town gets" is a quick response. My beer bringer goes on to tell us in brief about a short parade, and how it brings out the people from the town and immediately surrounding areas, but not much more. I throw out the usual, "yeah, beer and brats, that'll bring us Wisconsin folks out." The bartender adds cheese to my list, and honestly what was I thinking excluding it in the first place. I need more, he or someone listening has to know more, "so was there a UFO seen around here recently or something?." Between these walls my last bit of hope fades along with the bartenders sureness "yeah, there was a sighting awhile ago, like a long time ago by one of the cops and he got sick and eventually died." My response of "cool!" that immediately followed the bartenders "eventually died" was not how I hoped it just sounded to my ears. I was thinking of course on the large amount of data that a UFO experience like that leaves behind for investigators. That came out as "cool." I quickly move to damage control, attempting to explain my "cool" only a breath ago. "Well not 'cool' but very interesting," and I feel much better as my bartender agrees and assures me he understands my response. Our bartender moves off to tend to other bar things and leaves me to my own disappointed thoughts on the lack of a story I had turned up. I'm not to be left alone with my thoughts for too long as our beers are nearly empty.

Photo by Noah Voss of local eatery in Elmwood, Wisconsin.

Time-to-go for men in a bar is usually preceded with the "can I get you another round" from the bartender. Said men look at each other and then normally and accidentally respond in unison. For us with the quick read of body language, the fact that there was so much more to see in Elmwood and the long drive ahead, the answer was simple. We sat for another short while then, thanking our bartender we headed past the pool table, shiny Harley, and out the door. In front of us, if you'll allow me an obscure reference, was our friend "Ralph" from "Friday the 13th part II", no bicycle and not repeating "doomed, you're all doomed." Beyond that however, a dead ringer for him. Moving slowly we caught up in only a few steps and startled him as he scratched at a lottery ticket with nothing left on it to scratch. I, not desiring to be rude and still wanting to learn more about our new surroundings boldly asked if he knew "what that building was, or was for." I motioned across the street, several times till he and I were on the same page. After being informed that he had only recently come to town, I thanked him, and asked him to have a nice day. Only a few steps later and my mind is already running with follow up questions, "from where…why here…and for how long?" Consoling myself that those questions may have been to painful to actually ask, for him and I both, we moved on down main street and around the corner.

Pausing for some static pictures of Main Street Elmwood, we felt the need for food rise and went a few more doors down. When we reached the local eatery, it had been maybe 5 minutes between establishments and we were passed by only one slow moving car. The sign out front spoke of pizza and looked like a small dinner one might have found in many more cities during the 1980s.

Through the doors we went, Kevin following me. We took in the atmosphere of a diner that also rented VHS movies including the necessary cinematic snacks. Heading towards the menus posted on the back wall, we walked between the racks of snacks, and the different styles of tables. Reading through the menu, I proceed to place my order. While Kevin is placing his order for a fish sandwich I notice a small hand written sign next to the menus stating "UFO Wall" with an arrow motioning the reader around the corner.

"Finally" I think, "jack pot!" My excitement is for two reasons, the first being that Kevin has declined to take money for my food and the later that we have found someone with a UFO interest. I think, "at last some real stories" as I casually start to read through the postings. Most of them seem to be the same generalized overview that I have grown so accustomed to over the years after receiving them through UFOwisconsin.com. These are even further shortened as most have been reposted in the body of newspaper articles, speaking about the town's annual UFO Days.

I long for a detailed report of the events from 1975 and hopefully, newer, much more recent reports. I approach the business owner now in the kitchen working on our *Photo by Noah Voss, Kevin Nelson sitting past "UFO Wall" at local Elmwood Eatery.*

food. I point to the "UFO Wall" and ask, "so are you into this UFO stuff?" With an upbeat tone and a smile, I hope to put forward in my body language that I will not be ridiculing him if he says yes. I get a hesitant shoulder shrug as he moves closer, "well, I get people asking about it so I thought I would put that up," he sheepishly shares. I'm still standing in front of the UFO wall, as I ask "do you know any of the people involved in these stories?" He says that some of the kids mentioned in the articles are still in the area, and still very nervous to speak of their incident.

Our soon to be server and wait staff is referring to the event of March 2, 1975. Carol F. and her three children had been watching what they described as a bright star as they drove towards home. At some point the bright star lowered to the tree tops. She stops at a nearby house, fully aware that it is no ordinary star. That was the home of Roger W., who was the next to witness the UFO.

Back in the diner some 30 years later, I casually mention I am interested in the UFO phenomenon, and all types of mysteries asking if I might take some pictures. Finishing with my pictures I turn on the video feature of my digital camera and get some candid footage of the UFO wall and Kevin who has been taking in the view of Main Street from our table. Joining Kevin there I update him on my inside information as we settle back in our chairs watching "Grease II" on the nearby television. Our food arrives with a smile and we are brought two ice waters to-boot. The water is a welcomed treat as we were returning from giving a well received lecture at The Unexplained Conference one state over. As with most welcomed adventures we find ourselves celebrating as we did the previous night, drinking dehydrating drink.

Photo by Noah Voss, State Road 128 or County T south into Elmwood from the Interstate.

Finishing up our meal of grease and water, we head back out onto Main Street, only to find it still, quite still. Kevin and I take the opportunity to share with anyone watching the fact that we are at least on a certain level tourists, as we take turns posing for photographs.

We take some extra time shooting additional footage for a film I'm creating as a documentary on this book and my adventures had while writing it. A short walk down Main Street and one last chance for anything extraterrestrial or simply terrestrially interesting to happen, we reach the car.

The trip leaves me intrigued by the surface credibility of some witnesses. Officer George Wheeler and his some 30 plus years experience on police forces, along with his credentials as a World War II flyer should give pause to most that would attack the person instead of the event. Curious on how people living and working there today view the town's potentially perilous history. A sort of penchant pride with one mood and a nonchalant attitude of disinterest in UFOs the next. The people of Elmwood have not only the capability to understand the potential scope of a UFO sighting, but have gone further and come to a certain level of very practical terms. For many of them, they seem to be content with not investigating, researching, or knowing more about their own UFO history. Around this area people want what is within reach, and are happy with what they have. Having personally been able to spend at least some time in all but about four states of this great country, it is very much the same here as everywhere else in America. At the same time very unique to the environment that the Elmwood people are in. The history of events give the area a certain panache, an untouchable character, audacity maybe, or just plain pride. Whether that is something portrayed by the people living there or projected from the people visiting, is for you to decide the next time you find yourself looking for adventure.

Photo by Kevin Nelson, of Noah Voss standing off Main Street in Elmwood.

I am intrigued by most all things around me. My recent trip to Elmwood has not only given me few answers but thankfully added to my intrigue of life.

One way to visit: From Eau Claire Wisconsin take Interstate 94 West. Take exit 28, for State Road 128 or County T south. Or do as we have done, turn in the direction you think it is and hope you make it to the other side of the adventure!

#1 Long Lake, Wisconsin

Currently holding the number one spot is Long Lake Wisconsin. Situated in east central Wisconsin, not far from Lake Michigan this area is full of conventional Midwestern folks. Where as the other locations on the Top Five list are actual townships Long Lake is just that, a lake. This area has many things to offer locals and visitors alike. One of the states oldest campgrounds along historic Native American footpaths, thick forests, wide swamps, winding hiking trails through 30,000 acres of State Forests lining Long Lake help make this an option filled area to visit.

Oh yeah, and there are UFOs. From unexplainable lights in the nighttime sky, to daylight clear discs, UFO crafts sitting on the ground in front of you, or coming face-to-face with little green men; you can find or hear about it here.

The stories of unusual experiences didn't start in Wisconsin with the *X-Files* premier on FOX in 1991 or the series *In Search Of* over a decade earlier. For this story we must go back before European explorers not only "colonized" Wisconsin but most likely had even visited it

Native Americans or Indigenous peoples of what is now America are believed by some to have migrated here over 12,000 years ago, though this belief may be losing followers. These migrating peoples sometimes referred to as Paleo-Indian's spread over this land possibly from the Bering Straight Land Bridge. It seems at this time the more we learn of our ancient history of the Americas the more we find to rewrite. For example, each Indian cul-

Photo by Noah Voss showing the re-created wood structure near the tree line and a natural earthen mound in the foreground at Aztalan State Park Wisconsin 2002.

ture has its own story depicting their society's creation and development. It seems that most cultural oral histories predate the land bridge idea and to this day none of them mention it directly. A site in Brazil, South America, has had "an older radiometric date…" according to the authors of "Talking Rocks." The authors detail the "Geology and 10,000 years of Native American Tradition in the Lake Superior Region," and also the "Pedra Furada site in Brazil" as having dated materials approximately "30,000 and 50,000 years old." This certainly predates many older and possibly antiquated theories of the origins of Native American societies. Even beyond that, Native American lecturer Earth Walks spoke in the same book by George Carter. Mr. Carter along with Louis Leakey have suggested that the work on sites in the Mojave Desert date people present on our continent we call home, 100,000 years ago. Those, regardless of how and when they arrived, developed settlements that still have visible remnants in Wisconsin today. These centers, some of highly populated areas and complex structures such as those still found near Aztalan, Wisconsin hold remnants from the Mississippian Culture from around 1000AD.

The peoples who lived in the area of what is now called Wisconsin had at times tended crops, built wide-scale permanent fish harvesting systems across large rivers, created multilevel earthen mounds topped with structures, and white sand lined fire pits. These were complex society centers with full language, able to identify over 200 forms of native plant life, as Earth Walks said in "Talking Rocks," "Each adult knew which plants to eat, paint with, or use as medicine; when to pick it, whether to use the root, stem, leaf, flower, fruit, or seed; whether to make a tea with it, a poultice or a seasoning in a stew." The settlement structures found re-created today in Aztalan, Wisconsin, were surrounded with nearly 3,000 feet of large wood barricades, featuring watch towers, and disguised entries.

Photo by Noah Voss of re-created wood barricade without the filler normally between the wood, Aztalan State Park Wisconsin 2002.

These centralized settlements were what we could perhaps loosely compare today to city or urban centers. Just as our farms today are along the edges of our developments, supplying the required food; residences then were also set near the city centers. While their population centers may have arguably grew more out of necessity, ours may currently grow more out of practicality or luxury. These urban centers gave early people of the land the comfort and opulence then, which we hold dear today. During certain cultural periods they slept on beds raised up off the floors of their Hogan, or Long Style homes, using food storage caverns carved inside their dwellings to keep food accessible as our cupboards today. Despite these characteristics that we might call advanced, looking back from today it is just beyond difficult attempting to pinpoint the time and location most oral traditions are referencing.

Whether you call it "Miskwasiniing" as is done in some native Algic language, "Ouisconsin" to the French by 1634, 'Wiishkoonsing' to some current Ojibwe nations, I grew up knowing home as Wisconsin. Whatever it has been or will be called, boarders it is given, or people living within them, it would seem that there have always been experiences of flying objects and unexplainable situations. Events that people living here have remembered and attempted to explain. We find our next story as we meet up with two

Chippewa men. They are traveling across the countryside, maybe even early Wisconsin.

Our two Chippewa friends came upon someone "sitting on the grass. It was a man." As the two approached, he "halted them by raising his hand." The visitor said, "I don't belong here. I dropped from above." The oral belief goes on to say after the Chippewa men invited the stranger home, he requested they return there first and clean the place he was to stay. The two Chippewa men did as he asked. Returning home, the pair described the new visitor to the other people of their nation, "a nice-looking man, clean and shining bright." Once the Chippewa had completed their new cleaning task, they welcomed the stranger, turned friend, into their home. He in return shared his story. How "he had been running in the sky. There was an open place, he couldn't stop running, so he dropped through." The Chippewa over time came to call this visitor "Sky-Man." At night, the Chippewa's Sky-Man would intently watch the dark sky. They said he spoke in a clear voice "Something will come down, I will go up." Sky-Man was right. One afternoon he said "Now it's coming" and with that the Chippewa all gazed to the sky. None of the villagers could see anything. Then, the man who had been staying with him spoke up, "a brilliant star shining way up in the sky." he shared. All the Chippewa, who had now gathered, were able to see it as it grew nearer the ground. None had ever witnessed anything like it before. The nation's people agreed that it was the nicest thing "in the world." Upon reaching very near the ground "two men got a hold of it and pulled it down." With that, "Sky-Man got into it." The Chippewa said they did not want the Sky-Man to leave, but he responded that he "must go." The Chippewas continued saying "it rose and he was gone." They believe "He is up there yet. You can see him on clear nights."

This is such a wonderful story that I dare not say too much and ruin its beauty. The Chippewa Nation still has a noticeable presence in Wisconsin with land covering two separate areas in the north. Indeed today Wisconsin is proud to host the most Native Reservations East of the Mississippi River according to authors Bobbie Malone and Zoltán Grossman.

If we pressed further and looked at the 'Sky-Man' experience with today's eyes, what could we make of the Chippewa oral tradition that refers to a visitor from above?

He told them to go home and clean the place where he was to stay. Why was that? The stranger from above would return with them only after this was completed. After they had done this, they came back for him. This may seem like an odd request for that time, however, now we could possibly attribute, admittedly with many assumptions, that this star person was able to appreciate hygiene, bacteria, and viruses. His body may have not been introduced to all micro-organisms and hence he wished to keep it that way. Why he had not been introduced to those microbes could be further speculated upon. Perhaps he was a time traveler from a future where diseases had been whipped out. Maybe it was Sky-Mans first visit to Earth having lived his life on a far off planetoid. We could also interpret the request to "clean" the place he was to stay as, clean it out of all their belongings. This would help minimize the cross contamination of things he interacted with during his stay as these were the same objects his hosts would have to touch after he had left. As a result passing along any micro-organisms he had onto his hosts. Or was this perhaps only a story concocted to teach cultural practices even back then? Showing young native children, you must clean for company, and present a nice place for visitors. Be kind to strangers, an early golden rule? Maybe none of these fit, and why not even more than one. Perhaps the golden rule we know today started as a result of this real life visitor to the Chippewa peoples.

The descriptions of the Sky-Man have a fair amount of similarities to our current NASA astronauts and various projects that did not take shape until 1947. The star-man legend above was documented in 1930, by Charles Brown, once director of the Wisconsin State Historical Society. He did so before our NASA program really took off and people gained a familiarity that we now have with clean shinning bright space suits.

Mark V spacesuit typical used during the 1960s aboard Gemini space missions. Image credit: the National Aeronautics and Space Administration NASA

Not just Chippewa but other Native cultures that once flourished in what is now America held their own beliefs about what came from above. The Cherokee people's oral traditions spoke of the stars and how they are living creatures covered with luminous fur or feathers.

The Menominee or Mamaceqtaw once occupied over 10 million acres in what is now Wisconsin and the U.P. of Michigan. They share there own oral tradition and are still prevalent in the Long Lake region. One such tradition is told of a Menominee chief recounting his vision of "a huge flock of ravens" flying past him as he stood on the shore of Lake Michigan. He noted that these ravens were "unlike ordinary ravens" in that they were "shining brightly with color." One of these ravens "landed and turned into a naked man." He instructed his people to "give him clothing, for he deduced that" the naked man "was a great chieftain." The legend goes on to say that the rest of the ravens landed and turned into another tribe that lived also in Wisconsin.

By the 1830s the Oneida Nation had moved into Wisconsin. They too share poignant oral history. Theirs speaks of Atahensic or Ataensic who was a "sky goddess." They share that she fell to the "Earth during creation." The story goes on to say that she died during child birth, leaving behind a living legacy.

Is our current understanding of the UFO phenomena a clear result of culture creating phenomena or perhaps something more? Something that is not yet graspable by the inhabitants of this place we call Earth. Each culture living here attempting to explain their surroundings and experiences with the traditions of its people, and the scope of understanding held at any given time. What were solely gods and chieftains, to the indigenous peoples of Wisconsin is now to some, otherworldly alien races zipping about in their advanced technology. I wonder what it will be after my time?

From Native American oral tradition to frontier folk lore. This number one UFO Hot Spot has afforded me the opportunity to mix two of my many passions in the paranormal. Combining, ghostly tales of dark nights, and thick woods with possible otherworldly creatures moving through our sky. Perhaps not the clearest-cut ghost story as you will ever hear, you soon will read. As with any experience there can be both numerous causes and effects. For some experiencers who live to tell the tale, those can be unequivocally clear. This 'ghost story' however may also fit another genre closer to our UFO story line. Where it best fits, I aim for you to be the judge here again.

It's hard to distinguish when any good legend or lore begins. Perhaps that is part of the appeal. One thing can be sure this story starts long before it ends. The legend was known as the "Night Rider" back when everyone in Fond du Lac County knew someone who had first hand experience with it.

What "it" was exactly was as varied as the people who experienced it. Uncle John who was already grown and well on in years by 1962 recounted an experience he had as just a newlywed. John and his wife Em would make the short mile walk, nearly nightly, to his parent's home. One evening John was walking solo, returning a lantern, and the normal cream that would then go on the next morning with his dad to the creamery. The shortest route and the one most welcome by John, was the path through the woods between properties.

John was taking in the new landscape caused by the usual winter storm. Enjoying and even being comforted by the wind moving through the forest that moon filled evening, John paused for a moment beside a creek bed and took in all that was clearly illuminated by the bright moon. At that moment by the waters edge, the noise from the woods first caught his attention.

He thought it might be the wind picking up strength, but as he listened it was noticeably different. The forest around him didn't move a bit, no wind to speak of. The "wind" noise however was changing as he described it "like many ponderous things rolling over something big and hollow." He thought maybe "gigantic wagon wheels on a big, wooden bridge." No such bridge was around and as he struggled to place the noise he remembered the accounts of the "Night Rider."

He meant well for it to not scare him, as he heard it do to so many others. This however did not last long as he soon "heard woeful wailing like unnumbered soles in agonizing torment." The sound distant at first, quickly became "louder and closer with the other noise, now roaring and crashing." As he recounted, his ears began to actually hurt as it was "all around," surrounding him inside and out. He could brave it no longer, and began to run. Legs pumping, he noticed the air had grown denser, as if he was "trying to run against a strong wind." The woods around were him barely rustling in the breeze. In his haste to gain ground on the noise engulfing him, he dropped the cream, and lantern. His arms and legs grew "very weak." The force pressed against John's throat and chest as he ran and increased the whole time. So noticeable was this force John thought he "would surely strangle." He neared his fathers house as the force pressing against him grew to the point where he was pushed down "crawling on hands and knees."

His dad, hearing the "weird commotion in the sky" had come outside to watch for John. He met his son as John neared the house, lifting him to his feet he "half-dragged" him back to the doorway. John's mother met the two there and helped them inside. John shared that he "felt thankful to be alive and safe" after his experience with the enveloping noise that came from the air and woods. He slept heavy that night and returned home to Em along the same path the following day. He saw his footprints near the waters edge. John looked at the very place where the cream and lantern were dropped to hasten his exit. The marks were still in the snow from the cream container and lantern, but they were nowhere to be found. His anchoring objects from the night before were gone with not another footprint or mark in the area. Adding to the mystery, only a few hours had passed.

The woods of Wisconsin are home to many a legend and lore. Was John lucky to have out run a loud UFO looking to abduct any unwilling victim? Did John allow his emotions to rule over reason? Is there a big bad creepy crawly monster in the woods surrounding Long Lake? We may never know, but it was simply too good a story to leave out, and I thank John and his family for bringing the experience to me. Our next story doesn't leave the nearly claustrophobic confine that nature's thick forests can create. The next two witnesses also feel lucky to have escaped its grasp and what may hide within its leafy walls as well.

It was an average September evening in 1975 and the many woods surrounding Dundee were flourishing with all sorts of life. A pair of hunters wrapped up after a day of grouse hunting, and while heading back to their car they found hovering in a meadow before them an "orange" light appearing with two "objects." The most direct way out of the woods was to their cars, but that would take them right to the crafts in the process. They were so surprised and frightened by what was in front of them that they ran under several nearby "pine trees to take cover." Their new perspective on the objects was not enough to calm their nerves, "it scared the living hell out of us." They kept low and moved through the woods hunched over, even crawling at times. Anything they could do to stay out of sight from the objects, was done. The pair of hunters moved around the objects at a safe distance till they reached their car. When all of a sudden the two objects "jetted up and looked like shinning stars just sitting there." The hunters did not wait around to see what happened next and had no more experiences to share after that frightful day. The witness had this ominous insight to leave us with, "there is something very strange happening in Dundee Wisconsin." Our neighbors to the north in 1967 had a sighting with similarities worth mentioning here.

Way north, in Manitoba Canada skeptic Stepehn M. witnessed strange cigar shaped objects flying above after he happened to look up at some Geese making noise. One object reportedly moved quickly to the ground, where he slowly approached. Smooth silver skin covered the now saucer shaped object, just as our hunters in Long Lake had described. Stepehn attempted communication in several languages, even offering help in English as he temporarily assumed it was an advanced U.S. project.   Receiving no response, he slowly moved closer, and touched the craft with his gloved hand. The craft shot up into the sky leaving behind a severely burned and disoriented Stepehn. He stumbled to his vehicle and later to a hospital where doctors were not able to identify the burns appearing on his abdomen. The dot style burns were reportedly similar to radiation burns and plagued him with hampered health the rest of his life. Though his approaching the parked UFO provided an excellent case for ufologist to study, I'm glad our hunters remained out of potential harms way.

Just six miles southeast of Long Lake lay Campbellsport. On July 31st in 1976 a local youth watched what he could only compare to a meteor. According to the *Fond du Lac Reporter*, Mike T. reported that he saw what "looked like a big meteor," however he was adamant that it wasn't actually one. He was driving just south of Dotyville when he had his sighting on County W. I've said it before and I'll say it again, I appreciate when witnesses point out the obvious explanations for their own sightings. This additional effort made by any reporting witness shows that they are at least aware of what the sighting sounds like on the surface.

However as they were there watching with their own eyes, they at least have personally ruled out any great likelihood of it. This is a sensitive area for the ufologist. It is a balancing act between two stances. One stance where a debunker might overtly conclude all eyewitnesses have misidentified their UFO sighting because not everyone can be an expert on everything they might ever encounter in the sky. The stance balancing oppositely has a devout believer blindly following every detailed recounted to them as unequivocal fact.

It seems to mean so much more for the witness to cast their own logical doubt on terrestrial potential explanations, rather than have an investigator bring them up only to have them shot down by the witness. At that point it is easy to postulate that the witness has some vested interest in keeping their original story line intact, if for no other reason than not to look unintelligent for not thinking of the mundane possibilities being put forth by someone else. Of course when dismissing accepted possibilities such as "meteors," it is ideal that the witness give qualified observations that led them to dismiss the meteor possibility. This report was to have additional data become available later the same night. Approximately one hour later and only seven miles to the north Orville and his son were finishing up chores on the farm.

Orville first noticed moving lights in the sky that were "going around," and changing color. He called to his son Mark who came outside to watch the lights. Orville thought the lights were "kind of low" and "kind of big." The father and son watched as the lights moved in closer, rounding the new silo, and landing in the hayfield just out of sight. Mark estimated the object to be "small camper-trailer" in size. From their stationary perspective they couldn't see anything more. For Mark, this wasn't enough.

He hopped in the farm truck and went for a closer look. Before Mark was able to reach the object his attention instantaneously turned to that of the two green figures suddenly illuminated by the trucks headlights. They were solemnly standing in the field before him. Mark estimated that one was taller than he; the other figure was smaller. He instinctively switched the headlights to high. The figures raised their arms in response. With that Mark said they "disappeared somehow." According to the *Fond du Lac Reporter* Mark was significantly "scared" by the experience and wasn't able to recall any further details on the figures and never saw the craft on the ground. The father and son both mentioned that they had actually seen this same UFO earlier, but never the figures that seemed to come with this one. Does this experience had by father and son help to rule out the meteorite potential from Mike's account an hour earlier? It would seem to show there was something in the area as substantiated by potentially three individuals over a time period of an hour or more. I wonder how many other sightings I receive that could have a second eyewitness from a different perspective. If they were to report their observations it might either reveal an accepted terrestrial cause, or support a more mysterious UFO experience. Moving from two farmers in a field farther to the north a bit, we find two law officers and a wife.

February 15, 1984, Jenny was driving with her husband and a friend on a rural road outside Johnsburg. Jenny contacted UFOwisconsin.com herself to relay their experience. They were about 15 miles north east of Long Lake when she noticed a "very bright light." She thought at first it was maybe the "landing light of an airplane" but as she continued to watch she asked her two companions what they thought it might be. As they came around a curve in the road, they observed that the light didn't move. Curiosity got the better of them and they pulled onto the shoulder for a better look. They turned off the car and listened. No sound could be heard coming from the UFO. As they exited the car to listen closer and for a better view the "one light suddenly broke into two-horizontally." The three stood on the side of the road and watched as the objects "raced off" right over their heads. Jenny went on to share with UFOwisconsin.com that none of them bothered reporting their experience to the authorities as her husband was Captain of the Traffic

Department for a local County, and the friend present that evening was a State Trooper. She did say that over the years she has verbally shared their experience but this was the first time she had reported it to anyone on an official capacity.

Our next witness posted his experience to ufologist Peter Davenport along with calling CUFOS. The witness was on his way to a photography convention in Indiana very early on November 20, 1985. His friend and fellow professional photographer was driving the car when he noticed something unusual as they passed by Cedar Grove. The driver observed a "greenish glowing orb" in the sky. It appeared to be over Lake Michigan from their position just 15 miles east of Long Lake. The passenger "couldn't believe" his eyes as they pulled to the side of I-43 for a better look. Both exited the car and watched the light, trying to figure out its size and location. The passenger held his hand out at arm's length and reported "the object was almost the same size as my closed fist." Approximately four minutes later the object appeared to "increase rapidly in size." Applying the same outstretched arm technique at this time showed it to be "about the size of an open hand with the fingers fully extended."

To best place the possible size of what they were seeing that night, simply extend your arm, and place your open hand so it blocks an object from view. If you are able to clearly identify an airplane in the sky, try the same technique noticing how little of your hand it actually takes to block out the plane. Perhaps only a finger tip can cover an airplane in flight. Using these observations, even at night, there is a certain distance that an airplane can be readily identified while being covered with a small portion of an outstretched hand. For an entire hand to be needed to obscure a conventional airplane the observer would need to basically be at the airport. Going on a few assumptions of the accuracy of the previously mentioned technique, we have two clear paths to follow from the observation. The first is that the previous witnesses watched an extremely large object and at an extreme distance from their location. This would allow for its actual identification to be obscured by the great distance, even though it appeared extremely large. The second clear option would be that the object was of normal aeronautical size. With this option however, the proximity of the object would most likely have caused it to have been close enough to be readily identified as something known. For example: imagine if you are standing at the end of an airport's runway. There are airplanes lined up in the sky on final approach. You hold out your arm and open your hand. Covering an average sized airplane would be easily done with your outstretched open hand, until the plane was only several hundred feet away. By this time you would easily be able to identi-

fy the object as some type of airplane. This technique allows for rough estimates of size and proximity of objects in the sky and is discussed in much
greater depth in my following book's UFOlogy 102 chapter. Of course as
with any report there always seems to be a however. We could discuss the
possibility of the hand not covering the entire object but rather the light being
emitted by the object. On a dark night this light and surrounding halo could
be several times the size of the actual object emitting it. Couple that with the
perhaps unusually busy and loud interstate obscuring any normal aircraft
noise.

As the object appeared to grow in size both men's fear did the same. The
driver hopped back in the car, grabbed his camera, and snapped a couple pictures. They were quick to point out that without a tripod and an extended
exposure on the correct film, not much would show up. They watched the
light for several more minutes until "it seemed to expand outwardly and
dematerialize right in front of our eyes." The passenger had the foresight to
look at his watch in the beginning and end of their experience. They first
noticed the object at 4:15 am. Ten minutes later it was gone. The interviewer on the phone at the CUFOS informed the witness at the end of their conversation that he had received three other reports of similar sightings from
separate pilots in the area around the same time. No further information is
yet available on these other reports. Bird flocks, bug swarms, swamp gas,
military flares, or ball lightning may have once allowed some debunkers a
quick dismissal for every UFO experience. Many of them felt no need to dig
any deeper on the reported experiences. It has been my experience that if
you do, you will undoubtedly come up with more data that doesn't fit any of
those easy explanations. However I was not able to obtain any supplemen-
tary information on this event.

A granddaughter and friend were crossing the street from one home to the
other. They lived just 20 miles or so north of Long Lake in Chilton. As they
came out of some pine trees near the road they "heard a loud
humming/buzzing sound from above." As they moved onto the open road
"we both looked up and saw a large boomerang shaped flying object." They
saw "small towers at the three ends or arms that stick out" on the object.
Quickly moving back into the trees for safety sake, the two also noticed a
"slightly larger tower in the center" and that the "color was a very light blue."
The pair watched as the object moved above the church they frequented,
down the street, and back. "I remember a lot of little flashing lights on the
top of it." as it moved "very slowly" out of sight. They thought it was probably less than 1,000 feet up in the air and remembered it would "rotate as it
moved." Being younger, they didn't feel comfortable sharing the experience
with their parents until years after the June 15, 1986, sighting.

The area between Long Lake and Lake Michigan was all abuzz with UFO sightings the night of August 16, 1988. They made John's cows noticeably nervous, more so than he had ever seen them before. It was 11:15 pm. John walked around a nearby building to get a better look. Off to the east there was "this big, oval or saucer-shaped thing with orange lights." It was also reported in The Wisconsin Reporter that it was estimated to be "1,000 feet up and…100 feet in diameter." John watched for "15 to 20 seconds" however, it "didn't move and there was no noise associated with it." He shared with the newspaper that even though it was a hot night he "got chills looking at it." John ran to get his wife, "I wanted someone else to see it, I didn't want anyone to think I was crazy." By the time the couple had returned, the object was no longer visible. John had this to say in closing, "It was definitely not an airplane. I've seen lots of jets fly by with their landing lights on. I've never seen anything like this before."

Kate L. and her son described them as "50 to 75 times the size of lights you would see on a plane" while out on an evening walk. She reported to the Associated Press at the time "the lights stretched out, expanding outward, and then appeared to fall in toward the center…one of them disappeared. It all happened within seconds."

The Associated Press and The Wisconsin Journal also reported on one person's sighting as he stood in a group of four people who had similar sightings of the event from the city of Sheboygan. The anonymous witness reported "as many as 10 lights followed by a 'V' formation ... I don't know what I was seeing. Not planes, not helicopters. I just don't know. There were no sounds."

Corrine R. who was camping just a few miles north east of Long Lake watched presumably the same lights for an hour and a half.

Farther East and still several miles from Lake Michigan motorists "believed the lights were coming directly at them."

For those of you that crave closure, Sergeant Craig Dooms who held the position of public information specialist for the Eaker Air Force Base in Arkansas heard your call. He shared with the public that there was a B-52 bomber over Lake Michigan on the night of August 16th just after 11 pm. The purpose of the bombers flight was reported to be "testing its war-time defense system against heat seeking missiles" by dropping flares.

Corrine later shared that she "is skeptical that the Air Force maneuvers could account for everything she and the other campers saw." The Air Force did go on to state that they had "no explanation for other UFO sightings in the Sheboygan area Tuesday night between 9 and 10 pm" It was reported in The Wisconsin Journal that the earlier reports were "consistently mentioned a soundless swift cluster arrangement of lights followed by a semi-circle of three lights" and "of moving red lights spaced over a large area moving at extraordinary speeds."

Those still seeking my professional insight, yes a B-52 is a sight to be seen. This could be used to explain some of the experiences had that evening "just after 11pm." Key words being "some" and "just after 11pm" Could the rest of the witnesses be confused on the day or time of their experiences? Those sightings that don't easily or at all fit for that matter, a flare drop far out over Lake Michigan are then left to be just wrong with their observations? A debunker would have you believe so. Always striving to be an open minded skeptic, I can't draw any hard and fast conclusions with the above scenarios.

Six years later, Chris N. was returning home from a days work in West Bend. Much of Fond du Lac County is dotted with parts of the expansive Kettle Moraine State Park, including the eastern shore of Long Lake. Around 7:20 that May evening, Chris was driving on County Road F nearing a portion of the park just southeast of Long Lake. An unusual light in the sky grabbed her attention. She was so intrigued by this "huge pure white light" as she described it to UFOwisconsin.com; she pulled the car over on a blind curve. She had to have a better look at this object. Next she noticed that the UFO was silently "hovering right over the trees." She estimated the size to be that of a football field, and could see "windows in it that were lit up." Watching for movement in the windows yielded no results. Chris did feel compelled to share with us that two weeks later she found out she was pregnant. How this may relate to the story we may never know. Chris did not make note of any time loss, or abduction memories in the report she filed with us that would then possibly let us speculate further. Chris could not be reached for further clarification.

July 4th, Independence Day 1997. Numerous UFO reports were made by people attending a fireworks show just a few miles East of Long Lake. Along with the normal awe inspiring fireworks display, they had noticed two large triangular shaped crafts in the sky. Witnesses reported bluish lights on the bottom of the objects that made them appear to be in the shape of an arrow. People witnessing this event were able to view them for around 40 minutes before they streaked away.

These triangular shaped UFOs dotted with blue lights were to return and this time to dozens of witnesses in 2004.

A quaint restaurant and bar perched on the north shore of Long Lake, Benson's Hideaway is home of the Annual UFO Daze. It was here in September 1998 that Bill B. watched an interesting cat and mouse game, play out in the skies above. He reported to UFOwisconsin.com that, "very short-ly after" noticing a "strange red light" after which, "four jets began pursuing it." When Bill spoke of the red light he saw in the sky he said that it was "obviously not the normal red airplane light." "Whatever it was" when the "jets approached the object, it would quickly move away from them." Bill noted that the red light would "shrink to nothing" and reappear in another location. This continued until shortly after being sighted hovering above a nearby house. At this point the object "suddenly shot straight up into the air." The jets reportedly followed and nothing else was seen again that evening.

Our next witness was quick to point out that he was "a skeptic and always thought people were exaggerating when they told of sightings." That was until the evening of March 3, 1999. It was just six miles from Long Lake and dark around nine o'clock. They reported seeing "6 red lights…3 on one side and 3 on the other" apparently all coming from one craft. None of the lights were reported as blinking, including the one yellow light towards the back of the object. It was dark and in part the placement of the lights led the witness to perceive that the "craft was triangular in shape." Our self-pro-claimed skeptic watched as the "huge aircraft" with "little sound" turned from an eastwardly path towards Lake Michigan, 180° back, due west. They included that from Campbellsport, where they were watching, they could see "four airplanes traveling east together" when "this craft came from the east." They felt compelled to find out more after having their breath taken away and left "in awe" of the experience. So compelled, that they spent addition-al time searching out pictures of stealth aircraft and reporting the sighting to NUFORC.

A family camping in the Kettle Moraine Park was preparing for bed on that quiet April evening in 2000. Phillip, not yet tired chose to relax a bit on the picnic table to enjoy the stars. As his eyes adjusted and there became too many stars to count, he started to focus on one area. One star in particular grabbed his attention. He reported that maybe 10 minutes had passed when "a light turned on brighter than the star" he was watching. Phillip told UFOwisconsin.com that he watched as this new light made a "half circle around the star I was looking at" when all of a sudden "two spikes of faint light shot towards the round light." The light that had appeared, now vanished. Phillip theorized that it either just "turned off or left the atmosphere." He watched for awhile longer but nothing else ever appeared. Phillip went to bed puzzled as to what it was all about.

In 2000, brother and sister Jean and Jim Aho both had an amazing UFO sighting. They were both very similar looking pyramid objects, but one was seen in Wisconsin and the other in Pennsylvania. Could the fact that they are brother and sister mean the same UFOs were intelligent and watching them both despite the sightings being six months apart and hundreds of miles between them? Jim was not alone during his sighting as numerous people were gathered at Benson's Hideaway on the shores of Long Lake. The evening marked the 10th annual UFO Days event held every July.

Bonnie, also in attendance that evening, reported the sky was clear as they sat "by the lake watching for UFOs," when "all of a sudden there was a craft." She reported that it was "mostly blue in color although at times it looked many different colors." Bonnie watched as the "triangular" shaped craft began "to rotate and tumble" over the center of Long Lake. As soon as it began to move and tumble about "we realized it was not flat but it looked just like the pyramids in Egypt do." She went on to further describe how it "looked like two pyramids-one was on top of the other with the flat bottoms together so that there was a point at the top and the bottom." It moved off to the west, "rotating and tumbling at the same time." Another reporting witness to the evening's events was Diana.

She estimated for UFOwisconsin.com that, "there were about 15 or 20 witnesses to this sighting." As she faced south by southeast Diana noticed "a couple of orange lights then we saw a light with a bluish 'cloud' around it." She reported the same "pyramid shape with three lights across the base." Diana noted the "lights were purple, white and blue" and that some recalled "a diamond shape that was tumbling" and that others, a "pyramid facing downward." It moved slowly across the sky giving all watching "a good long look." Much with another sighting four years later, it moved "straight overhead and behind us until the trees...blocked our view."

Jim Aho described a "triangular shaped craft." He was fortunate enough to have been able to view this object through a pair of binoculars. With the binocular aided eye he clearly saw "three lights at the corners - blue, purple and green." He said the whole object had "a faint blue outline." Then Jim noticed a "ball of light" approach the "triangle from the right, and when it got near the triangle the light changed both course and appearance."

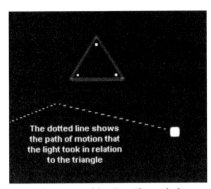

The dotted line shows the path of motion that the light took in relation to the triangle

A graphic created by Jim Aho to help visually depict what he experienced that evening in July, 2000.

He noted that the ball of light turned from one to "two lights: one red and one flashing white." Jim made the observation that had you just then noticed the light in the sky "it could have even been mistaken for an airplane even though before it changed you could see that it obviously wasn't an aircraft." This was an excellent observation that helps clarify the point I was making during the farm experience that had two beings sighted in the field. Any sighting witnessed by one person, from one perspective at any given moment, may be easily categorized as say a meteorite or airplane in Jim's previous observations, however when viewed from a different set of perspectives, everything could change. After "5 or 10 minutes" Jim noted, "the triangle craft started moving in a tumbling motion like it was almost rolling away to the right." As the triangle started to roll he noticed that it was more three dimensional "like a pyramid" with "three sides and a bottom."

Though a bit outside the boarders of Wisconsin under the guise that we truly do not know all the variables or potential connections in the UFO field let's take a look at another sighting. Jim's sister Jean was living in Pennsylvania during this encounter and witnessed the following just six months before her brother's.

The two hadn't discussed this sighting until after Jim had his in July. Jean was on her way home from school heading south on Highway 81. She was passing a nearby airport and watched as what she at first took to be an airplane. Keeping a watchful eye on the plane ensuring it wasn't "going to crash on me" she noticed it was "moving really slow" and had "different color lights on the corners of it." As it neared Jean she "saw that it was not a plane at all, but a pyramid shaped object." She slowed to about 40mph on a highway that normally holds cars moving 65mph or more. Jean was willing to risk the slower speed to get a better look at the object.

Jean's speed on the expressway perhaps earned her an unwanted distraction in the form of a tailgater. She sped up to make her exit and as she looked back up at the object she saw "the pyramid was moving really fast to the south" back the direction she first noticed it coming from. She thought that the size would be "larger than my hand at arms length." She got the odd feeling that the object was "checking me out to see my connection" to her brother Jim. They had discussed the UFO phenomena in the past but their conversation reportedly never reached descriptions of UFOs. Jim has reported continual experiences with UFOs however Jean said shortly after this experience "it all stopped" and has no more sightings to report.

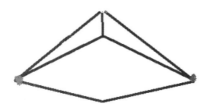

Jean's drawing of the object she saw while driving home an evening of January 2000.

UFO Days 2001 brought in a whole new batch of sightings. Multiple lights in the night sky are well documented. Many people attending the gathering watched for hours as different lights behaved according to the witnesses, unique from any known aircraft.

Later that same year, on November 10th a husband and wife left their home early in the morning. They were off to do some hunting when about 5:30 am they noted "two stars, one brighter and one smaller and not as bright." Sharing with UFOwisconsin.com that the "smaller star started to move in a perfectly straight line to the east." The witnesses stated that they had watched the "space lab" traveling in the night time sky years before and that the moving star acted in a similar fashion. Watching for a few moments the star "disappeared." They felt it did not "go behind a cloud because there was another small star next to where it disappeared" that could still be seen, even though the other one was not. The witness was nice enough to share their prior experience with observing space objects from the ground. I myself have done this on numerous occasions, some without aiding the eye. It is an enjoyable and sometimes well publicized opportunity, even catching notifications on the evening news. Some additionally rare observations but all together as predictable, are satellite flares. The most common and predictable are flares from a communication series satellite called Iridium. They have become a common name in ufology known as Iridium Flares, and are at times so bright that they can be witnessed during daylight hours. While noticeably more visible at night these bright streaks of light flash across a small portion of the sky in a few seconds as their mirror-polished door size antennas reflect sunlight directly back to Earth.

The triangle sightings were not done yet as the next sighting came in around St. Cloud Wisconsin. On June 28, 2002, Jim W. was able to catch a glimpse of one moving out of view. It was around 9 pm when he was "getting the kids ready for bed." This is when a "weird triangular object in the sky" caught his attention. He called for his kids to "come and see." After they got a brief glimpse, he then sent his kids off to quickly get the camera. Unfortunately, by the time they returned "it was gone." They described the object as "reddish-orange" in color and "moving very fast." Perhaps it was moving off to Long Lake just miles to the south.

July 14, 2002, Danny was doing some early morning fishing. Sitting on a public pier at a Long Lake campground he reported seeing "a large sphere with green, blue and possibly red lights spaced evenly on it." It was "high in the sky and moved slowly to the east." Then, looking to the south he noticed additional strange lights. He saw "several white blinking lights," then distracted by potential lunch showing interest in his fishing lure, he looked away. Turning his attention back to the sky moments later, the white blinking lights had disappeared. Now however "there was another object moving in the same direction." Fisherman Danny reported the now almost common object that was "triangular in shape." He noticed that it had "lights in rows of 1,3,5,7 in red, orange and yellow colors." It moved off to the east and as the early morning light rose, there were no more sightings.

There are known patterns even in the unknown, such as these elusive flying triangles in the UFO field. But what can we make of any observable patterns at this point? Just days after our last sighting Jack S. was relaxing at Bensons Campground near Long Lake. He was watching the stars when suddenly one started to move. He remembers "thinking it was a plane or satellite" so he kept watching when unexpectedly "it stopped." After that it "moved across the sky in jerks." It continued to move across the sky in this abrupt fashion growing dimmer with each movement until it "faded from view or disappeared after covering about 10% of arc across sky." Was this observation merely one of the nearly 3,000 satellites currently orbiting the Earth? The unusual movements reported don't match how most satellites are able to be observed from our terrestrial point of view. It seems at this time we are again left with no clear explanation.

That brings us back around to another year of UFO Daze at Bensons Hideaway. Once more the annual event brought a flurry of sightings. Wendy K. another self proclaimed "skeptic" had her mind made up that there was something unusual going on here. People come from near and far, the furthest we heard from for 2002 was a 1300 mile round trip. Most folks were not disappointed when the nighttime lights visited for a show.

July 20, 2002, Dundee, Long Lake UFO Daze. Photographer K. Sturges.

So who's looking into this entire phenomenon as far as local Wisconsin is concerned? The folks at the Paranormal Investigating Researchers Organization or P.I.R.O. have held several research and investigation trips to Long Lake and the surrounding areas. Just who are they? Well back before it was in vogue to have a "ghost group" this organization was spawned from me and my associates. In the 1990s we were a group of friends who were passionate about adventures and learning more on the paranormal. Gaining access to specific places with historic or active legends was difficult to say the least. It did however make it noticeably easier to approach potential 'clients' touting credentials and offering easily remembered acronyms. Things have changed considerably since then. I have directed my resources from supporting an organization to now working more with individual research while being supported by networks of industry contacts.

P.I.R.O.'s archives contain hundreds of files each listing different local and national experiences that all have a mysterious overtone. One such experience that caused us to continually make the excursion into the wilds surrounding Long Lake was the sighting we

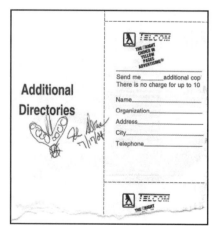

Sketch by John Albrecht on a motel phonebook page drawn on July 17, 2004.

had in July 2004. P.I.R.O. has this case listed as "open" in their archives and has turned up intriguing but circumstantial data thus far. Attempting to counter the lack of resources needed for such a large undertaking; P.I.R.O. continues to work in conjunction with independent researchers and investigators along with several organizations in order to put continued joint efforts into this mystery. Long time P.I.R.O. member John Albrecht was witness to the July, 2004, incident while near Long Lake on a professional capacity. John, a Whitewater resident, recalls seeing, "a light visible in the night sky

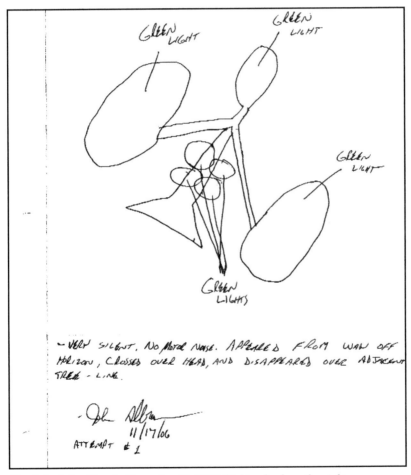

Sketch by John Albrecht November 17, 2006 thinking back on the night.

on the northern horizon." John goes on to share that the light "moved in closer until" he was "able to view to briefly what looked to be a silently flying bent cross-shaped object."

My friend and associate was kind enough to take part in the following little experiment. I asked him to re-create from memory only, the UFO he saw in July, 2004. The following sketch is from over two years after the original sighting, and I can attest that I had the only and original drawing by John, so he was indeed forced to re-create the image from memory only.

John included: "Very silent. No motor noise. Appeared from way off horizon, crossed over head, and disappeared over adjacent tree-line" in his quick visual rendering above. He went on further to share that he was working away from the equipment and had only a simple digital camera on his phone at the time, "I lifted the camera and noticed that there was nothing visible through the viewer and for some reason I didn't even try to take a picture, I'm not happy about that odd decision." Thanks for putting yourself 'out there' John.

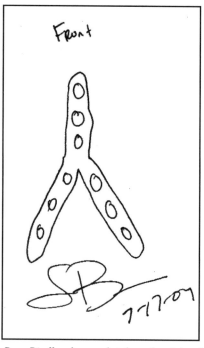

Sean Bindley drew a sketch on the night of July 17, 2004.

Another witness present to this same unexplained sighting was Sean Bindley. In 2004 he was also near Long Lake on a professional capacity with GetGhostGear.com and shared with us his experience. "I was only able to view the object as it moved over head...I noticed something that looked like the inside of a peace sign." Sean went on to share, "it had blue-green lights at each point of the structure as it moved almost floating, silently over."

Same thing here, I had to take some advantage of the unique situation as a UFOlogist to try this little experiment. I made the same request of Sean and below is his, from memory only, re-creation of the July 2004 sighting.

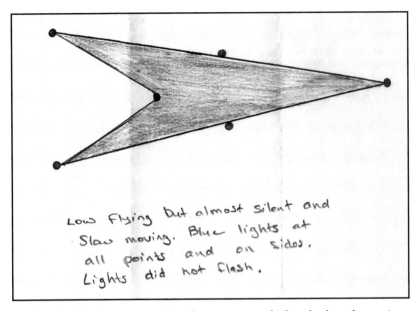

Mr. Sean Bindley drew a second sketch at my request thinking back on the evening in July, 2004.

The notes on his sketch read: "Low flying but almost silent and slow moving. Blue lights at all points and on sides. Lights did not flash." Thank you Sean for putting some added effort into your re-creation, it looks sharp. Now for my fine artistic drawing recorded that very night on a complementary envelope at our nearby Motel.

I have not included a second, from memory, re-creation of the UFO that I sighted that evening for several reasons. During countless interviews for radio, periodicals, books, websites, and so on, I've rehashed the sighting. I've also been working on this book project and came across the original sketches several times each year since they were first created. The problem this has caused me, is I have a better mental picture of my sketch than I do of the object that night.

Now that we have all seen John's, Sean's, and my own re-creation we must bring up some of the common group sighting variables that might help to explain any immediately noticeable variations that we had in our sketched observations. We did discuss the experience that evening however, only after we put our sighting down on paper. After that the three of us were all open to discuss how and why we didn't recall the exact same thing. There were many reasons we were able to list: location during the sighting, duration of the sighting, other witnesses next to each of us discussing aloud what they were seeing as we were seeing it, and not surprising those around us all saw it slightly different too. To fully understand some of the largest variables that were different let's re-examine that night in greater detail. An option often not had.

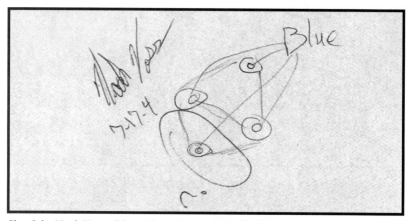

Sketch by Noah Voss of the sighting had on July 17, 2004.

Looking back into the stores of my vault like memory, I recall I have no such memory. Glancing over my notes on that night, it would seem best for me to start from the beginning. It was eight o'clock Saturday morning, 2004. Early mornings were not unusual for myself and Sean Bindley, but with no doubt we anticipate this to be the start of a long one. Sean has been many things over the years, this 17th of July he is friend and associate.

Sean and I had been working towards this day for weeks: creating a new product catalog for GetGhostGear.com, revising the brochures for UFOwisconsin.com and W-Files.com both, updating the information on the websites, responding to personal inquiries about the event that we had been marketing for months, making sure we had batteries for the gear, film for the cameras, and fuel for our bodies. Heck, we even printed out company logos and ironed them on three Hawaiian shirts that we hoped would fit the laid back lake side environment. Closer to the final weekend, we had a long Friday full of our nine-to-fiver, normal daily duties, and of final preparation for that year's UFO Daze on Long Lake.

The night before we used my small apartment to try out the next day's setup. We had a lot to place in a little area. An impressive six-foot folding table, two smaller four-foot collapsible tables along with a couple black mesh director chairs and less expensive matching stools. To set these up, in my apartment we used my 'office', living room, dinning room, and kitchen. If you count the items that we had to move to make space for the set-up you'd have to include the balcony and bedroom too.

Back to early Saturday morning, I was very happy to have the option of an elevator in my building. Utilizing a three shelf, multidirectional ball-bearing, fully stainless steel kitchen cart I made short, yet sweaty work of loading my small Toyota Celica. The cart was a bonus find in the corral of my apartment's dumpster. Having spent many years in many kitchens I quickly appreciated the trashed treasure and still have the cart to this day. After Sean showed up we finish loading the larger items in his much appreciated pickup truck. John Albrecht has been a friend since early grade school and that day when he arrived, he was also an associate. We all hoped this day was going to be fun and we'd try our best to keep it that way, however we all knew it would be work too. The plan was for Sean and John to help me put a good face on GetGhostGear.com Enterprises which included UFOwisconsin.com, among other endeavors. I was to be making the introduction for the annual events along with Bill Benson, owner of Benson's Hideaway. Sean and John prepared themselves for the never ending barrage of questions, along with running the booth while I was off speaking and giving interviews. The three of us headed out of the apartment parking lot in two vehicles. Stopping for gas and caffeine we hit the road only to arrive a couple hours later in the gravel parking lot at Benson's Hideaway.

Perched on the shores of Long Lake, Bill Benson has become well known for his openness, and interest in the possibility of other worldly life. This is not my first time to the Hideaway, but reflecting back on the first trip it was a motivational experience. When arriving at the bar and eatery it's hard to miss the picturesque setting. With a marsh to the North, Long Lake opening to the South, and surrounded on all other sides by flourishing forests. Walking through the main entrance at the Hideaway guides you in-between a pool table and bar. Every where else you look, furnishes a window into the owner's psyche. Sean, John, and I stroll into Bensons. Admiring the UFO paraphernalia plastered everywhere, we find Bill hurriedly preparing for the busy day ahead. He's looking forward to the day and says the local Lions Club will be along cooking brats and burgers soon. I make sure that the earlier chosen site for our booth is still ideal and the three of us move outside to unload the vehicles. We make short work of setting up the tent and securing it with stakes, and ropes for even the toughest of Wisconsin weather. It's still eleven something and people begin showing up and milling about. The bravest of the bunch timidly approach and quietly ask the occasional question as we finish setting up. We fill the three tables with books, investigating equipment, GetGhostGear.com catalogs, UFOwisconsin.com brochures, raffle prizes, a television set with DVD including 6 speaker surround sound, and stacks of business cards. Then we wait. The three of us have little time to rest back into our chairs before the usual questions start flying. Between each question I revert back into my own world. I review over some notes for my short lecture. Bill and I are co-hosting the opening welcome behind a wood podium set up in the corner of his main dinning room. All sorts of people come by the booth throughout the day. Most are hesitant at first. Understandably so, as this is nearly all visitors first time to Benson's along with their first time to anything remotely close to a paranormal focused event. It is an interesting dance, we as humans need to partake in when encountering something new. It is the norm for a person to slowly approach us, avoiding any long eye contact. My simple response to anyone's discrete approach is "let me know if you have any questions" which of course must be said with a smile. People are gauging me, and sizing up the things displayed before them. The people hesitantly look on determining if I am going to try to get them interested in my cult — really there's no cult. Some are quite conspicuously divining my stance on life through what is on a party table from the local superstore. It seems humorous at times. Don't get me wrong most people are sweet and go out of there way to avoid stepping on toes, usually stumbling over their own words until they're reassured it is okay to speak freely. It is a foreign experience for most, one where even at the root is me, them not even knowing what to call me. Some assume that I hold a doctorate and am working off a grant from some prestigious Ivy League school. Others outright attack a stance they assume I have from either my initial greeting, or one of the dozens of items I have laid out before me. Others hit us up for the answers to a few of life's greatest mysteries. We all take our turns doing the best we can answering questions with what limited knowledge we have on "what the government might really be doing?" or "where exactly the aliens are from that visit here?." My observations from over a decade of being a sounding board for paranormal experiences is that it is a very therapeutic process for people at these types of events to share their normally unique experiences. I and my colleagues all take great efforts to remain approachable at these events with this in mind. For most people attending that day it was the first and perhaps only time in their entire life that they would share their experience. That comes with some responsibility on our part. We try to afford the visitors an opportunity to share their very personal experiences with someone who was not going to judge, joke, or for that matter even ever have to be seen again.

Most enjoy the films being showcased on the TV from Totally Confused Productions. One other viewer condescendingly corrects the editing on "trial" instead of "trail." But hey, "these were rough draft, preliminary, short film format versions of the full featured documentaries soon to come," I think quietly in my mind as I thank her with a smile on my face. Then humbly make a note on some paper to fix it as soon as I get home. Some day I'll finish up shooting for the Ridgeway Phantoms. I guess I can console myself by remembering that progress comes to those who don't stop, not to only those who finish first. Many stop by for a break from the Sun of mid July in Wisconsin, in the shade provided by the tent.

There is no escaping the heat and humidity however and back on the shores of Long Lake, the smell of grilled brats and beer mix with lake water and woods. The three of us talk with some old friends, meet some new acquaintances, and laugh with those just passing by for the beer and entertainment. Through the afternoon we sold maybe $40 on raffle tickets, and gave away over $150 worth of prizes. I was happy to see friend and author Linda Godfrey win first prize. She took home a nice EMF meter from GetGhostGear.com. One that she still uses on her research and investigation trips to this day, I'm happy to report. Linda wasn't there presenting that day, but enjoying the atmosphere and no doubt doing research for her next project. Inside Benson's Hideaway just after Bill and I briefly gave our words, there was a barrage of speakers mainly from area UFO groups. Each had their own perspectives drawn on from their very specific life experiences. Some were hurriedly setting up projectors to show presentations completed earlier that day. Others were recounting the information that they had come across in their research as long as it wasn't too "…over-the-head of [the audience]." The atmosphere outside was that of T-shirt sales, diverse conversations, beer, and brats along with stories being shared in the "experiencer" tent. Between newspaper, radio, TV, and magazine interviews I was able to talk some with my associates, meet some new people, and hear of many new sightings. Upon night fall the crowd again increased in numbers and diversity. As the evening wore on, the alcohol consumption grew along with the unruliness. There were many more people there who were from the surrounding communities. Those folks seemed to show up for the novelty the evening provided. For many it was simply a new atmosphere to drink old beer in. As the condensation grew on the booth our energies shrunk. Sean, John, and I had packed up most of the equipment and assorted wares. Our friends had either left for the evening or were intermixed through the crowd that had filled the space from boat dock to bar stool. Taking a break from working the booth Sean and I separated in the crowd. I wanted to blend in a bit and get some video footage that wasn't a static tripod shot from the back of the booth, of which I had several hours of at that point. I returned awhile later to find my friend of 20+ years, obviously stressed to me, but remaining professional to a fault as far as everyone else was concerned. John screamed, "I need to get out of here!" by calmly saying he "needed to get something out of his car." That's one bonus of knowing someone for that long; you can usually read between the lines. His quick exit is even more quickly explained by the swaying young woman yelling at the TV set on our table. My second indication that this is not going to be pleasant is that the TV is off. With my new presence she has someone fresh to focus her misdirected hostilities on. She wastes no time in doing so. It is at this point I feel it very necessary to mention to you the reader, a gentleman who must have been witnessing the barrage of near outright insults thrown upon John. This gentleman quite considerately attempted to come to my rescue. He was successful in distracting her momentarily and ended up being sterner than I was, but looking back now, still far less than we both should have been. It was at this most unfortunate point in the night that I started to catch murmurings from the crowd that something was 'coming'. Being we were at a UFO festival, outside in the open air, and under many a wet drink along with the history of previous years yielding UFO sightings this is not a unique thing I'm hearing. Throughout the evening, many people took the opportunity to try their comedic timing with, "what's that!" or "in the sky!" or "UFO!" or, well you get the picture. My reaction is less than quick, or logical. In defense my mind was full of adrenaline, frustration, and on the swaying visitor's group of large men she came from.

Where in my younger years I had put myself in scraps with far worse odds, I was, among other things not in the mood. My patience paid off and as the UFO murmuring grew to a full conversation volume level, she ran off and fell down somewhere. It was at this point that Sean's reality started to mix with mine. He had been calling my name and quickly walking towards the booth. He was pointing up into the sky as I stepped out from our covered display tent to see what at. What I remember first about the experience was the bluish green lights. From the absentee stars I observe what seems to be perhaps a triangle shape.

The fact that I'm not witnessing this alone comes crashing back when someone near the Shore of Long Lake trains their spot light on the UFO above. I want to say that I can recollect a dim and dull illumination from the spotlight reaching the side of the UFO facing us. If this memory is accurate then that would certainly lend some insight as to the altitude of the object. It moved in a floating fashion on the same course until it disappeared over the tree tops. When it was all said and done, I probably witnessed the UFO for less than five seconds. My final conclusion: the woman drawing our attention pretending to be drunk was actually an alien and distracting us from taking readings and acquiring data while her mother ship flew over. Now of course I'm having a bit of fun, therapeutically for myself at the expense of someone else, who obviously was not an alien but rather a government official, propagating disinformation to throw us off the real trial...trail...ehh.

In all seriousness, let's take a moment now and apply further scrutiny to my experience. Feeling that any quality ufologist is faced with a nearly insurmountable number of variables when researching and investigating let's do our best to focus on perhaps the most poignant ones. At least the ones that I have the resources to freely examine. The first thing I noticed was the lights. They appeared to be nearer the edge of the object and on the 'points' saving one. The lights totaled four, one on each point, and another around the center. I am forced to speculate as to the lights location on the object itself. Not being able to see the actual object with great clarity but by noticing that the stars above were blocked out, presumably by the object's body behind the bluish green lights. I also can not be certain that the center light was actually on the entire time, but most likely at least the short duration I was looking at it, as others have said there was none. Another potential enters when we examine the witness sketches prior. You may notice Sean has a light placed towards the 'backside' of the triangle shaped craft but at an indentation. Was this perhaps what I was observing and only placed in the center of the craft? Perhaps since I didn't observe the object for as long I may have not had the opportunity to notice the possible indentation or triangle cut into the body of the triangle? Hey, maybe Sean got it wrong, and I got it right, or both wrong. Alright we could do that all day, so let's move on.

We are at the 14th annual UFO Daze event. The likelihood of someone attempting a hoax would certainly have to be increased during a venue of this nature, obviously. That being said, if this was a hoax, I'm impressed and would love to know how it was pulled off. Of course just because I'm not smart enough to figure how exactly what I saw could have been realistically hoaxed, doesn't discount the fact that it could still have been done.

I've been interested in UFOs for over two decades, that's a variable worth scrutinizing. Was I perhaps projecting the shape from the hundreds of reports of silently flying black triangles that I have encountered onto something less than extraordinary in the sky above me that one and only night? I would put more credence on this possibility that it was nothing out of the ordinary, had I been drinking, and alone. As it was I hadn't a drop all day and was in a group of at least 100 people, two of them who I can trust with my life, but none-the-less avoid that situation whenever possible.

There were no noticeable sounds or smells coming from the object. The lack of sound and scent could be attributed to the object being at great altitude. If scent or sound characteristics were present from the craft, it wouldn't have been detectable by my senses if it was at a great height. The apparent size of the object seemed to indicate to me that it was of average airplane size and altitude but silent, or of immense structure and of great height. Assuming for a moment that it was of average aeronautical size, but flying silently, and utilizing a fuel source that left no detectable trace, from an engine of unknown design, there was no interaction detectable between the terrestrial environment and the UFO. The lack of interaction between the UFO and the surrounding environment, such as the tree tops it disappeared over, could also indicate that it was simply not using any technology that would normally affect the tree tops and people below such as helicopter blades or burners used on dirigibles might. This could also indicate that the object was perhaps of a high enough altitude that any such technology if used, was simply not perceptible. Unfortunately this could also mean it was using gliding technology and if it even did have a self powering flight capability that it simply shut it off when it neared the event grounds, only to turn it back on after it was a safe distance away. There are many who speculate on the next generation of aircraft that are currently in the government's pipeline. Several model speculations are currently showing a new venting technology for advanced rocketry. Some reports show the exhaust comes out the top of these theoretical crafts. This is in effort, I am told by the people making these speculations, to enhance stealth capabilities. There are many design styles for aircraft that create different stealth qualities.

There is some documentation that shows Lockheed Corporation had designs for stealth blimp technologies as early as 1982. These are not your Goodyear styled blimps. Some such as National Institute for Discovery Science or NIDS, go as far as speculating the size to be approximately 600 x 300' x 40'. These suppositions made by NIDS, comes from observational sightings and documenting "triangles and the locations of Air Mobility Command and Air Force Materiel Command in the United States." With over 700 sightings plotted they constructed several theories behind what their data showed. Interestingly enough, after combining data from their own research and two of the largest archives of flying triangle sightings in the world they noticed an unusually high amount of triangle sightings over highly populated areas and heavily traveled sections, such as interstates. This they felt was "… certainly conceivable that deployment of low altitude surveillance platforms is routine and open." The United States currently has at least nine different aircraft projects known to be stealth capable, in service or flyable prototypes while holding at least some open records on six stealth aircrafts still in project phase. Just for some added plausibility, Russia, China, United Kingdom, France, Germany, Italy, Spain, Sweden, Greece, and Switzerland all have or had successful stealth programs of their own. We as researchers are obviously not as able to view private rocket and aeronautic industries secret development projects. However several colleges have been awarded financial backings from the United States Air Force such as Purdue and John Hopkins. These institutions remain slightly more transparent.

These universities and others have used smaller scale, workable prototypes as recently as 2005. The end goal of the blimps: to have the capability of continually monitoring one location for more than a year at a time, from a height of over 65,000 feet or near space levels. At least that is what most in the UFO field hear. The estimated size of the end project blimp is over 900' in length or nearly five times longer than the relatable Goodyear blimp and 100' longer than the infamous Zeppelins.

Back on the shores of Long Lake analysis of my own sighting must continue. Movement of the UFO was smooth, with purpose, and of a solid course or direction. It seemed to almost float overhead but not at the whim of the wind but rather with more precise power. I speculate this from the lack of bouncing or weaving as one may expect a smaller fixed wing craft to behave at lower altitudes having cross winds created by interaction with the ground and so on. Of course there is the potential of just a calmer atmosphere being present, as it was later into the evening and with the sun's warming rays gone, the air does traditionally become calmer. The UFO's movement reminds me now, of how a dirigible or more specifically a hot air balloon may float through the air. In a former life I crewed many different positions on several balloons, and was aloft over a dozen times in competition, commercial, or as the less glamorous counterweight capacity, and to an altitude of 5,000 feet. Drawing on those experiences I know that when a hot air balloon has been formed into an object other than a classic balloon shape, it does take some time to get used to the way it looks floating through the air. It can be very surreal to watch a giant can of beer, a star, or Snoopy creep silently over your head. That being said if this was a dirigible, under only wind power as most hot air balloons are, it would be beyond risky to pull off an ascent, and then landing without being detected or dying a painful death in the dark. Add to that the addition of a light rigging system to create the effect that people observed and the difficulty of the hoax grows. Now, a resourceful and dedicated ufologist would have exhausted all information gathering avenues. One that I regret not looking into greater was the FAA logs of scheduled departures and arrivals at all monitored air fields. This along with all recordings of applicable radar stations would certainly have

helped to remove certain obvious variables. That being said the existence of
no scheduled departures or landings, or simply the lack of data in the forms
of no logs would not have necessarily proved any one thing, short of control
to pilot radio recordings saying "I'm heading over to the UFO festival on
Long Lake to fool everyone into thinking I'm a UFO." There are of course
many long, wide-open fields for someone who would rather not use a monitored air field in pulling off a hoax. That also assumes that it was of the size
and technology that would require a long wide open space for landing and
take off. This is simply not known for any great certainty to be the case.

When any biological human being reads they start to automatically tone out
audible input. It's in most everyone's nature to one extent or another, it is
simply how the body functions. Nero bio-chemical inhibitors must be sent
to the auditory receptors of the brain when one reads. This allows them to
focus on one task with a great intensity, and some theorize may be in part an
issue with ADD or ADHD. The same occurs when we are visually taking in
information in the form of an experience. Witnessing something in the night
time sky as I did, is no exception. This is what was going on in my brain,
and looking back seems to have caused holes in the story line. For example
why do I struggle with remembering if someone on the shore shone a spot
light on the craft? I was very focused for the time on the UFO above. As
my attention instantly turned to the UFO, everything else around me sort of
faded away as a result of the normal biological response. Looking back however, it seems that I don't remember everything. I can start to doubt how I
remembered the craft, color of lights, who was standing next to me, and so
on. My mind was not on autopilot, but it had taken over with its automated
response to outside stimuli, as most everyone else's was too. Such a new and
unknown experience can draw parts of one's mind to sharp attention, while
sharply dulling others.

Chronologically speaking, right after I lose sight of the UFO over the trees,
John reappears. He, Sean, and I stood gathering our thoughts for a moment.
Sean started to discuss the event, as John, and I were still more distracted
than anything else from the mysterious disinformation government agent, or
was she just working for the aliens? On a serious note, it was interesting and
unnerving at the same time to see the lack of enthusiasm of what had just
occurred from the crowd. I remember having that stick in my mind. Reading
people's body language has always come naturally to me, and I was very
conscious of reading the crowd at that moment. I would have expected as in
the movies or in a great novel, for everyone to run and scream in panic.
Perhaps it being a UFO festival I may have half expected more to be yelling
at the craft "take us with you!" I've actually seen that before, so maybe I was

just expecting that response for that reason. Perhaps we as paranormal investigators were more quickly able to grasp the magnitude of what possibly just happened. However, just as easily could we not have been skewed from our paranormal pasts to make more of something that was really less? Despite what reality you decide we may have been in, the response to the UFO from the crowd was eerie.

Within a few minutes after the UFO had passed all was back to normal, with people falling, swaying, and being their normal rowdy selves. We were as a result additionally ready to pack up what was left of our display. Always on the lookout for a scam, we lowered our voices as we ran over aloud some of what had just happened. Was someone in the crowd waiting for our over reaction to the hoax they had perpetuated on the visiting UFOlogists? We were gauging the response of the crowd to help place what we had just experienced against every other experience ever had. I've reflected on my response from this point on in great length. John and I both were coming off of that almost high state caused by awfully awkward situations, this one brought on by our swaying guest. Now he and I both have worked our fair share of customer service and management positions and have dealt with far worse. It would have normally only taken a couple laughs and a few extra moments for us to regain full composure. Fate would seem, to have other plans for us that evening. No time to collect my thoughts instead I was ripped from that situation when I became aware of Sean moving towards me. From the moment my eyes made contact with the UFO, I was being pulled from one extremely stressful situation only to be poured blindly and backwards into an even more unbelievable scenario. Why not hop into the vehicles and tear out of the parking lot after the craft? Besides the parking lot being filled with inebriated people, not apt to move quickly out of the way, there are not many roads in those parts. There are even fewer bridges, actually none that would have taken you over Long Lake should the UFO have moved that direction and well frankly, it is a long lake and would have taken some time to drive around. Not to mention, much of the back roads around Long Lake are covered by tree canopies blocking out clear views of the sky. Of course there was the swaying guest and her many large friends to contend with, should we have left one person behind to tend to the equipment it took a life time to assemble. The real reason, or at least the most honest, was we simply had not enough left in our mind and bodies to really even discuss it aloud. That's right, the great paranormal investigators who had been everywhere, and done everything just didn't even bring it up as an option. Maybe we thought about it, but I don't recall anyone suggesting it. We were spent.

When we finally got things torn down, boxed up, and packed into the vehicles there were less than 20 people around. We picked up some trash left behind by the droves of people to help out Bill and his employees get out in a timely fashion. Sean made the trip home to his family, and John and I to a five star hotel to party like rock stars. After realizing neither of us were rock stars, nor had any of the funds to back up a pretend rock star life, we settled in at a very average motel in Fon Du Lac. We popped a bottle of champagne, nearly putting a hole in the ceiling and the two walls it bounced off of in the process. Normally beer drinkers, I had brought the Champaign to properly celebrate our first successful UFO Daze on Long Lake. Now one good thing that we had done regarding the UFO sighting is to keep the memory of the object itself as free of outside contamination as possible. We discussed everything but the craft itself up to this point. As a result John and I separated to opposite sides of the motel room. Now a huge five feet from John, I sketched my mental picture on a complimentary business envelope in the room and John on an advertising section torn from the motel's Yellow Pages. We didn't spend long with our artistic rendering, as is clearly seen when looking at them. Our physical and mental reserves were empty. We discussed in brief our interpretations of the craft as we exchanged sketches. There were differences in what we saw even at that time. This is quite possible the result of many things as stated in the beginning of the sighting. The easier variables to quantify and categorize such as I watched only for several seconds at the end, John from far off in the distance, till overhead. The less than easy variables are the conditions in which we all were when witnessing something currently unexplainable. John made it half way through his second 4oz plastic motel cup before passing out on his bed. I finished another glass or two while staring intently out the motel room window. I watched as a high, light cloud cover slowly blocked my star filled view. I reflected back on the night and our quick sketches we forced ourselves to draw before we discussed the sighting in greater detail with each other. A quick call to Sean to make sure he didn't fall asleep at the wheel or had gotten abducted on the way home without letting me know. I lie down in my bed, kill the lights. I think to myself how nice a shower and change of cloths would be. Too tired and ill prepared, I choose sleep instead.

Where does that leave us with my experience? I don't know. Since I have no other immediate data to help formulate a clearer view of the experience, I'm hoping that somehow my continual research and investigation into UFOs will help uncover some truth. It is in this truth that I hope helps clear some questions from my mind. If I were forced to state an opinion for the record I'm not sure what it would be. Thankfully, since this is my book I don't have to. However I have allowed myself to be painted into a corner on record giving as flaky as an answer I could come up with to avoid the dreaded quotable three second sound bite clip. It is quite humorous to listen to some of my old radio appearances in which I am posed a hard nosed question. I can hear my words falter as my mind races around to many variables. Struggling to be succinct for a society that demands it, in a field that in doing so only provides a disservice to it. I don't want to be the three second sound bite guy being made to sound like he has an alien in the attic. Any way, I don't have an attic. It is interesting for me to reflect back on some interviews and notice the simple lack of not yet having put my thoughts into words. It is difficult to express your belief system when your reality is no belief system at all, only possibilities. Perhaps the questions were posed to me before I felt comfortable disagreeing with someone nice enough to take an interest in my endeavors and have me on their program. I feel that for someone to have a belief system they have to have at some point, faith. That is to say, not religion, but the ability to make ones mind up without having all the information you feel may be available or at least necessary to take a definitive stance on an important issue. I don't have that blind resolve. When you do have a belief, your research and investigation can quickly fall into working around that reality. Whether this is a positive, negative, or something altogether different I'll let you decide from your own experiences. For myself I feel that with my current understanding of reality, and as one puts their resources into attempting to learn more about it, they will get out of it what they expect.

The more preconceived notions or beliefs one brings to any situation in life perhaps the less they get out of it. For example, I as a human being project my wants, desires, and versions of what I see as right, or fair onto everyone and everything around me. As a result I get disappointed when I interact with everyone and everything as they are most likely doing the same. The problem comes when their wants, desires, and versions of right, or fair differ from mine. To take the example further, I think that the person on the highway should have let me in because I had my blinker signaling my intent for a minute and a half. The person already on the highway doesn't want to let me in because I waited until the last two feet of the lane to try to get over, when everyone else was merging a mile back at the "Lane Ends" sign. If I had already come to the belief that aliens are real and visiting the Earth, then when I witnessed the triangle shaped UFO I could have easily used it to back up my belief system with "see there is one of their craft." So my belief system is no belief system. Sure, I'll entertain that as one of many possibilities, however until that craft lands, an entity emerges, communicates with me, and before leaving gifts me quantifiable evidence of its existence along with the resources to verify it, I simply can't have the belief. Of course this is an exaggerated example of what it might take to form one belief system.

Should I for another example see a strange UFO such as that on UFO Daze in 2004, I will and am entertaining further specific realities of beliefs such as there is more to this stuff than swamp gas. I try to look at each situation or experience I encounter from as many perspectives and with as much information I have available, realize that it is not everything needed to make a finite determination, but move forward with the lesson in my mind. I can say that, from much of the data I have come across in my endeavors that I think the UFO phenomenon warrants much further review. This is not a popular answer with the devout believers nor good enough logic for the debunkers. It is also not one that most media folks are looking for as it doesn't fit well in a headline.

The subjectiveness brought into any experience is overwhelming and infinitely incalculable at this time. I currently feel it must be a variable in all investigation and research placed along with all other data and when applicable, calculated out to statistical probability.

Until an era when the above calculations can be objectively made are we left with only, the simplest of answers is usually the most accurate? This is known to many as Occam's razor, an idea whose credit for creation is given to William of Occam who lived in the 1300s. It is often used in over generalizing terms. William of Occam was many things but as it might most closely relate here he was a logician. Logic can be considered a formal science or a theoretical study of more established systems. Many paranormal fields including the UFO phenomena could also have comparative qualities to this formal science.

The caveats that I enjoy pointing out with Occam's razor though a very weighty, yet very succinct, and normally argument ending statement are the semantics. First your starting with "simple" which to me denotes using as little of data as possible to arrive at an answer. Not complex, but simple. Also, not something you want done when you have a vested interest, such as a visit to your doctor's office. I don't think it is good practice to have a physician who interrupts you with a diagnosis before you have finished explaining your symptoms. Doctors in the U.S. have been taught and perhaps fitting in most situations, that when you hear hoof steps think horses not zebras. Now if you can get past the "simple" usage, you are still left with a wishy-washy "usually." Indiscriminant and indecisive could also be used along with maybe, uncertain, possibly, and not all of the time, but none exude the confidence in truth. I do feel that Occam's razor touches on unifying theories and can hold a solid logic when used in conjunction with the newer understandings of physics. Scientists working towards unifying theories of everything prior to the 1980s are thought to simply not have had enough discovered information to do so. I think sometimes this is where the UFO field currently is in its evolution. We as UFOlogists know there is something going on that doesn't have a definitively clear and singular explanation. I also feel that we do require additional knowledge to be discovered in order to form a clearer and additionally decisive theory on the UFO phenomenon.

Someone using the Occam's razor principle could say that the UFO sighted could have been a misidentified airplane, and since that is the simplest answer and holds the fewest assumptions that must be what was seen. This logic has its use, such as in logic based computer programming that may someday produce artificial intelligence. This is fitting as computer programmers can use a set of axioms or fixed grouping of rules that all actions are weighed against before responding. This and other similar sets of logic based formal sciences are considered bivalent. This can also be looked at in my mind as the ultimate black and white. There is no gray in this logic, either something is true or it is not true and leaves no possibility for logic tolerant to contradiction. As anyone familiar with physics will quickly point out some of the most advanced theories the smartest minds on the planet are currently working on are filled with paradoxes or some form of contradiction. Some of these newer practices of logic are called ternary logic, multivalued logic, intuitionistic logic, modal logic, Bayesian probability, and fuzzy logic. All of these other forms of logic attempt to take into consideration the infinite number of varied levels of truth. Some such as the Bayesian probability works with a system of logic that holds the subjective truth value as how likely something may be to happen. This can also be justified objectively by introducing Cox theorem which has three primary and accepted assumptions itself. All of these different perspectives on reality through the use of logic and other hard to pronounce theories is human kinds attempt to place simply every experience had or that we could have into compartmentalized categories in hopes to gain some insight with the smaller viewpoint that could then even be formulized into mathematics. If it sounds complicated, that is because it is. These theories are also not, infinitely perfected methods rather the best we can do with the knowledge we currently have.

So where does that leave us really? For me it leaves only possibility. Anything is possible and anything could have possibly happened that very night. No matter how strongly I feel about what may or may not have happened that evening I know that I can't fully trust my own senses to ever fully and incontrovertibly explain it. For now, there is only possibility.

The experience was enough to warrant use of P.I.R.O. along with members of other area investigative organizations. To put it succinctly, we have yet to witness what is believed to be the same craft.

After months of festival preparation, an entire week of rent paying jobs behind us, coupled with the same in front of us and the 16 hour work day nearly done, a toll was taken on the three of us that 17th of July. We were all spent and looking back on our response to the situation of the UFO sighting was only more evidence of it. The sightings have certainly not ended there. Less than a year later UFOwisconsin.com received additional reports from that area.

May 31, 2005 had our next two witnesses fishing on Long Lake. Bob was focused on fishing when his son exclaimed, "dad what the hell is that!!." As Bob turned he saw "what looked like a silver (with gold around the edges) disk shaped object." It was around 10 in the morning and there was plenty of light. Father and son were able to view the object hovering nearby for "3 to 5 minutes." They reported hearing nothing unusual during the sighting and "then it just vanished." Bob went on to share with UFOwisconsin.com that he doesn't "believe in spaceships from outer space, but now I am no longer 100% sure." He thought it "couldn't have been a plane, blimp or balloon" though he couldn't rule out possibly "military in origin." They did notice a woman on shore taking pictures of the object "but were unable to locate her" after.

The summer in Wisconsin brings many people together to enjoy the warmer weather. Those who enjoy the warmer weather here feel it can be too quickly fleeting. Jennifer L. was partaking in just such an evening with her husband and two friends who were visiting their farm northwest of Long Lake. It was June 2005, on a dark and clear evening around 10 pm when "all of a sudden this white ball of light appeared" high in the sky. Jennifer went on to say "it seemed to hover for a few seconds" then it "seemed to explode, two separate explosions and split into three, side by side." The four of them watched as the objects "went up into the sky in a triangle formation, one on top, two on the bottom." She said they noted "a lot of sparks flying when they did this." The lights now moved towards them in an "eastward direction." When "a jet came in from the south, close to the bottom north object" it responded by taking off "at a rapid speed." Jennifer thought the jet "appeared to be chasing it, but the object appeared back in it's [sic] position on the bottom north end of the triangle within a few seconds." The object and jet continued on their path until "within minutes, the sky was filled with all kinds of jets." The "bottom north object disappeared, the bottom south and the top object took off to the east" all in apparent reaction to the presence of the jets. Jennifer described the lights as "leap frogging themselves until out of sight." The witnesses reported that the sky was "then full of jets and planes, the jets seemed to be doing some kind of grid over the area." This reportedly continued for about an hour. When closing her report to UFOwisconsin.com Jennifer shared "this was by far the wierdest [sic] thing I've ever seen and I'm glad I'm not the only one who witnessed this, this was very real and I don't really know what I experienced..." Whatever it was, the presence of airplanes or even more specifically jets, is by this point of the book not an entirely new occurrence. As discussed in Ufology 101 similar reports were common from across the nation in the 1952 summer UFO wave, again in the Long Lake sighting of September 1998, and the January 2003 Elmwood sighting. Are these multiple misidentifications of experimental crafts being escorted by conventional jets? Perhaps conventional jets on sortie runs sent to intercept advanced and possible alien technology filled crafts? Depending on from what reality and belief you are looking at it, anything may still be possible.

Long Lake in July 2005 brought another nighttime light sighting. The object was reported to UFOwisconsin.com as first appearing in the southern sky "right above the horizon." The "bluish green" object reportedly "shot up and stayed stationary for 10-12 seconds before moving to the right and then the left." According to our witness it remained nearly motionless for approximately one minute. Then it again "shot to the left quite a ways" and became motionless. When it did move the great distances it "seemed to have a trail or color stream behind it." There were several people witnessing this event and all seemed to agree "it looked like it had two 'dots' following it' one red and one blue." Standing next to our reporting witness was a "65-year-old retired commercial pilot" who "couldn't even talk." When he gathered his composure the retired pilot shared "there was NO explanation he could come up with especially the fact that it traveled from one horizon to the other over us and with no sonic boom." The bluish green color is certainly reminiscent of other reports in this area and others in Wisconsin, mine included. I appreciate the candor of the second witness with their piloting experience and professional observation. The great distances perceived traveled in short time and the apparent lack of sonic boom are not observations most reports contain. I'm very glad they shared.

In July 2006 while on a research trip with friends and associates in the paranormal field we found ourselves stopping by Benson's again. This time not for work but for beer and on the infamous UFO Daze none-the-less. My cohorts in crime were, in no particular order Todd Roll, co-founder of

Wausau Paranormal Research Society (WPRS) who has been quoted in all forms of the media on his work in the paranormal field over the last three decades. The same Sean Bindley who was with me on UFO Daze 2004 and an intrepid paranormal investigator along with intermittent MC for the traveling "Unexplained Conferences." Richard Hendricks, co-author of "Weird Wisconsin," founder of Weird-WI.com, and co-director of the Wisconsin Paranormal Research Center, WPRC. Myself driving and lastly but not least Mr. Kevin Nelson who you may have seen during his appearances on the Discovery Channel's Mystery Hunters, and Travelers shows, ABC's Scariest Places on Earth, and who you have already met if you read the Elmwood chapter.

We were yet again, given a show from above. This show notably less dramatic and presumably further off, distance wise. At one point during our drinks and conversation there appeared a pair of bluish lights to the north and west of Benson's Hideaway. They almost seemed to be tethered together or moving along a similar flight path but independently of each other. They were quiet, but moved erratically to me as one would expect a small aircraft of conventional technology to do. It is interesting to note that earlier that very same day we were tromping about several acres and many miles of woods during the hottest weekend in 2006. In the 100°+ bright sunny day we found our way to the shores of Lake Michigan in search of an old ghost town that used to go by the name of Ulao. We were successful in our exploration for Ulao and were also granted a show from two very low flying aircraft as they zipped down the coast of Lake Michigan not more than a stones throw above. There was also an annual air show, most likely where these two crafts came from, not far from where we stood or from Long Lake. Not to insinuate that these good folks, who I have quite clearly on video, would be as unscrupulous as to hurl a hoax upon the good people of the Long Lake area. However, seeing these two distant lights bob about in the air only several hours later I was quick to see numerous relations between the two. Could this have been merely a test run for the evening's big event only miles away, or just some good people out for good fun? There have been other reports of the sightings had that night. NUFORC holds one report that describes the object as "pulsating lights two per object, green in color, having length and shape similar to a pair of fluorescent ceiling lights." This witness was able to get a look at the objects through a set of "10x50 binoculars."

What have these witnesses above and elsewhere in this publication been witness to? With this book in hand check out these places where legal, I implore. See if you can experience something for yourself. One of the great things about this area that helps place it in the current #1 location: you can still visit Long Lake and find yourself next to other UFO enthusiasts who regularly visit the area. Mr. Benson always has an open ear for UFO researchers with cold beer on tap and hot pizza in the oven. There are state run and private campgrounds surrounding Long Lake that allow you to keep your eyes closer to the sky all night long. As always tell them UFOwisconsin.com sent you!

One way to visit: Situated between Fond du Lac and Sheboygan off of county road 67. The small town of Dundee cradles the south end of Long Lake. For directions to Benson's Hideaway visit www.UFOwisconsin.com.

Final Thoughts this Time Around

"Be ashamed to die until you have won some victory for humanity."
Horace Mann

The quote perhaps a bit dramatic, but a goal none-the-less. I tried, perhaps overtly at times, to keep ufology from appearing upon some unattainably mystical pedestal. Placing any observable event under the category of mystical, can be an easy excuse for avoiding pointed questions with sweeping, grandiose, faith filled anecdotes. I did not aim to demystify UFO phenomena, and as you are nearing the end of this book you know there is much mystery remaining. I did want to make this book an affordable and approachable introduction into Wisconsin's UFO phenomena.

I strive to empathize with my reporting witnesses, many never having shared anything like a UFO experience and some quite literally only share it with UFOwisconsin.com, ever. This requires some empathy on the reader's behalf, hopefully borne out of at least some perspective gained from this book. For example, how does one exactly explain in a detailed, yet succinct, and logical progression something that has completely bewildered the observer? Many of the witnesses and experiencers are so moved it causes them to question their fundamental belief systems, which for most, have been held for a lifetime. Just as I attempted to show in the Long Lake section with my own July 2004 sighting, trying to get your head around the experience just for yourself can be an undertaking of no small size. To understand your experience clearly enough to write it in a coherent form, and then share it with a complete stranger is yet another unique experience in itself. To reach people's minds, to move their hearts or open their opinion, one must write skilled enough to move their message successfully through every type of person that might read it. This is often a difficult process for the most seasoned of authors, let alone someone who may have not written much more than a grocery list in the last few decades. These monumental hurdles and complete lack of practice, explaining such a unique and confusing situation makes it most difficult to regurgitate the experience as to lend any level of due credibility. I have included where possible as many direct quotes from the witnesses or records of the experience to allow for an additional window into their personality. Somethings are universal such as spelling, correct word usage, and punctuation accuracy. However, and this is a big however, some of these witnesses have these reality altering experiences, then immediately sit down in front of their computer, and stumble onto www.UFOwisconsin.com. They share their experience sometimes with such raw emotion, that the least of their attention is put on the grammatical structure of their report. For me to start dismantling the reports I receive and some that have made it into this book without meeting with the person, completing thorough research and investigation on the area and people involved would be simply irresponsible. There are plenty of reports I have come across that would fit perfectly as a misidentification of many a mundane thing such as a conventional airplane, blimp, or satellite, however after meeting with the witnesses I have had to completely reconsider these options due to additional and overwhelming information not included in the initial reports. Of course if we allow, even just for this sentence alone, for the existence of these legitimate sightings, why can't the worst grammatical of us have a UFO experience. At this time no one seems to be exempt.

There are a plethora of possibilities. In most any facet of life, there are many possible causes for any given effect. Let's use an example with dice to help further clarify this point. Two die are rolled with the first outcome totaling 6 and 9 the next. What are the odds of a total of 6 or 9 coming up the next roll? The same and in fact statistically speaking the slate is wiped clean and any number possible is again back to the same probability potentials. Even though any number can come up, due to the number combinations on each side of the die remaining constant, a 7 is the most mathematically probable. Alright so why have we moved from UFOs to the gambling dice game craps? I'm attempting to use a poor analogy for the history of UFO sightings and theories. Even if you erased all the UFO pictures, reports, and experiences today, an actual otherworldly UFO sighting has a certain measurable possibility of appearing tomorrow. I am only attempting to show that even though a noticeable number of UFO reports may be found to have mundane explanations, the cause for the very next sighting may not. As any good craps player may share with you the roll of the dice does have probable outcomes that can be utilized for maximizing your risk-reward ratio, in other words how much you bet and when. For many ufologists it does come down to researching the most probable explanations for a sighting due to limited resources. Even as independent scientists we must maximize our risk-reward margins to use those limited resources where they have the best chance of recovering some useable data. So just as with craps, ufologists do not always place their wager on the right theory every time.

What truths have we humans known only to have them revealed false by the passing of time? Looking back through history there are some instances of similar inexistences we can learn from and maybe even apply to the current UFO field. The panda bear was known to local cultures in China for thousands of years. It was not accepted by western science until 1869, when a dead specimen was produced by explorers. It took nearly 70 years and over a dozen well equipped scientific hunting parties to produce a live specimen. Another dramatic example of accepted reality was the coelacanth. It was estimated from fossilized skeletons to have become extinct 80 million years ago. This estimate was made from unearthed remains dated to more than 360 million years old. That was until the Nerine pulled one up in its fishing nets. The year was 1938. Not another was caught until 1952. My college chemistry book copyrighted in 1989 lists 109 elements in the periodic table. As of closer to today's date we have an estimated 118 with one never having been actually created, just hypothesized. It will be amazing how these elements and the ones still certain to be discovered or created could affect our reality. Some may even aid in explaining facets of the paranormal, including UFO phenomena. It has been said before, that the lack of proof must not imply inexistence. To be fair, history shows this can go both ways, some things held to be true such as a flat Earth, may not stand up to further observation. Most witnesses truly believe in their experience and have nothing outwardly to gain by lying or knowingly perpetuating a hoax. That doesn't mean, however, that there are no other possible explanations for what people are experiencing. Dealing with so many variables takes great effort on the part of the ufologist.

On the surface, some UFO reports seem to have easy explanations and fit perfectly with Occam's razor. Simple misidentifications of known phenomena or technology that appears clear to most all who read the report. It has always been my perception that even though this may be the proper explanation of events in some UFO reports, they are still typically explanations based on theory and conjecture. Whoever is commenting, writing, or just forming an opinion on any specific UFO report be it the investigator, debunker, or journalist were not there, experiencing the sighting or events unfold. This includes you the reader. While it may sound just like an airplane, weather balloon or other, there is almost always the potential for it to not have been. It simply could have been something that appeared to be similar either by direct intent or mere coincidence. However, I find even though we may have found a great fit, statistically speaking, for some of the sightings others beg to be approached from a second angle or with a new thought. Even the least credible witness may have truly had a real experience worth investigation. Just because a sighting has an explanation that seems to fit, doesn't mean there are no other possibilities. Unless the fit does so because it has quantified facts created by undeniable data. For instance, the government may indeed have our pilots, at the controls of some of these crafts that are being reported as UFOs. We mustn't stop our critical thinking there. If we assume that past United States governmental actions are a fair and logical indicator of future trends and actions of government, then it stands to reason there are top secret Military Industrial Complex operations.

Perhaps we did engineer these UFOs from the ground up with some of the brightest minds from MIT or JPL and there is nothing else to it other than military and technological might we are securing for our national benefit. And perhaps these vehicles are still piloted by our human Air Force personnel who are being told the same. And perhaps they are reverse engineered from crashed, traded, or stolen alien technology. The data and facts are less to support anything past the conclusion the government has potentially held secret projects with advance technological aircraft in the past. Are you still with me? All I'm attempting to put forward with too many words and analogies is don't stop the critical thinking. Yes, our government may be testing crafts, with advanced technology. Does that explain all of the credible UFO reports? I can't answer that, but perhaps you with your sharpened critical thinking skill, can get involved and apply it to your interest accomplishing something beneficial for that interest and for us all. It is easy when one hears about UFO sightings to dismiss everything with a generalizing nomenclature of misidentified known phenomena from low IQ folks. If you feel that way, then pursue that possibility. You may uncover the next bit of data the field needs to put the puzzle completely together.

So this is it for now. After reading this cover to cover I may have left you with more questions. Not by design, rather, purely by the nature of the field, full of uncertainty. It would seem to me there are currently an increasing number of paranormal groups making claims on what they see to be truths in the paranormal field. As a result, I feel obligated to proclaim or profess what I believe in.

I believe what I know as a fact today, I may have to re-learn tomorrow, and most likely will. I profess that there are probably more questions than answers in the paranormal fields and most likely we are not even asking all the right ones yet, if we ever can. I proclaim I am very intrigued and motivated by the idea that I am able to research, investigate, and learn about this very puzzling and challenging area of study, simply by observing things around me no matter where I may be. If this were a math equation, I would be interested in the solution but also the adventure had while doing the math. This analogy brings into sharp focus for me another question. Does this mean just because someone is able to form a question that there must be an answer? What does 2+2 equal, how does a boat float, where do babies come from, and why is blue, blue? As you might see from these four questions the answers are available. The answers themselves we may not all be able to agree on.

Yes, to most, 2+2 is indeed 4 and simply put, a boat floats because it displaces more of something than it creates. When we start to look at questions and how they are worded or more specifically how they are perceived by different people encountering them, then the answers tend to change along with it, assuming the answers still exist at all. The problem grows more complex when we make the question a bit more subjective. As said earlier, subjectivity is at the same time the UFO field's greatest strength moving forward and largest limitation.

Such is the case perhaps with: where do babies come from? Some might say God, others by a natural process happening at the molecular level — biology nothing more. Would either be right, would either be wrong?

Moving quickly away from such a controversial topic, to calming, and relaxing, blue. Have you ever tried to define blue to someone? Go ahead, try now to yourself. Difficult maybe. At least to do a thorough job worthy of Webster's. Attempting to solve my rudimentary riddle one could unequivocally speak of primary colors and what precise percentages of other colors you need to form the pigment that will be visible as blue in color when exposed to certain light radiation. You could also name objects that traditionally show in blue as long as it has been. Did you go a different direction with the blue, as in an emotion? If you didn't, did you at least notice that the way I had written the question, it could have been either? Far beyond context and grammar, would any of these definitions be wrong? It is not for me to decide. Besides it is easier for me to suggest perhaps an unconventional way of thinking, theorizing, and observing the world around you. It is mind exorcises such as this, which I hope draw sharp into focus the variable of perception. Is it a subjective or objective question, answer, or experience that you are presented with drawing a conclusion on? Is there really a universally objective question? How can that initial observation help you in reaching some sort of answer?

So if we are going to find answers where might they be hiding right now? An area of science that currently holds many tantalizing hiding places for answers is physics. Simple physics is the scientific study of matter and how it moves including space and time. Physics, whether showing the future potential for the possible technology being witnessed by UFO reportees, to the misidentification of currently unknown or misunderstood natural phenomena, the theories seem to touch on our topic. There are many theories put forth by physicists and peer reviewed by some of the smartest minds in the world. Many of these theories deal with understanding the fundamental workings of every physical action in our known reality. We'll get into greater depth on theoretical physics including unifying theories, quantum gravity, and general relativity in my following UFO book. These and other heavier worded topics will be discussed along side additionally in-depth analysis of Wisconsin's most significant and well documented UFO cases not mentioned in UFO Wisconsin. If any of that sounds of interest to you, then we'll be seeing each other again soon!

As some philosophers have questioned long before my observations, is reality perception or is perception reality? We all make assumptions. There's nothing wrong with reaching for the car door and assuming you are going to feel a car door handle, and assume as it opens the door follows. We must make countless assumptions every day. You, something with an outside, assume there is an inside. Everything you've ever experienced has had a beginning and though you can't see the end you know on some level there will be one. We see an unidentified flying object and assume there is an inside, as we are looking at what we assume to be an outside. Is it a fair assumption? Arguably a logical one no doubt. Yet when we see a UFO can we apply our reality of physics and the understanding of our experiences onto something we know very quantitatively little, if anything about? Allowing your perceptions or assumptions to create reality, confines you to a world that is only within your current understanding, and scope of everything. If one could truly, simply perceive reality and the effect of it, one could become wholly objective and free to experience whatever may be possible. However even if that is accurate, I'm not sure complete objectivity is achievable. Physicists have long debated the effects of the experimenter on the experiment and further tests are still needed.

It is at this point that I must leave you. Leave you with the thought if I may, that the next time you find yourself puzzled, confused, or simply intrigued with something, anything, step aside for a moment with your mind and ask yourself some questions. More objective ones if you can, like: what is the question, how else could one read the question, view the answer, or perceive all the variables involved. What answer would you find acceptable? What answer would you not find acceptable? Are you prepared to find either-or and both? If not, I ask why look at all, you already have created your reality of acceptability and in doing so predetermined what answer you will find. Besides what makes 2+2 equal 4?

Simply put, what makes something so?

I hope *UFO Wisconsin* gave you the chance to learn something new about the industry, about the state, about anything in general. I have succeeded if you find yourself intrigued or motivated. If so, I would be delighted for you to follow your interests and learn more about what is taking place around the state and elsewhere. If taking your scientific, open minded and safety conscious self into your field of interest, you should always come away with something beneficial.

Above all else be inquisitive and have fun; remember adventures come to the adventuresome!

Thank you so much for your time!

Appendix A

Let's give some scope to this report by taking a look at the following Fire Fly Squid illustration.

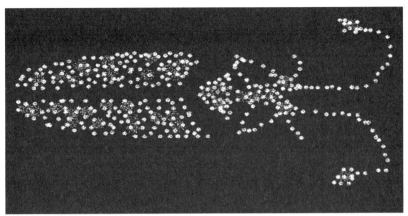

Reproduced image of the FireFly Squid, whose bioluminescent patterns are not fully understood by scientists. Image by Noah Voss.

So where's the connection right? I'm not implying that a six-inch Fire Fly Squid made the journey from its home off the coast of Japan to visit a sleeping young girl in Wisconsin. Looking into the future, basing our assumptions from what we now know from the past, perhaps, just maybe someday we visit an exoplanet. On this far off planet circling marvelously around its own star, we find it to be covered completely in liquid water. What a wonderful discovery this could be, for in the water we then find life! Wow, yes not only life but since this is liquid water, H2O just as here on Earth, the life is carbon based. Now on this far-off crazy water world, if the creatures have evolved to better live in their liquid environment, then might they not exhibit some characteristics of the life that we find in our deep and mystifying oceans? Since there is no land above water, perhaps in their history, potentially millions of years longer than our own, they have intelligently developed as water based creatures. Now these are all very big ifs, surrounded by even bigger piles of variables helping to make this potential fairly difficult to quantify. That being said let's reflect back on how far we as a human race have, shall we say, progressed with our technological advancements in even the last 100 years. From horse transportation, to space missions is a noticeable jump in the last century or so. I could imagine, maybe only six generations from now or about 200 years, how small a step that might seem. What will even the next century bring? The last year has brought the discovery of very a real exoplanet or planet orbiting a different star than our own.

The discovery of exoplanets has been theorized for many years, but the newest findings orbiting around a red dwarf star called Gliese 581 help bring the theories to a whole new stage. If you know your constellations you can see where Gliese 581 is located just off of Libra in our nighttime sky. I fell asleep staring up at this region of the sky on a recent research trip to great wooded wilds, pondering many what-ifs. What is so special about this star out of so many others? There is a planet orbiting around this red dwarf star and none-the-less in the zone that French and Swedish scientists are already speculating give it a climate of 32° to 104° Fahrenheit average. That temperature range should sound familiar to those reading this here on Earth. According to Discovery.com, Stephane Udry, the lead researcher with Switzerland's Geneva Observatory says, "Models predict that the planet should be either rocky — like our Earth — or covered with oceans." While Gliese 581c, the exoplanet's current name, is still a very great distance away from Earth, it is extraordinarily close in space terms. To place this distance into a relative area, we could look at all of the known hundred billion stars in our universe, Gliese 581 is the 87th closest one. If Gliese 581c turns out to be perhaps too hot for intelligent life as we know it then perhaps another planet in the same solar system by the name of Gliese 581d might just be cool enough. Astrobiologists are those who study life in the universe and have speculated this system will be of great interest in future interstellar exploration.

Our solar system is currently dated to be approximately 4.5 billion years old, whereas the Gliese system is approximately 4.3 billion years old. Speculation on any possible "life" there would be just that, speculation. Should life have formed there anything similar to our carbon based human type here on Earth, it can be fun to allow yourself to daydream on what it might be like. Going on the nearly blind assumption that it is exactly like ours, then what if their civilization's development, very roughly, follows our own and they were able to start even two hundred years earlier by some odd combination of variables. We know that here on Earth there have been several near global catastrophes that very well may have slowed down our development progress. Should Gliese 581c had only one less of these similar meteorite collisions, super volcanic eruptions or even one fewer ice age, who knows how many millennia that could have advanced any civilization.

Even two hundred years out of 4.3 billion seems reasonable on the surface, and what additional achievements might they have obtained in those two hundred years? If we again look back at our history of the last 200 years here on Earth, the implications of where we as a society could be in another 200 are mind boggling. As if that isn't enough, what if said society has an extra 2,000 years of societal and technological advancement on Earth? Think how things could potentially advance for humans in the next two millenniums. Of course, with the limited Gliese specific data we actually have to go off of in this fun mental exercise, their society could have started 200 or 2,000 years after ours did. Unfortunately with no additional data at this time, it's almost as possible that there are no intelligent life forms there at all, or they, like us, might not be able to sustain any one single political unit for more than 350 years.

Let's take just one more moment and look closer then. Are there any other potential planets of interest to those scientists who would openly pursue the possibility of life off our own? More accurately, not a planet but several moons, one of Jupiter's by the name of Europa. Having an atmosphere comprised in part of oxygen, this moon is widely theorized to have a liquid ocean beneath its icy surface.

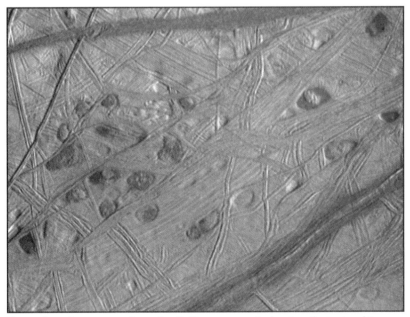

Europa's surface as seen from the Galileo spacecraft showing the textured icy surface. Image credit: NASA/JPL/University of Arizona/University of Colorado

Saturn's moon Titan, with its thick atmosphere, is the only known body other than the Earth to hold large liquid bodies on its surface. We may not yet have to travel light years to see how realistic such potentials are. The more scientists find out about the large bodies in our own solar system the more interest there is about what could be found when we get there with our technologies and someday, astronauts.

Image of Titan from Cassini first fly by in 2004 revealing the "dense atmosphere composed of nitrogen with a few percent methane." Image credit: NASA/JPL/Space Science Institute.

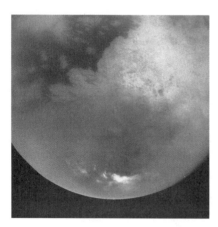

Image taken during the Cassini mission in 2004, revealing clouds on Titan. Image credit: NASA/JPL/Space Science Institute.

Several images of Titan taken by the Huygens probe during a mission by the ESA. Image credit: NASA's Descent Imager/Spectral Radiometer and the European Space Agency (ESA).

Appendix B

Photograph submitted to www.UFOwisconsin.com showing an object in the sky near the Wisconsin-Illinois boarder, not visible while the photograph was being taken on August 11, 2006 around 2 pm.

I enhanced and overlaid the image above, showing an original cigar shaped object magnified 300 percent. It seems to help reveal more detail, dare I say, it looks more like a traditional flying saucer silhouette. Though what looks like a pirate ship shaped cloud to one, might look like an insect shadow instead of a flying saucer to another. Similar photographs, when reproduced in similar conditions under high speed photography show how insects can produce very similar results. These experiments have been undertaken numerous times with nearly exacting results. A normal 35mm film camera, digital camera, high speed still camera along with standard video camera and high speed video camera all setup next to each other to document one event through several different perspectives. The varying technology gives varying results. The standard photography and video equipment show similar objects in frame as the above image. The advanced high speed equipment reveals a less mysterious culprit, typically insects. This has to do with current technology in video fields and frames along with the myriad of settings on standard still frame cameras. What does it mean that we are able to reproduce, similar results showing a mundane and known cause for some images? The presence of several possible explanations for one occurrence does not mean that the other alternative explanations are also not possible. We are however only able to test and experiment with what we have available. For example we are able to reproduce similar end data with insects as well as throwing any one of countless objects in front of the camera lens. Here we have two reproducible scenarios for this and other similar photographs. Just because one was used, does not make the other disappear. There is still the possibility that the above object was not a bug, not an object falling through the air, not even a known aircraft, but rather perhaps a true UFO.

Appendix C

Maybe we will happen upon a naturally occurring earthly phenomena in the future that would have this very similar blue light associated with it. In order to give scope to this supposition lets look at other natural oddities we have learned more about in recent history or simply just discovered.

At this time we know Earth Jets and Sprites are an unusual ocular phenomena happening in the upper atmosphere, one red and Jets blue. Picture a plume of water jetting out of a whales blow hole or the stream of mist from your cleaning solution bottle at home. This same misty looking spray is ejected in a luminescent cloud or vertical lightning discharging from the top of certain storm cloud systems.

To accompany these in your vocabulary we could also add trolls, halo, and elves all categorized under transient luminous events (TLEs). These are all different and equally magnificent phenomena that until relatively recently were more mysterious than understood. The first known filming of a TLE was not until 1989 when researchers from the University of Minnesota accidentally caught images on two frames in their film. Commonly found during severe thunderstorms scientists continue to learn and photograph these luminous events. On the surface of the reports this does not seem to be a probable fit or explanation for most UFO sightings.

Beyond how these TLEs could be interpreted, if you desire to view these events for yourself here are some techniques. First, these happen during storms, some severe. Educate yourself first on all manners of storms in your area and know the risks involved, because there are many and viewing these phenomena are not without danger. After all that the technique is really pretty simple. Block the lower level lightning from your eye's view. An outstretched hand could work, but again, this is all not without possible deadly consequences. With the lower altitude section of the storm covered, look above the clouds. This assumes two things, one you are able to see above the clouds. In order to have this situation you almost need a very large panoramic view and the good fortune to have a storm passing by in the distance allowing you to see stars above it. The second condition we are assuming is that the storm is powerful enough to be producing visually recognizable phenomena. These storms that are ideal for viewing the odd effects above are also the most dangerous, cumulonimbus clouds. Easily recognizable by their distinct anvil shape and high flattened altitudes they are also responsible for severe winds, flooding, hail and known to spawn a tornado or two. We are looking above all that secondary commotion and watching for a very fleeting effect of the charged atmosphere. TLEs are a fleeting phenomenon ranging in life from fractions of seconds to several short seconds. Setting up a secure tripod with a camera on an extended aperture setting could provide you a glimpse of the effects to hang on the wall. This could also land you in the category of having been struck by lightning, caught in a flash flood and so on and on. So practicing this is not without its calculable and incalculable risks. If you become learned on your surroundings and are willing to make an educated assessment of the risks involved, you just might be treated to one heck of a show. It is estimated that there are only 1,000 films that are archived with TLE phenomenon, far fewer than is speculated for UFOs on film.

Appendix D

The feelings shared during the last two sightings were both hovering around fear or at least great hesitation felt by the witness. The emotional reaction of fear could be a clue that allows us to postulate more information from the experience. The fear could also be nothing more than an understandable human reaction to such a unique event. After all, who hasn't seen a movie, read words, or watched television where aliens are depicted in a not altogether complementary light. There are many possibilities that an investigator could consider. Was the UFO emanating something with the intent of inducing fear, or was it by coincidence that the technology or maybe natural phenomenon was having this effect, or was the witness simply projecting their own fears onto the experience?

Certain radiating energy levels are known to have similar affects on human biology, especially the introduction of electromagnetic fields into the temporal lobes of the brain. Dr. Michael Persinger has been championing the lab setting experimentation regarding these effects and the direct correlation to reported paranormal experiences. Dr. Persinger is a cognitive neuroscience researcher that holds one of his degrees from the University of Wisconsin and as early as the 1980s was using double blind studies to recreate "an ethereal presence in the room" according to some participants in his test. Beyond what is happening in the brain of the experiencers, can we speculate that the previous sighted UFO may have been a terrestrial craft using a new propulsion technology? Was this technology emanating similar or as of yet to be known energy causing witnesses to have unusual feelings? Perhaps it was a normal aircraft that was testing some new "non-lethal" technologies on civilians before it was put into public riot use or even military application during engagements. To some, Dr. Persinger has proved that this technology can be applied to human biology with a known and repeatable outcome. As with everything in life there has been further research called for with this magnetic wave theory, including from Dr. Persinger himself. Closer to UFOs Dr. Persinger in 1975 put forth his tectonic strain theory. At the heart of this theory we have the seismic fault lines producing electromagnetic fields and perhaps causing the people nearby to experience the UFO in their brain or the related phenomena called earthquake lights. These lights have been witnessed up to 70 miles from the epicenter of earthquakes such as in the 1930 Idu earthquake and for up to several minutes in duration. There has been much public and professional criticism of this theory when used to explain all UFO sightings including several flaws in statistical methodology according to researcher Chris Rutkowski. There have been some connections made to this phenomena being at the root of at least some sightings. During the 1990s Mexico City had a well publicized UFO wave, and due to the volcanic eruptions taking place in the area some make the earthquake light connection to the UFO sightings.

If not an external stimuli, what about the possibility of self induced states giving altered perceptions? These different states of mind could be either unconsciously reached or consciously sought after such as a 2001 study of Tibetan Monks and Franciscan Nuns. Andrew Newberg, M.D. eventually published his findings in three books detailing some neurophysiological mechanisms that could start to clairfiy what, how, and why people have certain spiritual experiences. This moves us further away from the simple emotions and looks more into potential explanations or at least mental states during spiritual experiences possibly including some alien/human interactions.

At the end of the day, speculation is still speculation and ufologists are forced to make certain assumptions when forming thoughts and theories like I discussed in this appendix.

Our society does have a global economy, a networked community allowing instant access to vast reserves of information via the internet, a growing understanding of consciousness, and what might lie beyond the confines of our own planet. We as ufologists must continually document and investigate UFO experiences with the same grand scope of reality. Those UFO reports that have left us trace evidence, such as abnormally high radiation levels may help yield important information. This will help ufologists formulate additionally credible and sound theories as to exactly what people are experiencing and why. Less we make our selves obsolete by forming theories on narrow perceptions based on antiquated knowledge.

Appendix E

This wasn't the last time the unexplained loud noise or hum was to return to Milwaukee. The neighborhood is at the very least, somewhat accustomed to the average noises involved with living so near an airport. Are we then able to rule out any involvement of normal aircraft even given the proximity of the airport? If so, then what are we left with?

Well something not normal for starters, perhaps with the first description of a basketball sized or shaped object seems to fit nicely with ball lightning. I've remained brief on the ball lightning explanations in this book out of necessity. This was for the simple fact that there is no singular all encompassing explanation for this mysterious phenomenon. Sound familiar? Just as with the UFO phenomenon, ball lightning has many researchers that all hold varying theories, but still no empirical proof of one clear truth. John Abrahamson is a chemical engineer at the University of Canterbury in New Zealand. He recounted the general acceptance of ball lightning in the academic and professional fields recently for NewScientist, "I would say most scientists would accept that it does exist, based on about 10,000 carefully compiled case studies worldwide." Mr. Abrahamson believes "it occurs when ordinary lightning zaps the ground, freeing pure silicon from the soil and this glows as it reacts with oxygen in the air" as published in February 2000 Nature, an international weekly journal of science. It's a phenomenon that has been noted throughout history to behave quite unpredictably and in most weather conditions. Appearing and disappearing in closed rooms, moving almost intelligently through open windows, vanishing in loud explosions while some simply and silently fade away. For a simple visual explanation, picture a floating ball of light. However, there is little science behind replacing all UFO sightings with one, albeit controversial but mostly accepted rare phenomenon. That level of speculation has a better place between friends around a six-pack of beer or other preferred beverage.

One of the oldest ball lightning events recorded in history was during the infamous Great Thunderstorm of 1638. After this storm on October 21, a popular church in England would never be the same. The event was documented soon after in A true relation of those strange and lamentable Accidents happening in the Parish Church of Widecombe in Devonshire, on Sunday the 21 of October, 1638, by authors, Wykes and Rothwell. They reported the noise was "like unto the sound and report of many cannons." It was as "extraordinary lightning came into the church so flaming, that the whole church was presently filled with fire and smoke." The smell was that of "brimstone" as a "great fiery ball come in at the window." The authors quite vividly described the account in great detail and fervor describing one witness that "had her flesh torn about her back, almost to the very bones." The authors go on like this for many more grisly words and by the end of the event some reports have as many as over 60 injured and 6 dead.

As reported in a 2007 *New Scientist* article, it was in 1868 when Michael Fitzgerald reported a "glowing red orb" to the Royal Society of London for the Improvement of Natural Knowledge, founded in 1660. Fitzgerald's account is said to have recorded "no sound, no fire, no explosion – yet the ground beneath the red sphere's path has been turned up and torn to pieces." Fitzgerald observations as written for the article in NewScientist, noted where the orb first touched the ground it left a "square hole about 6 metres wide" then "ploughed up a 100-metre trench and torn away 25 metres of the bank of a stream." Plasma physicists Pace VanDevender from the Sandia National Laboratories in New Mexico, has constructed a unique theory on the source for this report and possibly many more archived ball lightning reports — black holes. To be more precise, microscopic primordial black holes that he speculates are left over everywhere in the Universe as a result of the big bang. His theory is currently supported by some data taken from the original location of Fitzgerald's 1868 sighting. From investigation done at the scene VanDevender believes that more than 100 tons of earth was displaced. The forces required to move that much earth are not readily found, even if we speculate that it was a more mundane form of ball lightning. There was no super heating and resulting steam explosion that could have possibly occurred with regular lightning or non-black-hole ball lightning. Even if the disturbed earth would have been caused by that method, neither of these noticeable events were reported by Fitzgerald. Speculation and coming to workable terms with a certain level of unknown in your research is not reserved for ufologists and paranormal investigators it would seem.

We are left to investigate the events as they are reported. Hopefully we can learn from the new investigations, not push our old understandings onto the findings. This is an imperative part of science, that someday new data will present itself to investigators that can help support a final answer to a specific question. Still later in 1994 a lightning tracking system at a University in Sweden reportedly recorded a lightning strike that was described by witnesses as a ball of lightning that moved through a closed window leaving a very round five centimeter wide hole.

However nicely ball lightning may fit one case, we can't simply ignore the other accounts of distinct craft shape descriptions sighted along with hums such as in Milwaukee on October 15, 1998, on February 5, in 2004, near Long Lake Wisconsin where several red lights were watched for nearly a half hour in formation and in conjunction with a hum, or June 15, 1986, where a hum was heard while watching a boomerang shaped object fly overhead of several witnesses, May 3, 2001, a witness reported a "can" shaped object moving erratically across the sky, while the room buzzed like the bass speaker was turned on.

This is a common situation to find in the UFO field, each case on the surface may seem plausibly discountable by some similar known phenomena but when taken as a whole, and held side by side other reports from over a span of decades the cases are not quite as easily dismissed out of hand. Or is this practice of looking at the big picture simply diluting the data pool and creating a situation where the experiences are made to be more than they are and reaching too hard for connections? What can we learn from this? Well at this time we can only speculate and maybe try some new breweries along the way. After all, it is Milwaukee.

Appendix F

From one remarkable sighting to another approximately one year later. Wauwatosa, a suburb of western Milwaukee holds our next sighting. Reported to NUFORC this witness was driving down the street when they noticed a "bird flying along about 50 feet above the ground." When, just like in the movies, they watched as it "stoped [sic] dead flight…like it hit a wall." The witness went on to stipulate, "there was nothing in the way that could disrupt" their view. They had a clear, panoramic view of the sky and were able to see it "flying swiftly threw [sic] the wind" just before "BAM." They felt that the bird hit something "transparent" whatever it was. Perhaps of interest they noted that the "street lights at this intersection where this occurred" have been "messed up for three days now."

Messed up indeed, most hoaxers fill out online UFO reporting forms in true 12 year old boy form; quick to include much potty humor and the occasional probe joke for the braver of the bunch. I've received my share of lower brow clear hoaxes that would better be labeled as simple jokes. It is reports, such as the one above, that contain fantastic claims but also include just a bit more than most people would bother to add in an average hoax, that give me the pause to further scrutinize the experience. The above report for example, in part describes a scene from the movie "Signs" released August 2, 2002 over a year before this report was made. Then again something experienced in life that imitates something seen in a movie, would make it no less real to the person who had the experience. After all, movies have been around for some time and as a result, many "real-life" situations have been covered on the big screen. Just because any one experience is portrayed in the movies, does not immediately make it exempt from actually happening, even if for the first time, in "real-life."

Appendix G

So you say we've been there right, how could there be something inhabiting the Moon or even oddities that we have not come to understand in the many years we've been observing it.

Bootprint from Astronaut Buzz Aldrin during Apollo 11 mission to the Moon. Image credit: NASA.

True enough, however there is a controversy surrounding the Moon and whether or not we have even reached it with astronauts. On the other side of the spectrum, there are many scientists that feel we know more about our Moon than we do about the deep Oceans on Earth.

The following example is not included to prove anything, simply to help give scope to the thought that things may not always be exactly what they seem. In his autobiography "My Life," former President Bill Clinton shared with his readers a story worth repeating here.

> Just a month before, Apollo 11 astronauts Buzz Aldrin and Neil Armstrong had left their colleague, Michael Collins, aboard space-ship Columbia and walked on the Moon, beating by five months President Kennedy's goal of putting a man on the Moon before the decade was out. The old carpenter asked me if I really believed it happened. I said sure, I saw it on television. He disagreed; he said that he didn't believe it for a minute, that "them television fellers" could make things look real that weren't. Back then, I thought he was a crank. During my eight years in Washington, I saw some things on TV that made me wonder if he wasn't ahead of his time.

I am less sure that President Clinton was directly referencing his stance on the Apollo program as he was perhaps using the opportunity to make a weighty analogy, easily related to many different and current realities.

Image taken of the Moon photographed by Expedition 10 while preparing for the eventual return of human astronauts slated for 2020. Image credit: NASA

Appendix H

While it does not seem that the last report was merely misidentified aircraft landing lights, we can use the opportunity to discuss them none-the-less. Discussed in several Federal Aviation Administration (FAA) manuals, hand-books, and regulations the aircraft landing lights have several uses. During takeoff and landing the lights can act just as those do on an automobile, to help see where you are going. They also serve to enhance the visibility of aircrafts, helping to avoid collisions especially in busy airport airspace.

Some FAA regulations require that these lights be turned on in specific situations or locations. There are some pilots who even keep them on during flight for an added safety measure. However, there are environments that can cause vision hampering reflections from these lights back into the pilot's field of view. This then results in them being turned off or on mid-flight with no obvious pattern to the casual observer. This could explain some UFO sightings being reported with lights just disappearing.

The number and type of aircraft landing lights in use are varied as well. I recently watched a mid-sized commuter, twin-jet landing with six forward-facing super-bright aircraft landing lights. The landing lights were white in color and matched with the normal red and green navigation lights along with additional wingtip strobes. Whether it is one aircraft landing light or six as I recently observed, they are made of different technologies as they become available.

Most of us are familiar with incandescent lights. We have them in one form or another around our house as the commonly referred to light bulb. This same technology can be used for aircraft lights or halogen lamps. Halogen lamps are slightly less common however you may also have one of these noticeably brighter lamps in your home also. Becoming more popular every day is the low wattage light emitting diode or LED. These are also being implemented in aircraft lights and of course can have their own uniqueness to the light they produce. Gas discharge driven lights cast a distinctive light depending on the type of gas used inside the lamp. Arc lamps are similar to gas discharge lights in that they can have specific individual light properties depending on the gas used.

The point I'm trying to drive home is that if you've seen one airplane at night you have not seen them all. Each aircraft itself can look extremely different between daytime and nighttime, as well as the different light technologies used amongst each aircraft and in a nearly never ending amount of combinations. I am also not attempting to disprove the entire UFO phenomenon as misidentifications, rather that some education and discrimination on the part of the people who might have an experience could go a long way in furthering our understanding of the mystery.

Appendix I

Obviously the witnesses didn't report that the object went over another object with its "searchlight beam," stop, go back, and then suck up the object to them, and disappear. This would have certainly lent some addition credence to the intelligent characteristics given to the UFO by witnesses feeling that it was searching for something. That being said who am I to say that it wasn't doing exactly that. Most people give in to their innate desire to relate to other human beings by going as far as overtly connecting to innate objects, such as naming a car for example. If not a name at least giving a gender to a genderless machine, "common old girl you can start this one last time," or "boy just a few more miles to the gas station." This anthropomorphic tendency is not always mislaid. Dolphins, chimpanzees, and even "man's best friend" the dog all have communicative skills that most humans would consider intelligent.

Proof positive is reached at many different levels depending on the person.

While some would consider the existence of a new photograph proof of an animal to still exist even though it was once thought to be extinct, photographs of UFOs do not hold the same weight. Photographs of UFOs are indeed, in my mind, not "proof" of anything one precise thing. I would concede it is vital data that should be used in conjunction to collaborate and substantiate other additionally sturdy data to show a potential evidence. For better or worse Carl Sagan would say, "extraordinary claims require extraordinary evidence."

Appendix J

In those cases we are left to speculate I tend to go with the most statistically probable explanation for UFO sightings or paranormal phenomena in general for that matter. There is a catch with this practice as there are very few truly controlled statistical analysis reports of UFO data. This practice then becomes a bit subjective, basing my understanding of someone's UFO sighting on the thousands that I have heard, read, or investigated.

SR-71 Blackbird was at one point cutting edge stealth technology and kept a well guarded secret for years. Image credit: NASA

Stealth is as loosely thrown about moniker as UFO. Stealth aircraft design has the goal of reducing as many observable characteristics of an aircraft as possible.

Not simply the black skin, oddly angled aircraft most of us are familiar with that focuses on radar return and electromagnetic covertness but also heat signatures, noise, affected air, or trail as well as visible light spectrum are all important variables addressed in stealth technology as it applies to aeronautics. Some of the earliest stealth adaptations were speed, height restrictions, and techniques such as simply painting the bottom of aircrafts to blend into the sky better.

By the 1940s observations started that had began to show the stealthy benefits of delta wing or triangle shaped crafts. Some of the first widely accepted modern stealth technology was possibly the "Have Blue" project in the 1970s. I had direct military application and was flown through U.S. air space during many test missions. The sighting above coming twelve years later would certainly allow for advancement from the maiden flight. Indeed the F117A Nighthawk, the one we're familiar with in the first Gulf War, may have had its first flight in 1981. This was still years before the above sighting, and quite possibly enough time to make it into Wisconsin skies. Continuing on with the known and generally accepted forms of Department of Defense and Intelligence aeronautic projects next we have the B-2. Estimated costs are around 2 billion dollars, per plane including the framework of creating a new industry to make the plane a reality. It has had many names through its design and testing phase: HAPB, ATB, or code name "Senior Cejay" to the current title B-2 Spirit bomber. Whatever you or 'they' call it, it is impressive with a 172 foot wingspan covering nearly 5,000 square feet. To see the B-2 all but silently floating through the air as it was designed capable of doing could be a striking sight. That sight could be forgivably mistaken for something of different size, and even origin. The issue comes in as a result of lacking details with some sightings of black triangle UFOs, mine included. Couple the detail lacking reports with the brief time span sighted, reports with no way of contacting the original witness, and an extreme lack of resources for learning more about the sightings. This all creates finding accurate explanations additionally difficult and makes great strides forward in the UFO field slow to materialize. The previous sighting has many potential explanations. It could have been merely one of the few crafts of many that we covered above. The UFO could have been any number of crafts that civilians are not yet fully privy to or indeed anything else. UFOs from Mars included.

Even if the above UFO was one of those two stealth aircraft, ironically enough ufologists such as John Greenewald have learned after obtaining manuals for both aircraft that they themselves have detailed procedures for reporting UFOs. Mr. Greenewald has the manuals for "F-117 Stealth Fighter

- AFI 11-2F-117 - 1 October 1998" and the "B-2 Aircrew Training Manual - AFI 11-2B-2V1" both listed on his website. Let's discuss this intriguing and seemingly paradoxical factoid in a greater detail.

The final thought on a government involvement with the UFO phenomenon brings us more paper work. Thankfully John Greenewald of TheBlackVault.com has done the lengthy researching and determined investigating for us. Mr. Greenewald shows on his website official government documentation he has compiled from over a decade of inquiries. The documents he obtained help to create a paper trail revealing procedures for reporting UFO sightings to the North American Aerospace Defense Command (NORAD). The most interesting findings were that these UFO reporting procedures are still printed in numerous manuals as recently as 2007. Not just outlining the FAA rules and Air Force procedures for doing so but Mr. Greenewald also holds copies of over 80 reports that had been submitted through the Canadian channels as recently as 2003. Through the Access to Information Act (AIA), and the Freedom of Information Act (FOIA), Mr. Greenewald was able to follow the documents and key words on a twistingly confusing journey through, Air Force Space Command (AFSPC), The Joint Army Navy Air Force Publication 146(E) (JANAP), Communications for Reporting Vital Intelligence Sightings (CIRVIS), National Technical Information Service (NTIS), and the Air Intelligence Agency. I know what you are thinking, as I was wondering, couldn't the listed procedures containing UFOs be excused away by NORAD simply needing to know when there is an unidentified aircraft inbound to the U.S? According to Mr. Greenewald this, "unidentified aircraft is already defined in the publication two items prior to Unidentified Flying Objects." Mr. Greenewald during a recent Coast to Coast AM radio show interview shared that when a UFO is witnessed by a pilot whether, "commercial, military, American or Canadian" the report is "funneled through NORAD." Admittedly to what end, we just don't currently know.

Appendix K

Well, the couple was certainly watching the round shaped stoplights and having the color green as they approached it. So there are the color potentials they spoke of in describing the UFO. To use a very thin analogy, have you ever looked at the sun? Yes I know you're not supposed to and please no hate mail, I'm not condoning it, but I'm also not denying that I have. When you look away from any bright light the rods and cones in your eye ball have become over excited and exerted thus will resonate the rough shape of said bright object. So the couple had this happen to them and interpreted it as a UFO. Yeah, like I said, thin. I look like an idiot and a debunker. It only partially explains some potentials. Most stoplights I've ever come across in my many a road trip have not been bright enough to leave a lasting impression. I'm sure the designers and manufacturers of the stoplights do not want their product even partially blinding those on the roadways.

Point being, that if you try hard enough and have a big enough venue with enough little letters before your name, some people can be led to a false explanation, no matter how illogical. As for this sighting, I have no good explanation, worldly or otherworldly.

Appendix L

The caveat even mentioned by the observer that he left before the lights disappeared. If the witness had stayed longer, perhaps they would have seen the train arrive.

Even if it was a mundane misidentified train crossing signal, and there are no great facts to support the train crossing lights supposition, what if no train were to have crossed such as the August 23, 1999, sighting listed earlier in the Milwaukee section? During that sighting several people watched as a train crossing signal seemed to react to the presence of a UFO. To completely speculate, even if the mysterious red lights had been identified by the onlooker as train crossing signals perhaps that might not have been the end. Wouldn't it be interesting if then no train were to appear but rather a UFO in the sky above. Perhaps statistically unlikely sure, but it has been reported before. I know in my busy life I may have well done the same if discovering the lights to be a train crossing signal. That is, not stayed to watch a train, thinking that it was perhaps farther up the line and simply stopped. If seemingly normal events were further scrutinized how many would turn up some level of mystery?

Appendix M

Some of the first forms of modern invisibility technology were simple projections of what was behind an object to the front of it. As you then looked towards the object, you would see a projection of the actual space behind it. Where are we now with this sci-fi sounding technology? That wonderful wizard Harry Potter may not be the only one with an invisibility cloak. In

2003, Time magazine included the invisibility cloak developed at the University of Tokyo in its "Coolest Inventions" section. They had developed a one of a kind material that did just as mentioned earlier, projecting the surrounding environment onto the outside of a cloak. The wearer in this case doesn't optically disappear, rather just becomes obscured behind an advanced camouflaging system. Professor Susumu Tachi developed this "Retro-reflective Projection Technology" at the University of Tokyo's Graduate School of Information Science and Technology. During several interviews showcased on the Grad School's website the professor shared his hopes that this new technology will someday help airline pilots view the runway beneath them, aid in medical diagnoses in the future and even appear in architecture. In early 2004 they were giving demonstrations around the world of the invisibility technology being used on several additional objects all treated with retro-reflectum. Could this or something like it be applied to the body or at least bottom of our stealth aircraft?

Not satisfied, don't worry there is another promising invisibility technology already in the works. Duke University working with scientists around the globe theorized to the Journal Science in 2006 that they could create a functional invisibility technology by means of metamaterials. According to an Associated Press article posted May 25, 2006 on Wired.com, "The Pentagon's Defense Advanced Research Projects Agency [DARPA] supported the research, given the obvious military applications of such stealthy technology." Only months later and whispers of additional funding from DARPA they had there working prototype. DARPA is a branch of the United States Department of Defense commonly used for among other things, advanced research and development of technologies with military applications. While the first known prototype has not caused anything to visually disappear, the cloaking device was obscured from microwave detection. This has noticeable potentials in the aereonautics field, where as the current known stealth technology minimizes the size of radar returns this could take it a step further. This is accomplished in practice now by specialized construction angles, minimized heat signatures and unique coatings. Could the previous UFO sighting be an advanced version of similar technology or perhaps just as easily a very misidentified satellite constellation? One certainty that could be agreed upon here is that no one perfect explanation is known for many observations reported on in UFO Wisconsin.

Appendix N

According to Kodak, unexposed film, film that has not yet been developed, is susceptible to fogging when exposed to varying levels of radiation. While trying to get in depth here for our topic, while at the same time staying away from the thousand page text books that cover every aspect of varying radiation fields and their sources, let's use some simple examples. You are at the airport and have a carry on bag that has several rolls of undeveloped film. The security x-ray machine at this location produces a radiation that is not powerful enough to fog or affect your film. If you however have checked your baggage with the unexposed film, you just might get a bunch of unrecoverable fogged film at your destination. Most airports have now implemented higher strength x-ray scanning machines that your entire suitcase moves through and in the process leaves your film fogged (can give the appearance of a very white washed photograph) and full of odd patterns (banding and stripping are typical) should you still try to use it. To add to the variables the higher speed films have a more noticeable response from a radiation source. The effect of scanner radiation also appears on the negatives and normally in a linear pattern through the entire roll when laid flat. This source of radiation interference would have then been noticed on the entire roll of film in the Belleville report. Instead the investigation from CUFOS showed that only the eleven frames were affected and those frames before and after had no detectable interference. The report called the affected frames completely white. There is the possibility if the radiation exposure was not of a high strength that depending on the subject in the photographs, the radiation interference would be difficult to detect. However as the eleven frames mentioned affected were completely rendered white a security scanning machine can all but be ruled out. But what else can we learn from the in-depth research film companies have compiled on their film?

Extreme temperatures can also have effects on film. Again these explanations all fail as viable explanation for the reported Belleville eleven frame whitening effect on that film that left the rest of the roll unaffected.

Radiation is present in most all parts of the world emanating naturally from the environment around us. It has been found that old film can show the effects of this ambient environmental radiation in the form of fogging. Different film is affected differently and according to Kodak.com the "faster silver halide grains" will be affected so the film starts to appear "grainier." This is again, noticed more pronouncedly in "800 speed or faster film." NASA has published some of its continuing research into the effects of space radiation on the film they use during space missions. The effects they have found on undeveloped film are similar to the fogging found from security x-ray machines. The industry lingo is "nonimage forming exposures" and is simply said by most of us as fogging. Even in their severe space environment the images were fogged having an "increase in minimum density and a decrease in contrast." We in the Belleville case could be looking at many radiation forms interacting with the film to one extent or another. During NASA experiments in the space environment they recorded most "forms of ionizing particles (alpha, beta, proton, etc.)." Again I find no parallel effects that would explain or at least show one known natural source for the eleven frames being completely white while the frames on either side remained normal. According to the same NASA report "188427" that detailed "The Effects of Space Radiation on Flight Film" they were able to categorize the radiation found in the films space environment into "(a) trapped particle radiation, (b) galactic cosmic radiation, and (c) solar particle radiation." These are all a natural occurring radiation, so the speculation still remains that a new technology, perhaps used to power a craft could have produced an undisclosed pattern or form of radiation that would explain the effects noted with the film from Belleville. Whether this unidentified radiation could be from a terrestrial or extraterrestrial technology is even further out of the realm of reasonable speculation. Unfortunately at this time, all we can do is speculate upon the limited data we as ufologists have.

Often in my research and investigation into unknown phenomena I am left with only ruling out as many known variables as possible. Those who follow this same procedure remain hopeful that by strictly eliminating all the known possible explanations and documenting all the possible variables involved, that they are at some point left with unknown and potentially paranormal possibilities. While this method may not have the surface sensationally poignant appearance of other techniques, it does create the opportunity to discover unknown knowledge.

Appendix O

I don't make great reference to annual meteor showers in the body of the book. I feel that mentioning those known showers in conjunction with any specific event immediately and inappropriately casts too much weight in either direction. Casting doubt and divining answers were not goals while writing this book. I hoped to increase people's awareness of the strange things taking place around them. Not to convince anyone of the existence of anything but perhaps open people's reality to new potentials. There does in my opinion need to be additional in-depth studies done on UFOs sighted during meteor showers. The data on whether the sightings increase or decrease statistically are not my main concern, rather what that data can tell us. There are many extrapolations one can make from the assumption that more UFO sightings are reported during a meteor shower such as the obvious misidentification of a natural phenomenon. If we open our reality up to an intelligent UFO possibility, does not the law of large numbers logically stand that a UFO could be sighted even during a known meteor shower? Besides that, if I had a top secret aircraft to test, I very well might choose just such a night, earthly technology or not. It would certainly add to the confusion and the credibility of the sighting should the wrong person report seeing my secret craft.

That is to say if the above sighting had occurred during the Autumn months perhaps it would be merely written off as a misidentification of the numerous meteorites entering our atmosphere during that time. Though this is still a viable possibility for explaining the experience, by not including the meteorite variable in every sighting I hope to allow for additional scrutiny of an event that might otherwise never get a second look.

To confuse things further, even if a UFO sighting does not occur during a known meteor shower, does not mean it wasn't a meteor. Meteors do enter our Earth's atmosphere on a very regular basis, with space arriving by the tons daily.

Sure the appearance of the previously mentioned blue orb moving upward could have been optically caused by the movement of the car or change in local terrain. I have been on gravity hills, several in Wisconsin alone. As you sit motionless in a very specific location on a gravity hill it can give the appearance from inside the car that you are rolling uphill. The illusion is typically ruined with the implementation of a level revealing that you are truly rolling down the hill, not up. Though I am quite certain they were not sitting stationary in the small area of only several of these hills that provide an optical illusion. The possibility does remain that they were mistaken with the observation of the object moving up, however I feel that from their report and all information included this report can be trusted with some face value. I would love to have had a chance to interview all the witnesses and provide video footage of some known satellites as they can appear from the surface of the Earth. This might have helped clarify some confusion as to if they could have misidentified a satellite or would have clearly known if that is what they were watching.

References

The Internet- To all those sites I have visited in the last twenty years, those that have come and gone, of the dedicated people that have played their role small or big, short or long, quality or confusing-I thank you.

People- To all those persons I have interacted with over my brief lifetime, conversations had in great depth or in short passing, new ideas introduced to me or old ones debated-I thank you.

Table Of Contents~
Allen, James. Fall of 2004. Carneades. *The Stanford Encyclopedia of Philosophy:*

Edward N. Zalta (ed.).
http://plato.stanford.edu/archives/fall2004/entries/carneades (accessed August 2007).

Introduction~
Zaadz. *Let's Change the World*: A Quote by John Henry Cardinal Newman on faults. http://www.zaadz.com/quotes/view/19835 (accessed August 2007).

Ufology 101~
Zaadz. *Let's Change the World:* Quotes by Charles Darwin http://www.zaadz.com/quotes/Charles_Darwin?page=2 (accessed August 2007).

Space Mission. http://www.NewScientist.com/Channel/Space-Tech/Astrobiology/dn7895 2014 (accessed June, 2007).

Wikipedia. Scientific Method. http://en.wikipedia.org/wiki/Scientific_Method (accessed October, 2006).

Cohen, Daniel. 1981. *The Great Airship Mystery: A UFO of the 1890s.* New York: DODD, MEAD & COMPANY.

Booth, B J. 1952 Washington D.C. Sightings. http://ufocasebook.com/washingtondc1952.html (accessed March, 2007).

Gross, Patrick. The Washington D.C UFO flap of 1952.
http://ufologie.net/htm/usa1952.htm (accessed March, 2007).

Fort, Charles. 1919. *The Book of the Damned*. Horace Liveright, Inc.

Secrecy Report Card 2006. Indicators of Secrecy in the Federal
Government.
http://www.openthegovernment.org/otg/SRC2006.pdf (accessed March,
2007).

U.S. Census Bureau. Wisconsin.
http://quickfacts.census.gov/qfd/states/55000.html (accessed December,
2006).

Roberts, Sam. Sam Roberts Photography. Sierra Nevada Gallery.
http://www.srobertsphoto.com/sierragallerypages/lenticularcloud.htm
(accessed April, 2007).

Hynek, Dr. J. Allen. 1972. *UFO Experience: A Scientific Inquiry.*
Chicago: Henry Regnery Company

Braid, James. 1843. *Neurypnology.* London: John Churchill.

Walton, Travis. Travis Walton's Home Page. An Ordinary Day.
http://www.travis-walton.com

Title 50 War and National Defense, Chapter 32 Chemical and Biological
Warfare Program, Section 1520a.
http://www4.law.cornell.edu/uscode/html/uscode50/usc_sec_50_00001520-
--a000-.html (accessed July 2007)

Milwaukee~ 29+ Reports Included

Voss, Noah. UFO Wisconsin: Milwaukee County UFO Reports.
http://www.ufowisconsin.com/county/milwaukee.html (accessed May
2006).

Lewis, Chad. 2007. *Hidden Headlines of Wisconsin: Strange, Unusual, &
Bizarre Newspaper Stories 1860-1910.* Unexplained Research Publishing
Company. 2007.

Newspaper Stories 1860-1910. Eau Claire: Unexplained Research
Publishing Company.

Jacobs, David, Michael. 1975. *The UFO Controversy in America.* Indiana University Press.

New Scientist Space. New crater revives Moon mystery. http://space.new-scientist.com/article.ns?id=dn3242 (accessed June 2007)

Michael, Donald N. 1961. Proposed Studies on the Implications of Peaceful Space Activities for Human Affairs. Washington

Discovery Channel, "New Earth-like Planet 'Habitable'" http://dsc.discovery.com/news/2007/04/24/earthlikeplanet_spa.html?category=space&guid=20070424164530 (accessed April 2007)

Filer, George, A. 2001. Filer's Files #12-2001/March 21, 2001. www.nationalUFOcenter.com (accessed June, 2006).

Mutual UFO Network. 1989. Wisconsin sightings. http://www.mufon.com/mufonreports.htm (accessed December 2006)

National UFO Reporting Center. March 13, 2001. State Report Index For WI. http://www.nuforc.org/webreports/ndxlWI.html (accessed November 2006)

Powell, Victor. *Neurotheology - With God In Mind* http://www.clinicallypsyched.com/neurotheologywithgodinmind.htm (accessed March 2008)

Rothwell and Wykes. *A true relation of those strange and lamentable Accidents happening in the Parish Church of Widecombe in Devonshire, on Sunday the 21 of October, 1638.* 1638. London.

Woods, M. Stephen. *Widecombe in the Moor.* 1996. Devon Books.

Devon Notes and Queries. Vol III. 1906. Exeter.

National UFO Reporting Center. October 3, 2006. State Report Index For WI. http://www.nuforc.org/webreports/ndxlWI.html (accessed December 2006).

Greenewald, Jr. John. Government Interest In UFOs - The Proof Exhibit. http://www.theblackvault.com/article7845.html (accessed March 2008).

Fawcett, Lawrence, and Barry Greenwood, J. *Clear Intent: The Government Coverup of the Ufo Experience.* 1984. Prentice Hall Trade.

WI Voice Journal. 1980. UFO's reported. August 7.

WI Advisor Press. 1985. August 29.

Trainor, Joseph. June 22, 1997. UFOs ACTIVE ON WISCONSIN'S LAKE MICHIGAN SHORE. UFO ROUNDUP. Volume 2, Number 25. http://www.ufoinfo.com/roundup/v02/rnd02_25.shtml

Hubler, K. Graham. February 3, 2000. *Lightning: Fluff balls of fire. Nature.* Page 487-488.

Muir, Hazel. January 3, 2007. "Blackholes in your backyard.". *New Scientist.* Page 48-51

Velikovsky, Immanuel. http://www.varchive.org (accessed July 2007)

NASA Image Gallery. Europa. http://www.nasa.gov/multimedia/image-gallery/image_feature_529.html

NASA Image Gallery. Titan. http://www.nasa.gov/multimedia/imagegallery/image_feature_199.html

NASA Image Gallery. Titan. http://www.nasa.gov/multimedia/imagegallery/image_feature_225.html

NASA Image Gallery. Titan. http://www.nasa.gov/multimedia/imagegallery/image_feature_250.html

NASA Image Gallery. Boot-Print on Moon. http://www.nasa.gov/multimedia/imagegallery/image_feature_69.html

NASA Image Gallery. Moon. http://www.nasa.gov/multimedia/imagegallery/image_feature_246.html

Madison~ 26+ Reports Included
Voss, Noah. UFO Wisconsin: Dane County UFO Reports. Madison Area Locations.http://www.ufowisconsin.com/county/dane.html (accessed May 2006).

The Capital Times listing. 1938. Mercury Theater. Sunday Morning edition October 30, page 18.

United States Air Force. Project Blue Book. U.S. "UNKNOWN": Case Number: 2267

United States Air Force. Project Blue Book. U.S. "UNKNOWN": Case Number: 11383

Smith, Warren. 1976. UFO TREK. New York: ZEBRA KENSINGTON BUPLISHING CORP.

Rath, Jay. 1997. The W-Files: TRUE REPORTS OF WISCONSIN'S UNEXPLAINED PHENOMENA. Trails Media Group.

News-Sickle/Cross-Arrow. 1985. UFO sighting reported here. August 8, Dane County, WI.

News-Sickle/Cross-Arrow. 1985. Others concur on UFO sighting. August 15, WI Dane County.

Capital Times. 1985. A bird, a plane or real UFO? August 21, Madison, WI.

News-Sickle/Cross-Arrow. 1985. Many other UFO sightings are reported in Midwest. August 22, Dane County, WI.

Wisconsin State Journal. 1985. " Oh, oh, UFO: Two are sighted here." November 26, WI.

Wisconsin State Journal. 1985. "UFO sighting reports aren't so far-fetched." December 1, WI.

Capital Times. 1987. "UFO sightings puzzle cops in Waunakee." July 14, WI.

Wisconsin State Journal. 1987. "Officers sure they weren't 'seeing things'." July 15, WI.

Courier Hub. 1987. "Was UFO sighted in Stoughton?" July 16, WI.

Sparks, Brad. 2001. Comprehensive Catalog of 1,500 Project BLUE BOOK UFO

Unknowns: Work in Progress (Version 1.1, Nov. 26, 2001). http://www.ufo-casebook.com/bluebookunknowns.pdf (accessed December 2006).

The University of Tokyo. Graduate School of Information Science and Technology. http://www.star.t.u-tokyo.ac.jp/index.php (accessed July 2007).

Mutual UFO Network. 1989. Wisconsin sightings. http://www.mufon.com/mufonreports.htm (accessed December 2006).

gopher://wiretap.spies.com:70/00/Library/Fringe/Ufo/mufon.89. January 13, 1989. Sun Prairie, Wisconsin sighting.

National UFO Reporting Center. State Report Index For WI. http://www.nuforc.org/webreports/ndxlWI.html (accessed November 2006).

International UFO Reporter, Vol 3, No. 8, Pages 11-15. August 1978.

National UFO Reporting Center. March 13, 2001. State Report Index For WI. http://www.nuforc.org/webreports/051/S51862.html (accessed July 2006).

NATIONAL AVIATION REPORTING CENTER ON ANOMALOUS PHENOMENA. Anon., Radar-Visual in Wisconsin: Case 3-8-24. International UFO Reporter, Vol. 3, No. 8, Pp. http://www.narcap.org/reports/airsafety_p2.htm (accessed July 2006).

Wisconsin state, United States. http://www.answers.com/Wisconsin (accessed July 2006).

NASA Image Gallery. SR-71 Blackbird. http://www.nasa.gov/multimedia/imagegallery/image_feature_622.html

Belleville~ 17+ Reports Included
Voss, Noah. Dane County UFO Reports. Belleville Area Locations. http://www.ufowisconsin.com/county/dane.html (accessed May 2006).

The shared archives of Richard Heiden.

The public archives of the Paranormal Investigating Researchers
Organization-P.I.R.O.

Monroe Evening Times. 1987. "Belleville site of UFO investigation."
March 28, Monroe, WI.

Monroe Evening Times. 1987. "Some UFO reports notable." January 24,
Monroe, WI.

Monroe Evening Times. 1987. "Midwest hot spot for UFOs." February
12, Monroe, WI.

Monroe Evening Times. 1987. "Lights in Belleville a mystery." February
12, Monroe, WI.

SN 1987A. Hubble Site. Mosaic of Supernova 1978A.
http://hubblesite.org/gallery/album/entire_collection/pr1999004e/
(accessed March 2008).

SN 1987A. Hubble Site. Supernova 1987A: Halo for a Vanished Star.
http://hubblesite.org/newscenter/archive/releases/1995/49/image/a/format/w
eb_print/ (accessed March 2008).

News-Republic. 1987. "UFO center probes abduction reports from
Belleville, New Glarus areas." June 26, Baraboo, WI.

Monticello Messenger. 1987. "Additional winter UFO sightings revealed."
June 17, Monticello, WI.

Monticello Messenger. 1987. "They're still around! UFO sightings continue in area." March 11, Monticello, WI.

Capital Times. 1987. "Belleville residents report UFO." March 10,
Madison, WI.

Recorder. 1987. "Night-time UFO Sightings Continue In This Area."
January 29, Belleville, WI.

News-Chronicle. 1987. "UFO center investigates sightings in Dane
County." January 28, Green Bay, WI.

Post. 1987. "Area farmer reports UFO observations." July 29, New Glarus, WI.

Post. 1987. "UFO sited in area by Belleville policeman." January 21, New Glarus, WI.

National UFO Reporting Center. State Report Index For WI. http://www.nuforc.org/webreports/ndxlWI.html (accessed November 2006)

NASA Image Gallery. BESS-Polar Scientific Balloon. http://imagine.gsfc.nasa.gov/Images/news/bess_launch_med.jpg (accessed March 2008).

NASA Image Gallery. InFOCuS Scientific Balloon Experiment.

http://www.nasa.gov/images/content/68066main_infocus_launch5.jpg (accessed March 2008).

Elmwood~ 20+ Reports Included
Blum, Howard. 1991. Out There. Pocket Star Books.

Chronicle. 1988. February 24, Melrose, WI.

Argus. 1976. June 3, Elmwood, WI.

Voss, Noah. Pierce County UFO Reports. Elmwood Area Locations. http://www.ufowisconsin.com/county/pierce.html (accessed May 2006).

Case records of the Paranormal Investigating Researchers Organization. P.I.R.O.

Pierce County Herald. 1988. August 24, Ellsworth, WI.

Vallee, Jacques. 1969. *Passport To Magonia: from folklore to flying saucers.* H. Regnery Co.

Vallee, Jacques. 1991. *Confrontations: A scientists Search For Alien Contact.* Independent Publishers.

Chronicle. 1988. February 24, Melrose, WI.

Connors, Wendy. *Night Journeys in Ufology: Cops & Saucers. Officer Wheeler Sighting.* Albuquerque, New Mexico. MP3 audio format on CD.

Argus. 1976. "Whatever 'They' Are, They Are Still Around Here." June 3, Elmwood, WI.

Chronicle. 1988. "UFOs - Seeing is Believing for Local Resident." February 24, Melrose, WI.

Elm Leaves. 1980. "UFOs in Village?" January 24, Elm Grove, WI.

Pierce County Herald. 1980. "Area residents witness UFO." October 30, Ellsworth, WI.

Pierce County Herald. 1988. "Strange lights, craft seen near Bay City Saturday night. March 9, Ellsworth, WI."

Pierce County Herald. 1988. "UFO sightings, suspicions reported around county." April 27, Ellsworth, WI.

Journal. 1988. "More unusual lights are spotted in PC skies." May 5, River Falls, WI.

Pierce County Herald. 1988. "Strange lights, unusual marks reported in area." August 24, Ellsworth, WI.

Kramer, William M. PhD, and Bahme, Charles J.D. 1992. *Fire Officer's Guide to Disaster Control.* 2nd Edition. Fire Engineering Books & Videos, A PENNWELL PUBLISHING COMPANY.

Heavens Above. Iridium Flares. http://www.heavens-above.com (accessed September 2006).

Long Lake~ 29+ Reports Included Voss, Noah. Fond Du Lac County UFO Reports. Long Lake Area Locations. http://www.ufowisconsin.com/county/fond_du_lac.html (accessed December 2006).

Voss, Noah. Sky-Man: The Indians' Alien. http://www.w-files.com/files/ceindiansalien.html (accessed October 2006).

Barnouw, Victor. 1977. WISCONSIN CHIPPEWA MYTHS & TALES: and their relation to Chippewa life. THE UNIVERSITY OF WISCONSIN PRESS.

Morton, Ron, and Gawboy, Carl. 2000. TALKING ROCKS: GEOLOGY AND 10,000 Years of Native American Tradition in the Lake Superior Region. Minneapolis/London: University Of Minnesota Press.

HO-CHUNK NATION: PEOPLE OF THE BIG VOICE. ABOUT US. http://www.ho-chunknation.com/AboutUs.aspx (accessed October 2006).

The Menominee Indian Tribe of Wisconsin. MITW History - Early Menominee's. http://www.menominee-nsn.gov/history/earlyMenominees/earlyMenominees.php (accessed October 2006).

National UFO Reporting Center. March 13, 2001. State Report Index For WI. http://www.nuforc.org/webreports/023/S23296.html (accessed December 2006).

National UFO Reporting Center. March 13, 2001. State Report Index For WI. http://www.nuforc.org/webreports/051/S51377.html (accessed December 2006).

Final Thoughts~
Zaadz. Let's Change the World: A Quote by Horace Man. http://quotes.zaadz.com/Horace_Mann (accessed August 2007).

Al-Khalili, Jim. 2004. Quantum: A Guide for the Perplexed. Weidenfeld & Nicolson.

Notes on Craps. http://www.mathproblems.info/gam470/games/craps/notes-craps.html (accessed January 2007).

Burns, Philip R. http://www.pibburns.com/cryptost/panda.htm (accessed January 2007).

Burns, Philip R. http://www.pibburns.com/cryptost/coelacan.htm (accessed January 2007).

Kaku, Dr. Michio. Theoretical physicist, Author, tenured professor, and co-founder of string field theory. http://www.mkaku.org (accessed June 2007).

References~
The Chicago Manual of Style Online. Chicago-Style Citation Quick Guide. http://www.chicagomanualofstyle.org/tools_citationguide.html (accessed August 2007).

Chicago Citation Style. The Chicago Manual of Style, 15th edition. http://www.liunet.edu/cwis/cwp/library/workshop/citation.htm (accessed August 2007).

For Further Information
Ufology 101~
Busby, Michael. 2004. *Solving the 1897 Airship Mystery.* Pelican Publishing Company.

Chariton, Wallace, O. 1990. *The Great Texas Airship Mystery. Republic of Texas.*

Chronology of UFO History. 1952. http://www.ufoscience.org/history/timeline-ufo-history.html (accessed March, 2007).

Darling, David. New-formed crater found on the Moon. http://www.daviddarling.info/archive/2002/archiveDec02.html (accessed June 2007).

Milwaukee~ 29+ Reports Included
Neurotheology. http://en.wikipedia.org/wiki/Neurotheology

Sandles, Tim. Jan Reynolds and The Devil. http://www.legendarydartmoor.co.uk/jan_reynolds.htm (accessed March 2008).

Nabeshima, Ricki. Goodness gracious, great (and small) balls of fire. http://www.telegraph.co.uk/connected/main.jhtml?xml=/connected/2006/10/10/ec light10.xml (accessed March 2008).

Madison~ 26+ Reports Included
Hendry, Allan. June 24, 1978. Radar-Visual In Wisconsin. The Center for UFO Studies CASE # 3-8-24; UFO of High Merit. International UFO Reporter, Vol. 3, No. 8. http://www.nicap.org/rvwisc1.htm (accessed July 2006).

Weinstein, Dominique, F. February 2001. UNIDENTIFIED AERIAL
PHENOMENA EIGHTY YEARS OF PILOT SIGHTINGS: Catalog of
Military, Airliner, Private Pilots' Sightings from 1916 to 2000. 6th edition.

http://www.ufoevidence.org/newsite/files/WeinsteinPilotCatalog.pdf
(accessed December 2006).

International UFO Reporter. June 24, 1978. Radar-Visual In Wisconsin.
The Center for UFO Studies. Vol. 3, No. 8, Pgs 11-15.

Steiger, Brad. 1976. *PROJECT BLUE BOOK: The Top Secret UFO
Findings Revealed.* New York: Ballantine Books.

Belleville~ 17+ Reports Included
Holly, H. Mark. 1995. The Effects of Space Radiation on Flight Film.
http://ston.jsc.nasa.gov/collections/TRS/_techrep/CR188427.pdf (accessed
March 2008).

Elmwood~ 20+ Reports Included
APRO Bulletin, Vol. 24 No. 10 (Apr 1976)

UFO Evidence. Police officer has repeat sighting. http://www.ufoevi-
dence.org/cases/case341.htm (accessed September 2006).

George Wheeler's close encounter, 1976. http://ufologie.net/htm/wheel-
er76.htm (accessed October 2006).

UFO Days. http://www2.jsonline.com/lifestyle/parenting/mar01/airtrav-
el031401.asp (accessed December 2006)

ASSORTED UFO CASES FOR 1989.
http://www.textfiles.com/ufo/UFOBBS/2000/2620.ufo (accessed December
2006).

Colares Brazil UFO flap of 1977. http://ufologie.net/htm/colares.htm
(accessed July 2007)

Foster, James L and Owe, Manfred. Goddard Space Flight Center:
Determining the Altitude of Iridium Flares.
http://pumas.jpl.nasa.gov/PDF_Examples/07_13_99_1.pdf

Iridium Flares. http://en.wikipedia.org/wiki/Iridium_flare (accessed January 2007).

Long Lake~ 29+ Reports Included
http://en.wikipedia.org/wiki/Ho-Chunk_mythology (accessed October 2006).

The Ho-Chunk Nation - A Brief History. http://hocaklanguage.com/HTM%20All/Ho-Chunk%20history.html (accessed January 2007).

Indian Country: Ho-Chunk History. http://www.mpm.edu/wirp/ICW-150.html (accessed January 2007).

College of Menominee Nation. http://www.menominee.edu (accessed October 2006).

Godfrey, Linda S, and Hendricks, Richard D. 2005. *Weird Wisconsin: Your Travel Guide to Wisconsin's Local Legends and Best Kept Secrets.* BARNES & NOBLE BOOKS.

Final Thoughts~
Hill, Paul R. *Unconventional Flying Objects: A Scientific Analysis.* Charlottesville, VA: Hampton Roads Publishing Co. 1995.

Hynek, J. Allen. *The UFO Experience: A Scientific Inquiry.* Chicago: Henry Regnery. 1972.

Clark, Jerome. *The UFO Encyclopedia.* Detroit, MI: Omnigraphics. 1998.

About the Author

Noah's endeavors into the paranormal fields have been included in such books as, *Hidden Headlines of Wisconsin, Hunting the American Werewolf, Weird Wisconsin, Haunted Houses, Strange Wisconsin, The 13th Planet, Legend Tripping Wisconsin, Monsters,* and *Milwaukee Ghosts.* Noah has worked with such companies as the History Channel, the Sci-Fi Channel, The CW network, Triage Entertainment, and Lions Gate Films on projects ranging from UFO documentaries to ABC's *Scariest Places on Earth.* Noah is a regular presenter and lecturer with the Unexplained Conferences, the longest running paranormal program of its kind in the World, and largest in America. Noah has also appeared on national and international radio programs broadcasted in over 40 countries, such as *Wake Up America, A UFO Study, The Kevin Smith Show, Uncanny Radio,* and *The Unexplained Radio Show.* Noah takes great pleasure in traveling and thus far he's had the good fortune to travel to all but four states in America, along the way-researching ghostly St. Augustine Florida, investigating the mysterious Winchester Mansion in California, haunted highways in Hawaii, looking for Bessie in Lake Erie, scanning for flying saucers on the summit of Mt. Saint Helens, werewolves in Wisconsin, ghosts of Alcatraz in San Francisco Bay, the Historic Bullock Hotel of wild-west Deadwood, Voodoo in Jamaica, UFOs in Mexico, and searching for Sasquatch in British Columbia.

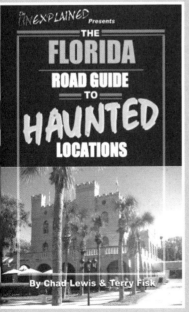

Presents

HIDDEN HEADLINES
Strange, Unusual, & Bizarre Newspaper Stories 1860-1910

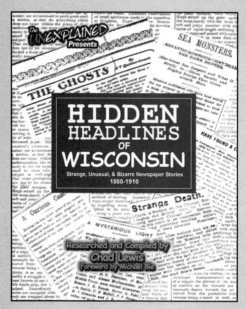

HIDDEN HEADLINES OF WISCONSIN
by Chad Lewis
Foreword by Michael Bie

EXTRA! READ ALL ABOUT IT!
- Mysterious Thing In The Sky
- Chicken Has Human Face
- Toads Tumble From Sky
- Yawns Herself To Death
- Woman Vomits Up Live Lizard
- Cows Bark Like Dogs
- Sea Serpent Seen By Campers
- Farmer Shot An Alligator

ISBN: 978-0-9762099-6-6

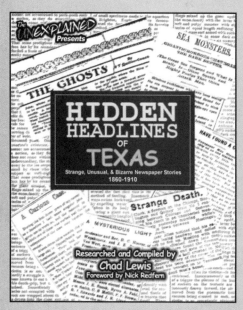

HIDDEN HEADLINES OF TEXAS
by Chad Lewis
Foreword by Nick Redfern

EXTRA! READ ALL ABOUT IT!
- Ghosts In The Alamo
- Lemonade Death
- The Dead Do Walk
- Nail Found In Heart Of A Cow
- Monster Tape Worm
- Eighteen-Horn Cow
- Sea Serpent Has Been Seen
- One-Eyed Wild Man

ISBN: 978-0-9762099-8-0

www.unexplainedresearch.com

HIDDEN HEADLINES

Strange, Unusual, & Bizarre Newspaper Stories 1860-1910

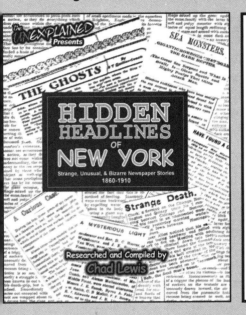

HIDDEN HEADLINES OF NEW YORK
by Chad Lewis

EXTRA! READ ALL ABOUT IT!
- The Sleeping Beauty
- A Petrified Giant
- Digging His Own Grave
- Sea Serpent Spotted
- Frightened To Death
- Half Human-Half Monkey
- In Her Coffin Alive
- Made Insane By Ghosts
- An Odd Freak

ISBN: 978-0-9762099-9-7

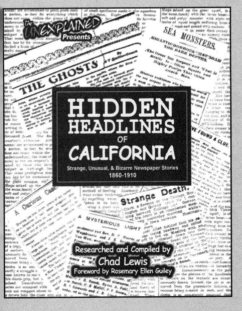

HIDDEN HEADLINES OF CALIFORNIA
by Chad Lewis
Foreword by Rosemary Ellen Guiley

EXTRA! READ ALL ABOUT IT!
- Frightened To Death
- Killed By The Bite Of A Fly
- Ghosts Inhabit House
- Crazed By Religion
- Wondrous Airship
- What Freak Beast Is This?
- Tanning Of Human Skin
- Victims Of Black Art

ISBN: 978-0-9798822-0-3

www.unexplainedresearch.com

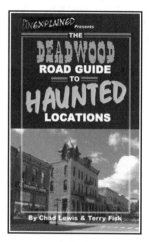
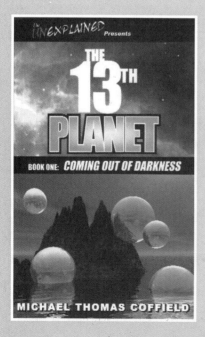